CONTENTS

OVERVIEW

U.S. Production Declines in 2004 Even as Sales Rise

The U.S. automotive industry held on in 2004 for a strong year in sales.

Excess inventory led to even more generous subsidizing of sales than in past years, especially at the end of the third-quarter and in December, to allow the year to end above 2003 in sales.

However, the solid gain was not enough to lift U.S. production above 2003 due to the high inventory levels, which for a while during the year topped 4 million units for the first time ever, and because more output was sourced from outside the country led by increased imports from Canada and South Korea.

In the two other North American markets, sales declined in Canada for the second straight year while rising in Mexico to an all-time high.

Thanks to demand in the U.S. market, Canada production recorded an all-time high. In fact, the province of Ontario for the first time became the No. 1 producer among any North America state or province for a calendar year. The shift knocked the state of Michigan out of first place, possibly for the first time ever. It was another indication of the decline of the long-time U.S.-based manufacturers — General Motors Corp., Ford Motor Co. and the Chrysler Group of DaimlerChrysler Corp. — and of union-made vehicles.

Overall, U.S. output totaled 11.96 million units, 1.1% below 2003's 12.09 million, and 2.6% short of 2002's 12.28 million. U.S. production of just cars fell to a decades-long low of 4.23 million, while trucks recorded a new high of 7.73 million.

GM, Ford and Chrysler still remain the Big Three in terms of volume, but their share of U.S. production declined to a new low of 69.3% in 2004 from 72.3% on 2003.

Accordingly, production by foreign-based manufacturers, among them Toyota Motor Mfg. U.S.A. Corp, Honda of America Mfg. Inc. and Nissan North America Inc., and their non-union plants, continued to rise. Nissan recorded the biggest increase among the major U.S. producers with a robust 44.5% rise over 2003, and a production share of 6.3% vs. 4.3% the prior year.

Overall, North American production increased slightly to 16.224 million units in 2004 from 16.215 million in 2003. But it was well below the last peak of 16.713 million in 2002.

Furthermore, U.S. production fell to 18.7% of total world output, following 20.0% in 2003, 20.8% in 2002 and 20.4% in 2001.

With U.S. output accounting for nearly three-fourths of North American output, production on the continent suffered the same trend in comparison to global output. In 2004, North America output accounted for 25.4% of global production, down from 26.9% in 2003.

Meantime, global assemblies totaled 63.96 million in 2004, a strong 6.0% increase above 2003's 60.33 million, and well above the 58.97 million and 56.07 million of 2002 and 2001, respectively.

Asia was the main impetus for the global production growth.

Production in the Asia-Pacific region, including Australia, leapt 12.0% to 24.32 million units from 2003's 21.72 million.

By country, all eyes were on China.

Output in the emerging giant topped 5 million units for the first time in 2004. That was more than double production as recently as 2001.

Western Europe's place as a world production center also was waning somewhat.

Production was nearly flat in 2004 from 2003: 17.72 million units vs. the prior year's 17.70 million.

Slack times in Western Europe were largely due to headier days in Eastern/Central Europe.

Although still a small amount by regional standards, production in the Eastern/Central Europe grew 18.5% in 2004 to 3.15 million units led by gains in Poland and Russia.

Automakers in that part of the world continue to take advantage of lower cost labor and the eagerness for investment by countries in the Eastern/Central Europe region — not in the established manufacturing centers of Western Europe.

South America also contributed to the declining, albeit still integral, role of North America and Western Europe as major auto manufacturing centers.

Led by Brazil, which accounts for close to 90% of production in the region, car and truck output in South America grew 25.0% to 2.55 million units in 2004. A good turnaround since production bottomed out at 2 million units in 2002, but still between one-half and two-thirds of the region's annual production capacity.

In other highlights from *Ward's Motor Vehicle Facts & Figures*:

The number of cars and trucks operating on U.S. roads reached 231,398,281 as of July 1, 2004. The number was 2.4% above the prior year total, and the largest increase since 2.5% in 1996. The number of trucks increased to 42.6% of the total, and has increased every year since 1963 when the share was 15.8%.

Toyota Motor Corp. became the No.2 global producer in 2004, knocking Ford to the third slot. GM remained in No. 1 by producing some 1.2 million vehicles more than Toyota. Volkswagen AG, DaimlerChrysler and PSA Peugeot Citroen kept the Nos. 4, 5 and 6 slots, respectively. However, Honda Motor Co. Ltd. came in at seventh by pulling Nissan down to eighth place. Hyundai Motor Co. Ltd. (including Kia) and Renault SA rounded out the Top 10.

Silver was the most popular color on cars sold in the U.S. in the '04 model year as it was for '03. It was the second popular color for light trucks behind white. ❑

U.S. Production and Factory Sales of Passenger Cars, Trucks and Buses

ANNUAL U.S. MOTOR VEHICLE PRODUCTION AND FACTORY SALES

Year	Production Passenger Cars	Production Commercial Vehicles	Production Total	Factory Sales Passenger Cars	Factory Sales Commercial Vehicles	Factory Sales Total
2004	4,229,625	7,730,729	11,960,354	N.A.	7,466,739	N.A.
2003	4,510,469	7,576,559	12,087,028	N.A.	7,143,429	N.A.
2002	5,018,777	7,260,805	12,279,582	N.A.	6,963,720	N.A.
2001	4,879,119	6,545,570	11,424,689	4,884,313	6,223,586	11,107,899
2000	5,542,217	7,231,497	12,773,714	5,504,385	7,022,478	12,526,863
1999	5,637,949	7,387,029	13,024,978	5,427,746	6,699,113	12,126,859
1998	5,554,373	6,448,290	12,002,663	5,676,964	6,435,185	12,112,149
1997	5,933,921	6,196,654	12,130,575	6,069,886	6,152,817	12,222,703
1996	6,082,835	5,747,322	11,830,157	6,140,454	5,775,730	11,916,184
1995	6,339,967	5,655,281	11,995,248	6,309,836	5,713,469	12,023,305
1994	6,601,220	5,638,068	12,239,288	6,548,562	5,640,275	12,188,837
1993	5,982,120	4,873,342	10,855,462	5,961,754	4,895,224	10,856,978
1992	5,666,891	4,024,552	9,691,443	5,685,299	4,062,002	9,747,301
1991	5,439,864	3,349,976	8,789,840	5,407,120	3,387,503	8,794,623
1990	6,077,903	3,689,536	9,767,439	6,049,749	3,725,205	9,774,954
1989	6,821,291	4,035,501	10,856,792	6,807,416	4,061,950	10,869,366
1988	7,137,433	4,084,575	11,222,008	7,104,617	4,120,574	11,225,191
1987	7,099,854	3,812,074	10,911,928	7,085,147	3,821,410	10,906,557
1986	7,829,271	3,490,853	11,320,124	7,516,189	3,500,933	11,017,122
1985	8,186,043	3,452,094	11,638,137	8,002,259	3,464,327	11,466,586
1984	7,773,332	3,151,449	10,924,781	7,621,176	3,175,835	10,797,011
1983	6,781,184	2,443,637	9,224,821	6,739,223	2,433,876	9,173,099
1982	5,073,496	1,912,099	6,985,595	5,049,184	1,906,455	6,955,639
1981	6,253,138	1,689,778	7,942,916	6,255,340	1,700,908	7,956,248
1980	6,375,506	1,634,335	8,009,841	6,400,026	1,667,283	8,067,309
1979	8,433,662	3,046,331	11,479,993	8,419,226	3,036,706	11,455,932
1978	9,176,635	3,722,567	12,899,202	9,165,190	3,706,239	12,871,429
1977	9,213,654	3,489,128	12,702,782	9,200,849	3,441,521	12,642,370
1976	8,497,893	2,999,703	11,497,596	8,500,305	2,979,476	11,479,781
1975	6,716,951	2,269,562	8,986,513	6,712,852	2,272,160	8,985,012
1970	6,550,128	1,733,821	8,283,949	6,546,817	1,692,440	8,239,257
1965	9,335,227	1,785,109	11,120,336	9,305,561	1,751,805	11,057,366
1960	6,703,108	1,202,011	7,905,119	6,674,796	1,194,475	7,869,271
1955	7,950,377	1,253,672	9,204,049	7,920,186	1,249,106	9,169,292
1950	6,628,598	1,377,261	8,005,859	6,665,863	1,337,193	8,003,056
1945	83,786	701,090	784,876	69,532	655,683	725,215
1940	3,728,491	784,404	4,512,895	3,717,385	754,901	4,472,286
1935	3,252,244	694,690	3,946,934	3,273,874	697,367	3,971,241
1930	2,784,745	571,241	3,355,986	2,787,456	575,364	3,362,820
1925	N.A.	N.A.	N.A.	3,735,171	530,659	4,265,830
1920	N.A.	N.A.	N.A.	1,905,560	321,789	2,227,349
1915	N.A.	N.A.	N.A.	895,930	74,000	969,930
1910	N.A.	N.A.	N.A.	181,000	6,000	187,000
1905	N.A.	N.A.	N.A.	24,250	750	25,000
1900	N.A.	N.A.	N.A.	4,192	N.A.	4,192

N.A. - Not available. Production data does not include Buses.
SOURCE: *Ward's Automotive Reports.*

North America Passenger Car Production by Model

NORTH AMERICA PASSENGER CAR PRODUCTION BY MODEL

	Canada		Mexico		United States		North America	
	2004	2003	2004	2003	2004	2003	2004	2003
Ford Mustang	—	—	—	—	41,925	—	41,925	—
Mazda6	—	—	—	—	91,339	83,422	91,339	83,422
AUTOALLIANCE TOTAL	**—**	**—**	**—**	**—**	**133,264**	**83,422**	**133,264**	**83,422**
BMW 3-Series	—	—	—	308	—	—	—	308
BMW Z4	—	—	—	—	35,136	56,589	35,136	56,589
BMW TOTAL	**—**	**—**	**—**	**308**	**35,136**	**56,589**	**35,136**	**56,897**
300M	—	27,130	—	—	—	—	—	27,130
300 Series	144,376	—	—	—	—	—	144,376	—
Concorde	—	29,303	—	—	—	—	—	29,303
Neon	—	—	—	—	1,844	1,859	1,844	1,859
PT Cruiser Convertible	—	—	36,994	—	—	—	36,994	
Sebring Convertible	—	—	—	—	39,388	46,158	39,388	46,158
Sebring Sedan	—	—	—	—	77,269	64,308	77,269	64,308
Chrysler Total	**144,376**	**56,433**	**36,994**	**—**	**118,501**	**112,325**	**299,871**	**168,758**
Charger	56	—	—	—	—	—	56	—
Intrepid	—	83,916	—	—	—	—	—	83,916
Neon	—	—	—	—	139,004	150,957	139,004	150,957
Stratus Sedan	—	—	—	—	90,792	97,261	90,792	97,261
Viper	—	—	—	—	2,469	2,484	2,469	2,484
Dodge Total	**56**	**83,916**	**—**	**—**	**232,265**	**250,702**	**232,321**	**334,618**
CHRYSLER GROUP TOTAL	**144,432**	**140,349**	**36,994**	**—**	**350,766**	**363,027**	**532,192**	**503,376**
Crown Victoria	82,826	82,541	—	—	—	—	82,826	82,541
Escort	—	—	—	12,406	—	—	—	12,406
Five Hundred	—	—	—	—	42,782	—	42,782	—
Focus	—	—	58,475	59,875	184,805	204,328	243,280	264,203
Ford GT	—	—	—	—	500	—	500	—
Ikon	—	—	11,081	13,191	—	—	11,081	13,191
Mustang	—	—	—	—	69,704	154,937	69,704	154,937
Taurus	—	—	—	—	254,842	294,326	254,842	294,326
Thunderbird	—	—	—	—	10,716	18,837	10,716	18,837
Ford Total	**82,826**	**82,541**	**69,556**	**85,472**	**563,349**	**672,428**	**715,731**	**840,441**
Lincoln LS	—	—	—	—	27,146	39,579	27,146	39,579
Town Car	—	—	—	—	53,958	54,458	53,958	54,458
Lincoln Total	**—**	**—**	**—**	**—**	**81,104**	**94,037**	**81,104**	**94,037**
Grand Marquis	85,619	89,932	—	—	—	—	85,619	89,932
Marauder	1,964	2,208	—	—	—	—	1,964	2,208
Montego	—	—	—	—	7,448	—	7,448	—
Sable	—	—	—	—	44,216	55,215	44,216	55,215
Mercury Total	**87,583**	**92,140**	**—**	**—**	**51,664**	**55,215**	**139,247**	**147,355**
FORD TOTAL	**170,409**	**174,681**	**69,556**	**85,472**	**696,117**	**821,680**	**936,082**	**1,081,833**
LaCrosse	32,277	—	—	—	—	—	32,277	—
LeSabre	—	—	—	—	103,311	131,962	103,311	131,962
Park Ave	—	—	—	—	12,601	26,616	12,601	26,616
Regal	73,094	127,154	—	—	—	—	73,094	127,154
Buick Total	**105,371**	**127,154**	**—**	**—**	**115,912**	**158,578**	**221,283**	**285,732**
CTS	—	—	—	—	71,518	59,250	71,518	59,250
Deville	—	—	—	—	63,459	82,965	63,459	82,965
Seville	—	—	—	—	5	15,619	5	15,619
STS	—	—	—	—	20,496	—	20,496	—
XLR	—	—	—	—	5,314	1,731	5,314	1,731
Cadillac Total	**—**	**—**	**—**	**—**	**160,792**	**159,565**	**160,792**	**159,565**
Cavalier	—	—	7,968	23,614	180,175	282,424	188,143	306,038
Cobalt	—	—	—	—	25,994	—	25,994	—
Corvette	—	—	—	—	28,723	36,026	28,723	36,026
Impala	296,594	300,121	—	—	—	—	296,594	300,121
Joy/Swing	—	—	60,600	43,594	—	—	60,600	43,594
Malibu	—	—	—	—	315,171	184,155	315,171	184,155
Monte Carlo	57,820	71,173	—	—	—	—	57,820	71,173
Monza	—	—	22,551	14,350	—	—	22,551	14,350
Chevrolet Total	**354,414**	**371,294**	**91,119**	**81,558**	**550,063**	**502,605**	**995,596**	**955,457**

North America Passenger Car Production by Model

NORTH AMERICA PASSENGER CAR PRODUCTION BY MODEL — continued

	Canada		Mexico		United States		N. America Total	
	2004	2003	2004	2003	2004	2003	2004	2003
Alero	—	—	—	—	18,906	111,680	18,906	111,680
Aurora	—	—	—	—	—	1,786	—	1,786
Oldsmobile Total	**—**	**—**	**—**	**—**	**18,906**	**113,466**	**18,906**	**113,466**
Bonneville	—	—	—	—	31,693	22,649	31,693	22,649
G6	—	—	—	—	42,186	—	42,186	—
Grand Am	—	—	—	—	116,877	174,324	116,877	174,324
Grand Prix	143,867	119,701	—	—	—	18,687	143,867	138,388
Pursuit	—	—	—	—	2,575	—	2,575	—
Sunfire	—	—	49,562	24,703	21,298	52,393	70,860	77,096
Pontiac Total	**143,867**	**119,701**	**49,562**	**24,703**	**214,629**	**268,053**	**408,058**	**412,457**
Ion	—	—	—	—	110,902	138,008	110,902	138,008
Saturn L	—	—	—	—	11,729	45,440	11,729	45,440
Saturn Total	**—**	**—**	**—**	**—**	**122,631**	**183,448**	**122,631**	**183,448**
GM TOTAL	**603,652**	**618,149**	**140,681**	**106,261**	**1,182,933**	**1,385,715**	**1,927,266**	**2,110,125**
Acura CL	—	—	—	—	—	4,201	—	4,201
Acura EL	3,719	5,620	—	—	—	—	3,719	5,620
Acura TL	—	—	—	—	82,635	60,397	82,635	60,397
Acura Total	**3,719**	**5,620**	**—**	**—**	**82,635**	**64,598**	**86,354**	**70,218**
Accord	—	—	21,824	21,624	350,337	380,946	372,161	402,570
Civic	190,795	187,167	—	—	133,995	147,564	324,790	334,731
Honda Total	**190,795**	**187,167**	**21,824**	**21,624**	**484,332**	**528,510**	**696,951**	**737,301**
HONDA TOTAL	**194,514**	**192,787**	**21,824**	**21,624**	**566,967**	**593,108**	**783,305**	**807,519**
Stratus Coupe	—	—	—	—	23,035	18,056	23,035	18,056
Dodge Total	**—**	**—**	**—**	**—**	**23,035**	**18,056**	**23,035**	**18,056**
Eclipse	—	—	—	—	11,210	39,287	11,210	39,287
Galant	—	—	—	—	45,188	59,572	45,188	59,572
Mitsubishi Total	**—**	**—**	**—**	**—**	**56,398**	**98,859**	**56,398**	**98,859**
Chrysler Sebring Coupe	—	—	—	—	12,103	9,332	12,103	9,332
MITSUBISHI TOTAL	**—**	**—**	**—**	**—**	**91,536**	**126,247**	**91,536**	**126,247**
Altima	—	—	—	—	279,642	240,666	279,642	240,666
Maxima	—	—	—	—	87,129	81,402	87,129	81,402
Platina	—	—	51,681	53,500	—	—	51,681	53,500
Sentra	—	—	151,391	142,450	—	—	151,391	142,450
Tsubame	—	—	—	472	—	—	—	472
Tsuru	—	—	73,938	63,384	—	—	73,938	63,384
Nissan Total	**—**	**—**	**277,010**	**259,806**	**366,771**	**322,068**	**643,781**	**581,874**
Renault Clio	—	—	10,420	13,324	—	—	10,420	13,324
NISSAN TOTAL	**—**	**—**	**287,430**	**273,130**	**366,771**	**322,068**	**654,201**	**595,198**
Corolla	—	—	—	—	167,970	157,561	167,970	157,561
Voltz	—	—	—	—	201	1,733	201	1,733
Toyota Total	**—**	**—**	**—**	**—**	**168,171**	**159,294**	**168,171**	**159,294**
Pontiac Vibe	—	—	—	—	69,226	74,223	69,226	74,223
NUMMI TOTAL	**—**	**—**	**—**	**—**	**237,397**	**233,517**	**237,397**	**233,517**
Subaru Legacy	—	—	—	—	98,298	89,243	98,298	89,243
SUBARU TOTAL	**—**	**—**	**—**	**—**	**98,298**	**89,243**	**98,298**	**89,243**
Avalon	—	—	—	—	33,074	49,250	33,074	49,250
Camry	—	—	—	—	388,119	356,829	388,119	356,829
Corolla	141,445	135,428	—	—	—	—	141,445	135,428
Matrix	81,064	78,781	—	—	—	—	81,064	78,781
Solara	—	—	—	—	49,247	29,774	49,247	29,774
TOYOTA TOTAL	**222,509**	**214,209**	**—**	**—**	**470,440**	**435,853**	**692,949**	**650,062**
Beetle	—	—	38,847	50,318	—	—	38,847	50,318
Beetle Cabrio	—	—	38,857	60,276	—	—	38,857	60,276
Bora	—	—	2,226	—	—	—	2,226	—
Jetta	—	—	145,412	169,109	—	—	145,412	169,109
Sedan	—	—	—	7,550	—	—	—	7,550
VOLKSWAGEN TOTAL	**—**	**—**	**225,342**	**287,253**	**—**	**—**	**225,342**	**287,253**
TOTAL CARS	**1,335,516**	**1,340,175**	**781,827**	**774,048**	**4,229,625**	**4,510,469**	**6,346,968**	**6,624,692**

SOURCE: Ward's AutoInfoBank.

North America Truck Production by Model

NORTH AMERICA TRUCK PRODUCTION BY MODEL

	Canada		Mexico		United States		North America	
	2004	2003	2004	2003	2004	2003	2004	2003
Hummer H1	—	—	—	—	237	395	237	395
Hummer H2	—	—	—	—	32,597	37,857	32,597	37,857
AM GENERAL TOTAL	**—**	**—**	**—**	**—**	**32,834**	**38,252**	**32,834**	**38,252**
Ford Medium Truck	—	—	12,724	8,511	—	—	12,724	8,511
BLUE DIAMOND TRUCK TOTAL	**—**	**—**	**12,724**	**8,511**	**—**	**—**	**12,724**	**8,511**
BMW X5	—	—	—	—	108,780	109,501	108,780	109,501
BMW TOTAL	**—**	**—**	**—**	**—**	**108,780**	**109,501**	**108,780**	**109,501**
Equinox	126,621	—	—	—	—	—	126,621	—
Tracker	4,543	41,978	—	—	—	—	4,543	41,978
Chevrolet Total	**131,164**	**41,978**	**—**	**—**	**—**	**—**	**131,164**	**41,978**
Suzuki Vitara	26	8,986	—	—	—	—	26	8,986
CAMI TOTAL	**131,190**	**50,964**	**—**	**—**	**—**	**—**	**131,190**	**50,964**
Pacifica	91,252	83,542	—	—	—	—	91,252	83,542
PT Cruiser	—	—	119,637	137,345	—	—	119,637	137,345
Town & Country	124,913	118,512	—	—	35,004	14,429	159,917	132,941
Voyager	—	—	—	—	—	12,867	—	12,867
Chrysler Total	**216,165**	**202,054**	**119,637**	**137,345**	**35,004**	**27,296**	**370,806**	**366,695**
Caravan	130,068	84,829	—	—	166,809	210,610	296,877	295,439
Dakota	—	—	—	—	129,112	122,772	129,112	122,772
Durango	—	—	—	—	160,703	113,787	160,703	113,787
Magnum	64,613	—	—	—	—	—	64,613	—
Ram Pickup	—	—	185,173	171,067	332,400	341,491	517,573	512,558
Ram Van	—	20,294	—	—	—	—	—	20,294
Dodge Total	**194,681**	**105,123**	**185,173**	**171,067**	**789,024**	**788,660**	**1,168,878**	**1,064,850**
Grand Cherokee	—	—	—	—	194,227	224,823	194,227	224,823
Liberty	—	—	—	—	224,067	237,712	224,067	237,712
Wrangler	—	—	—	—	75,787	84,486	75,787	84,486
Wrangler Unlimited	—	—	—	—	21,914	—	21,914	—
Jeep Total	**—**	**—**	**—**	**—**	**515,995**	**547,021**	**515,995**	**547,021**
CHRYSLER GROUP TOTAL	**410,846**	**307,177**	**304,810**	**308,412**	**1,340,023**	**1,362,977**	**2,055,679**	**1,978,566**
Econoline	—	—	—	—	201,319	178,308	201,319	178,308
Escape	—	—	—	—	223,425	216,437	223,425	216,437
Excursion	—	—	—	—	19,541	25,619	19,541	25,619
Expedition	—	—	—	—	172,008	201,510	172,008	201,510
Explorer	—	—	—	—	370,990	424,015	370,990	424,015
Ford Chassis	—	—	—	—	10,630	6,980	10,630	6,980
F-Series	56,285	112,796	23,903	50,664	952,288	810,777	1,032,476	974,237
Freestar	128,864	56,668	—	—	28,954	—	157,818	56,668
Ranger	—	—	—	—	151,308	224,233	151,308	224,233
Windstar	—	108,825	—	—	—	—	—	108,825
Ford Total	**185,149**	**278,289**	**23,903**	**50,664**	**2,130,463**	**2,087,879**	**2,339,515**	**2,416,832**
Aviator	—	—	—	—	26,953	34,412	26,953	34,412
Navigator	—	—	—	—	38,489	40,505	38,489	40,505
Lincoln Total	**—**	**—**	**—**	**—**	**65,442**	**74,917**	**65,442**	**74,917**
Mazda Pickup	—	—	—	—	8,486	23,413	8,486	23,413
Tribute	—	—	—	—	46,716	61,827	46,716	61,827
Mazda Total	**—**	**—**	**—**	**—**	**55,202**	**85,240**	**55,202**	**85,240**
Mariner	—	—	—	—	17,614	—	17,614	—
Monterey	16,683	8,459	—	—	—	—	16,683	8,459
Mountaineer	—	—	—	—	49,767	48,808	49,767	48,808
Mercury Total	**16,683**	**8,459**	**—**	**—**	**67,381**	**48,808**	**84,064**	**57,267**
FORD TOTAL	**201,832**	**286,748**	**23,903**	**50,664**	**2,318,488**	**2,296,844**	**2,544,223**	**2,634,256**
Rainier	—	—	—	—	21,834	17,031	21,834	17,031
Rendezvous	—	—	66,061	77,330	—	—	66,061	77,330
Terraza	—	—	—	—	4,918	—	4,918	—
Buick Total	**—**	**—**	**66,061**	**77,330**	**26,752**	**17,031**	**92,813**	**94,361**
Escalade	—	—	—	—	40,437	38,800	40,437	38,800
Escalade ESV	—	—	18,392	16,294	—	—	18,392	16,294
Escalade EXT	—	—	10,952	10,617	—	—	10,952	10,617
SRX	—	—	—	—	35,725	15,404	35,725	15,404
Cadillac Total	**—**	**—**	**29,344**	**26,911**	**76,162**	**54,204**	**105,506**	**81,115**
Astro Van	—	—	—	—	38,342	36,181	38,342	36,181
Avalanche	—	—	89,926	100,293	—	—	89,926	100,293
Colorado	—	—	—	—	170,625	18,180	170,625	18,180
Express	—	—	—	—	124,966	119,154	124,966	119,154
Kodiak	—	—	2,017	3,029	16,064	9,289	18,081	12,318
S Blazer	—	—	—	—	24,628	66,207	24,628	66,207
S10 Pickup	—	—	—	—	628	97,787	628	97,787
Silverado	226,467	235,326	17,955	9,874	530,182	564,282	774,604	809,482
SSR	—	—	—	—	16,344	3,522	16,344	3,522
Suburban	—	—	91,937	91,243	39,318	65,945	131,255	157,188
Tahoe	—	—	—	—	191,541	232,843	191,541	232,843
Tiltmaster	—	—	—	—	1,809	1,620	1,809	1,620
TrailBlazer	—	—	—	—	209,392	231,720	209,392	231,720
TrailBlazer EXT	—	—	—	—	76,424	76,243	76,424	76,243
Uplander	—	—	—	—	18,879	—	18,879	—
Venture	—	—	—	—	70,800	117,055	70,800	117,055
Chevrolet Total	**226,467**	**235,326**	**201,835**	**204,439**	**1,529,942**	**1,640,028**	**1,958,244**	**2,079,793**
Canyon	—	—	—	—	46,524	5,459	46,524	5,459

North America Truck Production by Model

NORTH AMERICA TRUCK PRODUCTION BY MODEL - continued

	Canada		Mexico		United States		N. America Total	
	2004	2003	2004	2003	2004	2003	2004	2003
Envoy	—	—	—	—	81,185	96,714	81,185	96,714
Envoy XL	—	—	—	—	41,171	50,114	41,171	50,114
Envoy XUV	—	—	—	—	12,390	13,873	12,390	13,873
Forward	—	—	—	—	448	402	448	402
S Jimmy	—	—	—	—	2,928	2,154	2,928	2,154
Safari Van	—	—	—	—	10,714	12,450	10,714	12,450
Savana	—	—	—	—	48,678	42,195	48,678	42,195
Sierra	93,743	86,569	—	—	176,516	169,938	270,259	256,507
Sonoma	—	—	—	—	172	29,629	172	29,629
Topkick	—	—	—	—	17,624	11,310	17,624	11,310
Yukon	—	—	—	—	98,166	105,062	98,166	105,062
Yukon XL	—	—	29,573	29,715	49,134	53,539	78,707	83,254
GMC Total	**93,743**	**86,569**	**29,573**	**29,715**	**585,650**	**592,839**	**708,966**	**709,123**
Ascender	—	—	—	—	7,939	4,025	7,939	4,025
Ascender EXT	—	—	—	—	3,794	—	3,794	—
Isuzu Total	**—**	**—**	**—**	**—**	**11,733**	**4,025**	**11,733**	**4,025**
Isuzu NPR	—	—	—	—	1,962	1,753	1,962	1,753
Isuzu Truck	—	—	—	—	657	307	657	307
Isuzu Truck Co. Total	**—**	**—**	**—**	**—**	**2,619**	**2,060**	**2,619**	**2,060**
Bravada	—	—	—	—	500	7,120	500	7,120
Silhouette	—	—	—	—	2,209	16,276	2,209	16,276
Oldsmobile Total	**—**	**—**	**—**	**—**	**2,709**	**23,396**	**2,709**	**23,396**
Aztek	—	—	18,517	26,963	—	—	18,517	26,963
Montana	—	—	—	—	45,530	71,592	45,530	71,592
Montana SV6	—	—	—	—	10,107	—	10,107	—
Pontiac Total	**—**	**—**	**18,517**	**26,963**	**55,637**	**71,592**	**74,154**	**98,555**
Relay	—	—	—	—	7,705	—	7,705	—
Vue	—	—	—	—	100,209	99,349	100,209	99,349
Saturn Total	**—**	**—**	**—**	**—**	**107,914**	**99,349**	**107,914**	**99,349**
GM TOTAL	**320,210**	**321,895**	**345,330**	**365,358**	**2,399,118**	**2,504,524**	**3,064,658**	**3,191,777**
Element	—	—	—	—	56,736	84,280	56,736	84,280
Odyssey	7,621	14,911	—	—	151,891	167,925	159,512	182,836
Pilot	122,864	116,968	—	—	27,809	—	150,673	116,968
Honda Total	**130,485**	**131,879**	**—**	**—**	**236,436**	**252,205**	**366,921**	**384,084**
Acura MDX	67,529	67,564	—	—	—	—	67,529	67,564
HONDA TOTAL	**198,014**	**199,443**	**—**	**—**	**236,436**	**252,205**	**434,450**	**451,648**
Mercedes M-Class	—	—	—	—	73,500	84,100	73,500	84,100
MERCEDES TOTAL	**—**	**—**	**—**	**—**	**73,500**	**84,100**	**73,500**	**84,100**
Endeavor	—	—	—	—	21,744	47,452	21,744	47,452
MITSUBISHI TOTAL	**—**	**—**	**—**	**—**	**21,744**	**47,452**	**21,744**	**47,452**
Armada	—	—	—	—	39,976	18,065	39,976	18,065
Frontier	—	—	—	—	83,531	62,111	83,531	62,111
Nissan Chassis	—	—	20,026	17,656	—	—	20,026	17,656
Nissan Pickup	—	—	16,476	14,440	—	—	16,476	14,440
Pathfinder	—	—	—	—	25,309	—	25,309	—
Quest	—	—	—	—	47,113	40,445	47,113	40,445
Titan	—	—	—	—	104,045	9,745	104,045	9,745
Xterra	—	—	—	—	71,687	69,837	71,687	69,837
Nissan Total	**—**	**—**	**36,502**	**32,096**	**371,661**	**200,203**	**408,163**	**232,299**
Infiniti QX56	—	—	—	—	16,328	—	16,328	—
Renault Scenic	—	—	622	2,090	—	—	622	2,090
NISSAN TOTAL	**—**	**—**	**37,124**	**34,186**	**387,989**	**200,203**	**425,113**	**234,389**
Toyota Tacoma	—	—	—	—	143,281	161,566	143,281	161,566
NUMMI TOTAL	**—**	**—**	**—**	**—**	**143,281**	**161,566**	**143,281**	**161,566**
Axiom	—	—	—	—	1,840	4,998	1,840	4,998
Rodeo	—	—	—	—	11,310	20,241	11,310	20,241
Isuzu Total	**—**	**—**	**—**	**—**	**13,150**	**25,239**	**13,150**	**25,239**
Subaru Baja	—	—	—	—	7,252	7,750	7,252	7,750
SUBARU TOTAL	**—**	**—**	**—**	**—**	**20,402**	**32,989**	**20,402**	**32,989**
Sequoia	—	—	—	—	62,040	66,668	62,040	66,668
Sienna	—	—	—	—	189,343	119,188	189,343	119,188
Tacoma	—	—	238	—	—	—	238	—
Tundra	—	—	—	—	122,634	105,660	122,634	105,660
Toyota Total	**—**	**—**	**238**	**—**	**374,017**	**291,516**	**374,255**	**291,516**
Hino Truck	—	—	—	—	671	—	671	—
Lexus RX330	65,350	13,334	—	—	—	—	65,350	13,334
TOYOTA TOTAL	**65,350**	**13,334**	**238**	**—**	**374,688**	**291,516**	**440,276**	**304,850**
Freightliner	20,224	16,120	18,327	12,316	99,550	74,457	138,101	102,893
International	18,007	8,092	14,719	10,594	66,672	47,809	99,398	66,495
Kenworth	10,347	8,914	9,546	7,363	26,132	16,944	46,025	33,221
Mercedes Benz	—	—	3,940	3,773	—	—	3,940	3,773
Peterbilt	—	—	—	—	29,365	18,632	29,365	18,632
Scania Heavy Truck	—	—	168	23	—	—	168	23
Volkswagen	—	—	65	—	—	—	65	—
Volvo Truck	—	—	253	199	50,937	35,783	51,190	35,982
Other	—	—	—	—	790	805	790	805
TOTAL TRUCKS	**1,376,020**	**1,212,687**	**771,147**	**801,399**	**7,730,729**	**7,576,559**	**9,877,896**	**9,590,645**

SOURCE: *Ward's AutoInfoBank.*

U.S. Factory Sales of Trucks and Buses by Gross Vehicle Weight Rating

U.S. FACTORY SALES OF TRUCKS AND BUSES BY GROSS VEHICLE WEIGHT RATING

| | Gross Vehicle Weight Rating (Pounds) | | | | | | | | |
	6,000 & Less	6,001- 10,000	10,001- 14,000	14,001- 16,000	16,001- 19,500	19,501- 26,000	26,001- 33,000	33,001 & Over	Total
U.S. TOTAL									
2004	4,176,947	2,767,305	136,229	36,203	26,058	67,252	61,918	194,827	7,466,739
2003	4,238,125	2,503,395	116,416	26,888	20,086	46,211	56,225	136,083	7,143,429
2002	4,279,792	2,274,661	121,867	29,277	15,913	40,507	62,070	139,633	6,963,720
2001	3,915,731	1,968,010	66,787	29,876	22,616	35,815	69,749	115,002	6,223,586
2000	4,533,600	1,973,801	100,293	48,572	25,137	36,874	106,750	197,451	7,022,478
1999	4,876,534	1,891,397	116,868	44,250	19,699	25,528	122,411	248,332	7,345,019
1998	4,458,970	1,431,110	147,839	33,513	17,441	19,850	116,412	210,050	6,435,185
1997	4,377,340	1,366,899	47,022	32,286	4,056	16,687	128,245	180,282	6,152,817
1996	4,073,778	1,344,826	38,525	32,912	4,127	12,379	106,657	162,526	5,775,730
1995	3,742,739	1,583,878	901	37,073	1,549	16,369	125,703	205,257	5,713,469
1994	3,811,837	1,478,854	848	29,585	550	13,559	115,334	189,708	5,640,275
1993	3,488,278	1,124,106	—	8,149	—	21,943	93,939	158,809	4,895,224
1992	2,978,214	850,876	—	7,193	2	21,993	81,601	122,123	4,062,002
1991	2,533,904	658,425	—	3,820	56	19,498	77,850	93,950	3,387,503
1990	2,574,071	906,423	—	789	1,726	38,123	87,107	116,966	3,725,205
1989	2,657,084	1,130,606	11	146	4,593	37,788	90,440	141,282	4,061,950
1988	2,704,891	1,105,069	—	182	5,618	55,840	97,771	151,203	4,120,574
1987	2,475,402	1,052,958	—	366	6,085	46,473	103,188	136,938	3,821,410
1986	2,238,922	997,272	—	—	5,931	45,333	96,998	116,477	3,500,933
1985	2,095,856	1,057,556	19,463	—	5,345	53,471	98,406	134,230	3,464,327
1984	1,807,811	1,061,974	1,631	4	5,713	60,457	87,396	150,849	3,175,835
U.S DOMESTIC									
2004	3,795,422	2,530,711	131,889	33,870	23,702	65,869	56,579	164,711	6,802,753
2003	3,818,750	2,300,058	112,745	24,960	18,304	45,515	50,927	114,990	6,486,249
2002	3,827,782	2,073,553	117,927	26,986	14,279	39,607	56,691	120,409	6,277,234
2001	3,511,326	1,794,251	61,168	27,038	20,216	34,905	64,454	99,422	5,612,780
2000	4,070,026	1,757,683	97,697	35,407	22,602	35,752	100,175	171,565	6,290,907
1999	4,453,332	1,723,012	112,349	37,328	17,542	24,362	113,147	218,041	6,699,113
1998	4,053,521	1,303,786	141,781	29,629	15,779	18,989	105,874	177,852	5,847,211
1997	3,894,222	1,236,119	44,893	28,428	3,931	15,609	116,922	149,183	5,489,307
1996	3,699,385	1,225,792	37,559	30,309	4,056	11,717	97,720	141,941	5,248,479
1995	3,405,062	1,458,713	780	35,427	1,471	15,046	114,194	180,652	5,211,345
1994	3,475,044	1,353,576	848	28,437	533	12,123	102,745	165,375	5,138,681
1993	3,187,731	1,031,829	—	7,630	—	19,277	84,779	140,247	4,471,493
1992	2,711,172	785,198	—	6,612	2	19,160	71,899	108,003	3,702,046
1991	2,281,761	594,435	—	3,547	28	16,536	69,703	83,875	3,049,885
1990	2,383,892	848,690	—	693	1,644	34,141	78,553	107,025	3,454,638
1989	2,447,962	1,057,077	11	54	4,234	32,721	81,971	127,880	3,751,910
1988	2,496,648	1,020,515	—	86	5,238	49,670	87,994	135,163	3,795,314
1987	2,270,950	976,573	—	322	5,841	40,502	93,044	121,859	3,509,091
1986	2,072,880	927,462	—	—	5,749	40,353	87,831	103,990	3,238,265
1985	1,962,323	989,633	19,397	—	5,123	46,340	88,784	121,996	3,233,596
1984	1,711,345	997,626	—	4	5,502	52,053	78,977	139,135	2,984,642

SOURCE: *Ward's Database Opers.*

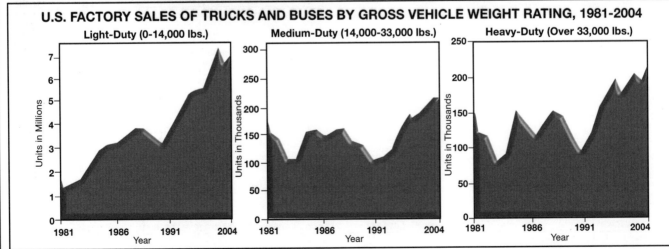

U.S. FACTORY SALES OF TRUCKS AND BUSES BY GROSS VEHICLE WEIGHT RATING, 1981-2004

Light-Duty (0-14,000 lbs.)

Medium-Duty (14,000-33,000 lbs.)

Heavy-Duty (Over 33,000 lbs.)

U.S. Factory Sales of Diesel Trucks and Motor Vehicle Factory Sales from U.S. and Canadian Plants

U.S. FACTORY SALES OF DIESEL TRUCKS BY GROSS VEHICLE WEIGHT RATING

	Gross Vehicle Weight Rating (Pounds)								
	6,000 & Less	6,001- 10,000	10,001- 14,000	14,001- 16,000	16,001- 19,500	19,501- 26,000	26,001- 33,000	33,001 & Over	Total
U.S. TOTAL									
2004	2,241	253,504	93,426	25,546	23,901	50,985	33,201	194,827	677,631
2003	2,445	256,122	79,054	19,865	18,518	35,633	26,393	136,083	574,113
2002	3,010	229,638	81,488	19,795	14,788	26,846	33,515	139,572	548,652
2001	1,935	244,805	41,958	27,188	20,434	24,932	41,201	114,657	517,110
2000	2,580	279,224	50,571	30,223	23,422	19,807	72,509	197,451	675,787
1995	5,995	225,968	150	25,241	1,346	11,403	93,237	205,254	568,594
1990	449	102,051	—	81	51	12,567	61,010	116,931	293,140
1985	15,447	132,871	5,870	—	—	16,537	57,238	132,429	360,392
1980	72,501	4,973	—	—	—	15,268	34,544	116,860	244,146
1975	—	1	—	—	159	5,651	11,819	84,878	102,508
1970	8	417	—	168	26	7,875	11,932	85,288	105,714
U.S DOMESTIC									
2004	231	212,652	90,331	23,305	21,660	49,803	29,287	164,711	591,980
2003	255	213,969	76,437	18,040	16,771	35,003	23,477	114,990	498,942
2002	241	190,754	78,721	17,778	13,170	26,014	30,057	120,348	477,083
2001	193	200,292	37,880	24,508	18,102	24,101	37,340	99,086	441,502
2000	271	221,830	48,911	26,997	20,921	18,812	68,678	171,565	577,985
1995	4,579	191,758	92	23,913	1,272	10,597	84,213	180,652	497,076
1990	337	94,030	—	55	51	11,458	53,957	107,002	266,890
1985	9,663	123,882	5,870	—	—	14,253	50,492	120,311	324,471
1980	68,868	4,397	—	—	—	12,337	30,958	98,002	214,562
1975	—	1	—	—	159	3,517	8,992	59,936	72,605
1970	—	268	—	165	—	3,158	10,245	77,965	91,801

*Reporting firms do not represent the entire industry.
SOURCE: Ward's Communications.

MOTOR VEHICLE FACTORY SALES FROM U.S. AND CANADIAN PLANTS

	U.S. Plants				Canadian Plants*			
	U.S Total	Exports to Canada	Other Exports	U.S. Domestic	Canada Total	Exports to U.S.	Other Exports	Canada Domestic
PASSENGER CARS								
2004	4,229,625	N.A.	N.A.	N.A.	1,335,516	N.A.	N.A.	N.A.
2003	4,510,469	N.A.	N.A.	N.A.	1,340,175	N.A.	N.A.	N.A.
2002	5,018,777	N.A.	N.A.	N.A.	1,369,042	N.A.	N.A.	N.A.
2001	4,884,313	258,724	195,585	4,430,004	901,075	833,109	6,851	61,115
2000	5,504,385	285,348	236,589	4,982,448	1,151,889	1,063,547	12,617	75,725
1995	6,309,839	265,594	256,422	5,787,820	1,028,970	912,939	22,128	93,903
1990	6,049,749	416,459	131,419	5,501,871	901,903	795,621	3,725	102,557
1985	8,002,259	635,546	29,978	7,336,735	1,068,420	878,052	5,878	184,490
1980	6,400,026	488,857	70,864	5,840,305	827,124	539,239	86,297	201,588
1975	6,712,852	549,353	90,199	6,073,300	1,043,245	713,407	58,149	271,689
1970	6,546,817	245,746	113,753	6,187,318	919,232	681,872	30,427	206,933
TRUCKS AND BUSES								
2004	7,466,739	419,384	244,602	6,802,753	923,873	837,521	8,542	77,810
2003	7,143,429	411,539	245,641	6,486,249	917,240	806,830	8,648	101,762
2002	6,963,720	446,775	239,711	6,277,234	1,003,861	845,602	8,187	150,072
2001	6,223,586	384,775	226,031	5,612,780	982,983	851,884	5,868	125,231
2000	7,022,478	410,698	320,873	6,290,907	1,161,653	954,641	8,899	198,114
1995	5,713,469	318,470	183,654	5,211,345	1,004,717	871,134	5,180	128,403
1990	3,725,205	207,559	63,008	3,454,638	8,124,697	660,176	26,441	125,850
1985	3,464,327	197,903	32,828	3,233,596	853,974	677,998	7,706	168,270
1980	1,667,283	86,420	117,055	1,463,808	525,968	290,529	47,228	188,211
1975	2,272,160	133,701	135,701	2,002,758	390,065	181,165	47,742	161,158
1970	1,692,440	53,646	73,125	1,565,669	252,079	157,532	32,429	962,118

N.A.-Not available.
*Reporting firms do not represent the entire industry.
SOURCE: Ward's Communications.

Passenger Car Production by City and State

PASSENGER CAR PRODUCTION BY CITY AND STATE, 2004

State/City	Model	Units	Percent	State/City	Model	Units	Percent
CALIFORNIA		**237,397**	**5.6**	Wayne	Ford Focus	184,805	4.4
Fremont	Pontiac Vibe	69,226	1.6	Wixom	Ford GT	500	—
	Toyota Corolla	167,970	4.0		Ford Thunderbird	10,716	0.3
	Toyota Voltz	201	—		Lincoln LS	27,146	0.6
	Total NUMMI	**237,397**	**5.6**		Lincoln Town Car	53,958	1.3
					Total Ford	**346,829**	**8.2**
DELAWARE		**11,729**	**0.3**	Hamtramck	Buick LeSabre	83,228	2.0
Wilmington	Saturn L-Series	11,729	0.3		Cadillac DeVille	63,459	1.5
	Total General Motors	**11,729**	**0.3**		Cadillac Seville	5	—
					Pontiac Bonneville	31,693	0.7
GEORGIA		**235,542**	**5.6**	Lansing	Chevrolet Malibu	88,107	2.1
Atlanta	Ford Taurus	197,842	4.7		Oldsmobile Alero	18,906	0.4
	Mercury Sable	37,700	0.9		Pontiac Grand Am	116,877	2.8
	Total Ford	**235,542**	**5.6**	Lansing (Craft Center)	Cadillac CTS	71,518	1.7
					Cadillac STS	20,496	0.5
ILLINOIS		**346,130**	**8.2**	Orion	Buick LeSabre	20,083	0.5
Belvidere	Chrysler Neon	1,844	—		Buick Park Ave	12,601	0.3
	Dodge Neon	139,004	3.3		Pontiac G6	42,186	1.0
	Total Chrysler Group	**140,848**	**3.3**		**Total General Motors**	**569,159**	**13.5**
Chicago	Ford Five Hundred	42,782	1.0				
	Ford Taurus	57,000	1.3	**MISSISSIPPI**		**59,892**	**1.4**
	Mercury Montego	7,448	0.2	Canton	Nissan Altima	59,892	1.4
	Mercury Sable	6,516	0.2		**Total Nissan**	**59,892**	**1.4**
	Total Ford	**113,746**	**2.7**				
Normal	Chrysler Sebring Coupe	12,103	0.3	**OHIO**		**797,009**	**18.8**
	Dodge Stratus Coupe	23,035	0.5	Lordstown	Chevrolet Cavalier	180,175	4.3
	Mitsubishi Eclipse	11,210	0.3		Chevrolet Cobalt	25,994	0.6
	Mitsubishi Galant	45,188	1.1		Pontiac Pursuit	2,575	0.1
	Total Mitsubishi	**91,536**	**2.2**		Pontiac Sunfire	21,298	0.5
					Total General Motors	**230,042**	**5.4**
INDIANA		**98,298**	**2.3**	East Liberty	Honda Civic	133,995	3.2
Lafayette	Subaru Legacy	98,298	2.3	Marysville	Acura TL	82,635	2.0
	Total Subaru	**98,298**	**2.3**		Honda Accord	350,337	8.3
					Total Honda	**566,967**	**13.4**
KANSAS		**227,064**	**5.4**				
Fairfax	Chevrolet Malibu	227,064	5.4	**SOUTH CAROLINA**		**35,136**	**0.8**
	Total General Motors	**227,064**	**5.4**	Spartanburg	BMW Z4	35,136	0.8
					Total BMW	**35,136**	**0.8**
KENTUCKY		**504,477**	**11.9**				
Bowling Green	Cadillac XLR	5,314	0.1	**TENNESSEE**		**417,781**	**9.9**
	Chevrolet Corvette	28,723	0.7	Spring Hill	Saturn Ion	110,902	2.6
	Total General Motors	**34,037**	**0.8**		**Total General Motors**	**110,902**	**2.6**
Georgetown	Toyota Avalon	33,074	0.8	Smyrna	Nissan Altima	219,750	5.2
	Toyota Camry	388,119	9.2		Nissan Maxima	87,129	2.1
	Toyota Solara	49,247	1.2		**Total Nissan Motor Mfg.**	**306,879**	**7.3**
	Total Toyota	**470,440**	**11.1**				
				TOTAL CARS		**4,229,625**	**100.0**
MICHIGAN		**1,259,170**	**29.8**				
Flat Rock	Ford Mustang	41,925	1.0				
	Mazda6	91,339	2.2				
	Total AutoAlliance	**133,264**	**3.2**				
Detroit	Dodge Viper	2,469	0.1				
Sterling Heights	Chrysler Sebring Convertible	39,388	0.9				
	Chrysler Sebring Sedan	77,269	1.8				
	Dodge Stratus Sedan	90,792	2.1				
	Total Chrysler Group	**209,918**	**5.0**				
Dearborn	Ford Mustang	69,704	1.6				

TOP STATES IN CALENDAR 2004 U.S. PRODUCTION

Rank	Cars	Rank	Trucks
1. Michigan	1,259,170	1. Michigan	1,339,218
2. Ohio	797,009	2. Missouri	1,226,300
3. Kentucky	504,477	3. Ohio	943,622
4. Tennessee	417,781	4. Indiana	674,294
5. Illinois	346,130	5. Kentucky	658,352

SOURCE: Ward's AutoInfoBank.

Truck Production by City and State

TRUCK PRODUCTION BY CITY AND STATE, 2004

State/City	Model	Units	Percent
ALABAMA		**253,200**	**3.3**
Lincoln	Honda Odyssey	151,891	2.0
	Honda Pilot	27,809	0.4
	Total Honda	**179,700**	**2.3**
Vance	Mercedes M-Class	73,500	1.0
	Total Mercedes	**73,500**	**1.0**
CALIFORNIA		**143,952**	**1.9**
Fremont	Toyota Tacoma	143,281	1.9
	Total NUMMI	**143,281**	**1.9**
Long Beach	Hino Truck	671	—
	Total Toyota	**671**	—
DELAWARE		**160,703**	**2.1**
Newark	Dodge Durango	160,703	2.1
	Total Chrysler Group	**160,703**	**2.1**
GEORGIA		**160,148**	**2.1**
Doraville	Buick Terraza	4,918	0.1
	Chevrolet Uplander	18,879	0.2
	Chevrolet Venture	70,800	0.9
	Oldmobile Silhouette	2,209	—
	Pontiac Montana	45,530	0.6
	Pontiac Montana SV6	10,107	0.1
	Saturn Relay	7,705	0.1
	Total General Motors	**160,148**	**2.1**
ILLINOIS		**50,698**	**0.7**
Chicago	Ford Freestyle	28,954	0.4
	Total Ford	**28,954**	**0.4**
Normal	Mitsubishi Endeavor	21,744	0.3
	Total Mitsubishi	**21,744**	**0.3**
INDIANA		**674,294**	**8.7**
Mishawaka	Hummer H1	237	—
	Hummer H2	32,597	0.4
	Total AM General	**32,834**	**0.4**
Fort Wayne	Chevrolet Silverado	193,228	2.5
	GMC Sierra	53,813	0.7
	Total General Motors	**247,041**	**3.2**
Lafayette	Isuzu Axiom	1,840	—
	Isuzu Rodeo	11,310	0.1
	Subaru Baja	7,252	0.1
	Total Subaru	**20,402**	**0.3**
Princeton	Toyota Sequoia	62,040	0.8
	Toyota Sienna	189,343	2.4
	Toyota Tundra	122,634	1.6
	Total Toyota	**374,017**	**4.8**
KENTUCKY		**658,352**	**8.5**
Kentucky Truck	Ford Excursion	19,541	0.3
	Ford F-SuperDuty	375,627	4.9
Louisville	Ford Explorer	237,360	3.1
	Mercury Mountaineer	25,824	0.3
	Total Ford	**658,352**	**8.5**
LOUISIANA		**217,149**	**2.8**
Shreveport	Chevrolet Colorado	170,625	2.2
	GMC Canyon	46,524	0.6
	Total General Motors	**217,149**	**2.8**
MARYLAND		**49,056**	**0.6**
Baltimore	Chevrolet Astro	38,342	0.5
	GMC Safari	10,714	0.1
	Total General Motors	**49,056**	**0.6**
MICHIGAN		**1,339,218**	**17.3**
Detroit	Jeep Grand Cherokee	194,227	2.5
Warren	Dodge Dakota	129,112	1.7
	Dodge Ram Pickup	159,131	2.1
	Total Chrysler Group	**482,470**	**6.2**
Dearborn Truck	Ford F-Series	89,550	1.2
Detroit	Ford Chassis	10,630	0.1
Wayne	Ford Expedition	172,008	2.2
	Lincoln Navigator	38,489	0.5
	Total Ford	**310,677**	**4.0**
Flint No.1	Chevrolet Silverado	123,631	1.6
	GMC Sierra	47,439	0.6
Flint No.3	Chevrolet Kodiak	16,064	0.2
	GMC Topkick	17,624	0.2
	Isuzu Truck	657	—
Lansing (Craft Center)	Chevrolet SSR	16,344	0.2
Lansing (Grand River)	Cadillac SRX	35,725	0.5
Pontiac East	Chevrolet Silverado	213,323	2.8
	GMC Sierra	75,264	1.0
	Total General Motors	**546,071**	**7.1**
MINNESOTA		**148,993**	**1.9**
Twin Cities	Ford Ranger	144,906	1.9
	Mazda Pickup	4,087	0.1
	Total Ford	**148,993**	**1.9**
MISSISSIPPI		**207,462**	**2.7**
Canton	Infiniti QX56	16,328	0.2
	Nissan Armada	39,976	0.5
	Nissan Quest	47,113	0.6
	Nissan Titan	104,045	1.3
	Total Nissan	**207,462**	**2.7**
MISSOURI		**1,226,300**	**15.9**
St. Louis North	Dodge Ram Pickup	173,269	2.2
St. Louis South	Chrysler Town & Country	35,004	0.5
	Dodge Caravan	166,809	2.2
	Total Chrysler Group	**375,082**	**4.9**
Kansas City 1	Ford Escape	198,090	2.6
	Mazda Tribute	46,716	0.6
Kansas City 2	Ford F-Series	248,242	3.2
St. Louis	Ford Explorer	133,630	1.7
	Lincoln Aviator	26,953	0.3
	Mercury Mountaineer	23,943	0.3
	Total Ford	**677,574**	**8.8**
Wentzville	Chevrolet Express	124,966	1.6
	GMC Savana	48,678	0.6
	Total General Motors	**173,644**	**2.2**
NEW JERSEY		**39,157**	**0.5**
Edison	Ford Ranger	6,402	0.1
	Mazda Pickup	4,399	0.1
	Total Ford	**10,801**	**0.1**
Linden	Chevrolet Blazer	24,628	0.3
	Chevrolet S10	628	—
	GMC Jimmy	2,928	—
	GMC Sonoma	172	—
	Total General Motors	**28,356**	**0.4**
OHIO		**943,622**	**12.2**
Toledo	Jeep Wrangler	75,787	1.0
	Jeep Wrangler Unlimited	21,914	0.3
Toledo North	Jeep Liberty	224,067	2.9
	Total Chrysler Group	**321,768**	**4.2**
Avon Lake	Ford Escape	25,335	0.3
	Mercury Mariner	17,614	0.2
Lorain	Ford Econoline	201,319	2.6
	Total Ford	**244,268**	**3.2**
Moraine	Buick Rainier	21,834	0.3
	Chevrolet TrailBlazer	209,392	2.7
	GMC Envoy	81,185	1.1
	Isuzu Ascender	7,939	0.1
	Oldsmobile Bravada	500	—
	Total General Motors	**320,850**	**4.2**
East Liberty	Honda Element	56,736	0.7
	Total Honda	**56,736**	**0.7**
OKLAHOMA		**133,779**	**1.7**
Oklahoma City	Chevrolet TrailBlazer EXT	76,424	1.0
	GMC Envoy XL	41,171	0.5
	GMC Envoy XUV	12,390	0.2
	Isuzu Ascender EXT	3,794	—
	Total General Motors	**133,779**	**1.7**
SOUTH CAROLINA		**108,780**	**1.4**
Spartanburg	BMW X5	108,780	1.4
	Total BMW	**108,780**	**1.4**
TENNESSEE		**280,736**	**3.6**
Spring Hill	Saturn Vue	100,209	1.3
	Total General Motors	**100,209**	**1.3**
Smyrna	Nissan Frontier	83,531	1.1
	Nissan Pathfinder	25,309	0.3
	Nissan Xterra	71,687	0.9
	Total Nissan	**180,527**	**2.3**
TEXAS		**202,841**	**2.6**
Arlington	Cadillac Escalade	40,437	0.5
	Chevrolet Suburban	3,726	—
	Chevrolet Tahoe	119,195	1.5
	GMC Yukon	35,799	0.5
	GMC Yukon XL	3,684	—
	Total General Motors	**202,841**	**2.6**
VIRGINIA		**238,869**	**3.1**
Norfolk	Ford F-Series	238,869	3.1
	Total Ford	**238,869**	**3.1**
WISCONSIN		**219,974**	**2.8**
Janesville	Chevrolet Suburban	35,592	0.5
	Chevrolet Tahoe	72,346	0.9
	Chevrolet W4 Tiltmaster	1,809	—
	GMC W4 Forward	448	—
	GMC Yukon	62,367	0.8
	GMC Yukon XL	45,450	0.6
	Isuzu W4 NPR	1,962	—
	Total General Motors	**219,974**	**2.8**
	Other Medium/Heavy Trucks	**273,446**	**3.5**
TOTAL TRUCKS		**7,730,729**	**100.0**

SOURCE: *Ward's AutoInfoBank.*

Factory Installations of Selected Passenger Car and Light Truck Equipment

FACTORY INSTALLATIONS OF SELECTED EQUIPMENT BY MODEL YEAR

	2004		2003		2002		2001	
	Units (000)	% of Total	Units (000)	% of Total	Units (000)	% of Total	Units (000)	% of Total
PASSENGER CARS								
Automatic Transmission	5,100	91.5	5,790	91.7	5,416	91.7	5,778	90.8
5-Speed Transmission	385	6.9	436	6.9	439	7.4	558	8.8
6-Speed Transmission	76	1.4	93	1.5	50	0.8	28	0.4
Four-Wheel Drive	79	1.4	119	1.9	95	1.6	99	1.5
4-Cylinder Engine	2,791	50.1	3,107	49.1	2,893	49.0	3,103	48.8
6-Cylinder Engine	2,366	42.4	2,704	42.8	2,532	43.0	2,689	42.3
8-Cylinder Engine	415	7.5	507	8.1	479	8.1	570	8.9
Traction Control	1,458	26.2	1,532	24.2	1,950	33.0	2,120	33.3
Anti-Lock Brakes	3,207	57.5	3,395	53.7	3,678	62.3	3,917	61.6
Power Door Locks	5,212	93.5	5,753	91.0	5,353	90.7	5,584	87.8
Power Seats, 4 or 6 way	2,515	45.1	2,673	42.3	2,739	46.4	3,044	47.8
Memory Seats	565	10.1	475	7.5	464	7.9	496	7.8
Power Windows	5,182	93.0	5,523	87.4	5,167	87.5	5,376	84.5
Sun Roof	1,400	25.1	1,568	24.8	1,639	27.8	1,496	23.5
Side Air Bags	1,545	27.7	1,291	20.4	1,585	26.8	1,421	22.3
Navigation System	88	1.6	45	0.7	11	0.2	—	—
Keyless Remote	4,762	85.4	5,158	81.6	4,339	73.5	4,355	68.4
Air Conditioning, Automatic Temp. Control	1,464	26.3	1,401	22.2	1,200	20.3	1,092	17.2
Air Conditioning, Manual Temp. Control	4,107	73.7	4,889	77.4	4,639	78.6	5,208	81.8
Limited Slip Differential	166	3.0	227	3.6	224	3.8	234	3.7
Styled Wheels	3,425	61.5	3,753	59.4	3,449	58.4	3,502	55.1
Adjustable Steering Column	5,474	98.2	5,941	94.0	5,609	95.0	5,951	93.5
Rear Window Defogger	5,574	100.0	6,244	98.8	5,800	98.2	5,995	94.2
Cruise Control	5,004	89.8	5,439	86.1	5,105	86.5	5,327	83.7
Anti-Theft Device	2,425	43.5	2,768	43.8	3,054	51.7	2,635	41.4
LIGHT TRUCKS (0-10,000 lbs. G.V.W.R.)								
Automatic Transmission	8,002	95.6	8,119	95.2	7,701	94.5	6,428	92.5
Four Wheel Anti-Lock Brakes	7,443	88.9	7,524	88.1	6,781	83.2	5,724	82.3
Rear Anti-Lock Brakes	414	4.9	420	4.9	569	7.0	579	8.3
Keyless Entry	6,722	80.3	6,328	74.1	5,528	67.9	4,977	71.6
Anti-Theft Device	5,694	68.0	5,273	61.8	4,660	57.2	2,546	36.6
Side Air Bag	2,254	26.9	1,868	21.9	1,551	19.0	681	9.8
Four-Wheel Drive	4,127	49.3	4,026	47.1	3,723	45.7	2,935	42.2
Diesel Engine	514	6.2	428	5.0	398	4.9	370	5.3
4-Cylinder Gasoline Engine	374	4.5	548	6.4	519	6.4	503	7.2
5-Cylinder Gasoline Engine	96	1.1	—	—	—	—	—	—
6-Cylinder Gasoline Engine	3,644	43.6	3,941	46.2	4,073	50.0	3,301	47.5
8-Cylinder Gasoline Engine	3,680	43.9	3,546	41.5	3,083	37.9	2,679	38.5
10-Cylinder Gasoline Engine	64	0.7	75	0.9	73	0.9	100	1.4
Air Conditioning	8,344	99.7	8,470	99.2	8,036	98.7	6,889	99.1
Cruise Control	7,466	89.2	7,455	87.3	6,954	85.4	5,993	86.2
Limited Slip Differential	2,857	34.1	3,130	36.7	2,773	34.0	2,233	32.1

*Based on production in the United States, Canada and Mexico for the United States market.
SOURCE: Ward's Database Opers.

Recreational Vehicle Shipments

U.S. RECREATIONAL VEHICLE SHIPMENTS BY TYPE

| Year | Total All Types | Travel Trailers | | Folding Camping Trailers | Truck Campers | Motor Homes | | | Multi-use Van Con-versions |
		Conven-tional	Fifth Wheel[1]			Type A Conven-tional	Type B Van Campers[2]	Type C Chopped Vans[3]	
2004	412,100	163,600	91,000	34,100	9,600	46,300	2,500	23,000	42,000
2003	377,800	139,800	74,600	35,700	8,800	41,500	2,100	18,300	57,000
2002	378,700	129,700	66,100	44,800	10,000	39,600	2,800	18,000	67,700
2001	321,000	102,200	54,700	40,800	9,900	33,400	2,600	13,200	64,200
2000	418,300	114,500	62,300	51,300	11,100	41,000	3,400	16,500	118,200
1999	481,200	117,500	60,500	60,100	11,500	49,400	3,600	18,600	152,600
1998	441,300	98,600	56,500	63,300	10,800	42,900	3,600	17,000	148,600
1997	438,800	78,800	52,800	57,600	10,300	37,600	3,800	13,600	184,300
1996	466,800	75,400	48,500	57,300	11,000	36,500	4,100	14,700	219,300
1995	475,200	75,300	45,900	61,100	11,900	33,000	4,100	15,700	228,200
1994	518,800	79,100	48,900	61,700	11,400	37,300	3,500	17,300	259,600
1993	420,200	69,700	43,900	51,900	10,900	31,900	3,000	16,500	192,400
1992	382,700	63,600	38,900	43,300	10,600	27,300	2,900	16,800	179,300
1991	293,700	49,300	28,300	33,900	9,600	23,500	3,500	15,200	130,400
1990	347,300	52,500	27,900	30,700	9,700	29,000	5,900	17,400	174,200
1989	388,300	53,500	29,400	33,900	9,900	35,400	5,000	20,800	200,400
1988	420,000	58,300	31,300	42,300	11,000	41,500	5,200	26,200	204,200
1987	393,600	59,100	27,100	41,600	10,100	40,800	6,600	26,400	181,900
1986	371,700	55,100	23,100	36,500	7,400	33,300	6,200	28,200	181,900
1985	351,700	54,700	20,700	35,900	6,900	33,600	6,700	28,400	164,800
1984	391,000	65,600	19,600	40,900	7,600	42,100	7,100	32,800	175,300
1983	350,800	64,700	18,100	37,500	6,800	34,400	5,600	30,500	154,200
1982	251,900	47,700	11,700	34,300	5,700	19,300	3,900	18,000	111,300
1981	233,400	48,500	9,600	35,000	5,100	14,300	3,800	17,300	99,800
1980	178,500	42,700	6,300	24,500	5,000	9,800	2,400	16,400	71,400

(1) To be towed by pickup truck with fifth-wheel hitch mounted on the truck bed.
(2) Panel-type trucks with interior converted to living area.
(3) Chopped Vans: (Mini) — unit over 8' high attaches to van chassis of 6,500 lbs. GVWR or more; (Low Profile) — unit less than 8' high attaches to van chassis of 6,500 lbs. GVWR or more: (Compact) — unit attaches to van chassis less than 6,500 lbs. GVWR.
SOURCE: Recreation Vehicle Industry Association.

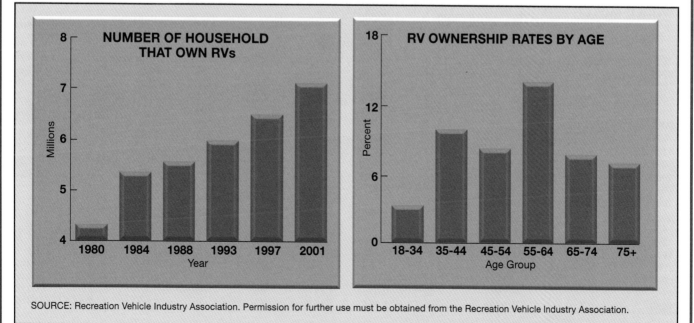

SOURCE: Recreation Vehicle Industry Association. Permission for further use must be obtained from the Recreation Vehicle Industry Association.

World Motor Vehicle Production by Country

WORLD MOTOR VEHICLE PRODUCTION BY COUNTRY, 2004

Region/Country	Cars	Commercial Vehicles	Total
North America			
Canada	1,335,516	1,376,020	2,711,536
Mexico	781,827	771,147	1,552,974
United States	4,229,625	7,730,729	11,960,354
Total	**6,346,968**	**9,877,896**	**16,224,864**
Western Europe			
Austria	227,244	21,474	248,718
Belgium	852,441	42,908	895,349
Finland	10,051	450	10,501
France	2,913,133	438,574	3,351,707
Germany	5,192,101	377,853	5,569,954
Italy	833,578	308,366	1,141,944
Netherlands	187,600	59,903	247,503
Portugal	150,781	75,947	226,728
Spain	2,402,501	609,673	3,012,174
Sweden	290,383	48,373	338,756
Turkey	447,152	376,256	823,408
United Kingdom	1,646,881	209,168	1,856,049
Total	**15,153,846**	**2,568,945**	**17,722,791**
Eastern/Central Europe			
Czech Republic	443,065	5,295	448,360
Hungary	118,590	4,076	122,666
Poland	515,779	75,740	591,519
Russia	1,109,958	275,476	1,385,434
Other	523,033	75,568	598,601
Total	**2,710,425**	**436,155**	**3,146,580**
Asia-Pacific			
Australia	340,954	64,360	405,314
China	2,316,262	2,754,265	5,070,527
India	940,068	571,103	1,511,171
Japan	8,720,385	1,791,133	10,511,518
South Africa	200,264	127,488	327,752
South Korea	2,053,668	1,415,796	3,469,464
Taiwan	299,639	131,175	430,814
Other	1,757,642	838,630	2,596,272
Total	**16,628,882**	**7,693,950**	**24,322,832**
South America			
Argentina	171,398	89,022	260,420
Brazil	1,756,166	453,896	2,210,062
Other	64,219	11,500	75,719
Total	**1,991,783**	**554,418**	**2,546,201**
TOTAL	**42,831,904**	**21,131,364**	**63,963,268**

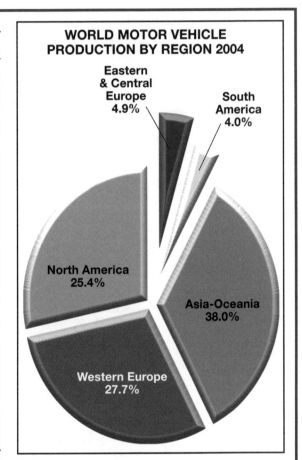

WORLD MOTOR VEHICLE PRODUCTION BY REGION 2004

- Eastern & Central Europe 4.9%
- South America 4.0%
- North America 25.4%
- Asia-Oceania 38.0%
- Western Europe 27.7%

WORLD MOTOR VEHICLE PRODUCTION (In Thousands)

Year	United States	Canada	U.S. & Canada Total	Western Europe	Japan	Other	World Total	Percent of World Total United States	U.S. & Canada
2004	11,960	2,712	14,672	17,723	10,512	21,056	63,963	18.7	22.9
2003	12,087	2,553	14,640	17,703	10,286	17,702	60,331	20.0	24.3
2002	12,280	2,629	14,909	17,295	10,258	16,511	58,973	20.8	25.3
2001	11,425	2,532	13,957	17,840	9,777	14,494	56,068	20.4	24.9
2000	12,771	2,962	15,732	17,161	10,145	14,490	57,528	22.2	27.3
1999	13,025	3,057	16,082	19,158	9,905	9,803	54,948	23.7	29.3
1998	12,006	2,173	14,179	18,137	10,050	9,732	52,098	23.0	27.2
1997	12,119	2,571	14,690	17,773	10,975	10,024	53,463	22.7	27.5
1996	11,799	2,397	14,196	17,550	10,346	9,241	51,332	23.0	27.7
1995	11,985	2,408	14,393	17,045	10,196	8,349	49,983	24.0	28.8
1990	9,783	1,928	11,711	18,866	13,487	4,496	48,554	20.1	24.1
1985	11,653	1,933	13,586	16,113	12,271	2,939	44,909	25.9	30.3
1980	8,010	1,324	9,334	15,496	11,043	2,692	38,565	20.8	24.2
1975	8,987	1,385	10,372	13,581	6,942	2,211	33,106	27.1	31.3
1970	8,284	1,160	9,444	13,049	5,289	1,637	29,419	28.2	32.1
1965	11,138	847	11,985	9,576	1,876	834	24,271	45.9	49.4
1960	7,905	398	8,303	6,837	482	866	16,488	47.9	50.4
1955	9,204	452	9,656	3,741	68	163	13,628	67.5	70.9
1950	8,006	388	8,394	1,991	32	160	10,577	75.7	79.4

SOURCE: *Ward's Database Opers.*

World Motor Vehicle Production by Manufacturer

WORLD MOTOR VEHICLE PRODUCTION BY MANUFACTURER, 2004

Manufacturer	Passenger Cars	Light Trucks	Heavy Trucks	Buses	Total
General Motors	4,502,680	3,530,767	33,089	—	8,066,536
Toyota	5,869,629	676,399	230,511	38,015	6,814,554
Ford	3,497,334	3,071,784	73,780	1,126	6,644,024
Volkswagen	4,892,529	168,840	29,212	4,899	5,095,480
DaimlerChrysler	1,913,693	2,368,437	298,708	47,045	4,627,883
PSA Peugeot Citroen	3,004,710	400,535	—	—	3,405,245
Honda	3,183,269	54,165	—	—	3,237,434
Nissan	2,423,893	615,628	146,353	4,345	3,190,219
Hyundai-Kia	2,377,546	146,883	128,655	113,237	2,766,321
Renault-Dacia-Samsung	2,163,620	308,034	—	—	2,471,654
Fiat-Iveco	1,583,501	385,207	119,821	31,188	2,119,717
Suzuki-Maruti	1,639,366	337,458	—	—	1,976,824
Mitsubishi	1,110,679	310,749	7,135	—	1,428,563
Mazda	1,042,849	228,069	4,162	—	1,275,080
BMW	1,250,345	—	—	—	1,250,345
Daihatsu	785,166	172,731	7,398	—	965,295
GM-Daewoo	869,382	15,002	3,761	10,795	898,940
Avtovaz	717,985	—	—	—	717,985
Fuji-Subaru	512,953	88,252	—	—	601,205
FAW(Excluding VW)	50,009	403,218	125,007	9,193	587,427
Beijing AIG	—	538,699	—	—	538,699
Isuzu	14,620	49,645	433,327	2,745	500,337
Dongfeng	—	251,769	180,437	9,821	442,027
Chana Automobile	—	418,587	—	—	418,587
Tata	179,046	130,646	9,539	59,301	378,532
SAIC	—	308,665	—	—	308,665
GAZ	65,686	148,565	—	—	214,251
Harbin Hafei Automotive	—	205,991	—	—	205,991
Volvo Truck	—	8,430	174,835	8,089	191,354
Mahindra & Mahindra	78,940	67,012	36,174	3,342	185,468
Ssangyong	131,536	4,260	—	8,562	144,358
Anhui Jianghuai Auto	—	119,223	—	12,077	131,300
Navistar	—	—	109,745	15,762	125,507
PACCAR-DAF	—	—	125,479	—	125,479
Jinbei Auto Holding	—	110,505	—	—	110,505
MG Rover	106,088	125	—	—	106,213
Changhe Aircraft Industry	—	104,289	—	—	104,289
Ijmach Avto	82,687	13,810	—	—	96,497
Hino	—	4,675	83,854	6,316	94,845
Nanjing Auto	94,551	—	—	—	94,551
Zhejiang Geely	—	91,744	—	—	91,744
Porsche	84,095	—	—	—	84,095
SAIC-Cherry Auto	79,565	—	—	—	79,565
MAN	—	—	64,093	6,389	70,482
Kamaz	41,207	—	29,243	—	70,450
UAZ	31,136	35,565	—	—	66,701
Scania	—	—	53,051	5,621	58,672
Soueast Auto Industrial	—	57,798	—	—	57,798
Great Wall Motor	54,904	—	—	—	54,904
Nissan Diesel	—	650	37,721	1,736	40,107

SOURCE: OICA

U.S. Retail Sales of Cars and Trucks

ANNUAL U.S. VEHICLE RETAIL SALES (In Thousands)

Year	Passenger Cars			Trucks			Total Vehicles		
	Domestic	Import	Total	Domestic	Import	Total	Domestic	Import	Total
2004	5,357	2,149	7,506	8,523	1,269	9,793	13,880	3,418	17,299
2003	5,527	2,083	7,610	8,111	1,246	9,357	13,638	3,329	16,967
2002	5,878	2,226	8,103	7,952	1,084	9,035	13,830	3,309	17,139
2001	6,325	2,098	8,423	8,048	1,002	9,050	14,373	3,100	17,472
2000	6,831	2,016	8,847	8,092	873	8,965	14,923	2,889	17,812
1999	6,979	1,719	8,698	7,922	795	8,716	14,901	2,513	17,415
1998	6,762	1,380	8,142	7,151	674	7,826	13,913	2,054	15,967
1997	6,917	1,355	8,272	6,632	593	7,226	13,549	1,949	15,498
1996	7,255	1,271	8,526	6,478	452	6,929	13,732	1,723	15,455
1995	7,129	1,506	8,635	6,064	417	6,481	13,193	1,923	15,116
1994	7,255	1,735	8,991	5,996	425	6,421	13,251	2,160	15,411
1993	6,742	1,776	8,518	5,287	394	5,681	12,029	2,170	14,199
1992	6,286	1,927	8,213	4,482	423	4,904	10,768	2,350	13,117
1991	6,162	2,028	8,189	3,814	550	4,365	9,976	2,578	12,554
1990	6,919	2,384	9,303	4,217	630	4,846	11,136	3,014	14,149
1989	7,098	2,680	9,779	4,405	661	5,067	11,503	3,342	14,845
1988	7,543	3,004	10,547	4,511	734	5,245	12,054	3,737	15,792
1987	7,085	3,107	10,192	4,059	942	5,001	11,144	4,049	15,193
1986	8,215	3,189	11,404	3,930	989	4,919	12,145	4,178	16,323
1985	8,205	2,775	10,979	3,905	841	4,746	12,110	3,615	15,725
1984	7,952	2,372	10,324	3,480	679	4,159	11,432	3,051	14,483
1983	6,795	2,353	9,148	2,663	500	3,163	9,458	2,853	12,312
1982	5,757	2,200	7,956	2,146	436	2,582	7,902	2,636	10,538
1981	6,181	2,308	8,489	1,821	468	2,289	8,001	2,777	10,778
1980	6,580	2,369	8,949	2,015	480	2,494	8,594	2,849	11,444
1979	8,341	2,332	10,673	3,010	470	3,480	11,351	2,802	14,153
1978	9,312	2,002	11,314	3,773	336	4,109	13,085	2,338	15,423
1977	9,109	2,074	11,183	3,352	323	3,675	12,461	2,397	14,858
1976	8,611	1,499	10,110	2,944	237	3,181	11,555	1,736	13,291
1975	7,053	1,571	8,624	2,249	229	2,478	9,302	1,800	11,102
1974	7,454	1,399	8,853	2,512	176	2,688	9,966	1,575	11,541
1973	9,676	1,748	11,424	2,916	233	3,149	12,592	1,981	14,573
1972	9,327	1,614	10,941	2,486	143	2,629	11,813	1,757	13,570
1971	8,681	1,561	10,242	2,011	85	2,096	10,692	1,646	12,338
1970	7,119	1,280	8,399	1,746	65	1,811	8,865	1,345	10,210
1969	8,464	1,118	9,582	1,936	34	1,970	10,400	1,152	11,552
1968	8,625	1,031	9,656	1,807	24	1,831	10,432	1,055	11,487
1967	7,568	769	8,337	1,524	21	1,545	9,092	790	9,882
1966	8,377	651	9,028	1,619	17	1,636	9,996	668	10,664
1965	8,763	569	9,332	1,539	14	1,553	10,302	583	10,885
1963	7,334	386	7,720	1,230	40	1,270	8,564	426	8,990
1961	5,556	379	5,935	908	29	937	6,464	408	6,872
1959	5,486	614	6,100	928	37	965	6,414	651	7,065
1957	5,826	207	6,033	878	16	894	6,704	223	6,927
1955	7,408	58	7,466	1,012	3	1,015	8,420	61	8,481
1953	5,775	33	5,808	965	N.A.	965	6,740	33	6,773
1951	5,143	21	5,164	1,111	N.A.	1,111	6,254	21	6,275
1942-1950	N.A.	N.A.	N.A.	N.A.	N.A.	N.A.	N.A.	N.A.	N.A.
1941	3,763	N.A.	3,763	902	N.A.	902	4,665	N.A.	4,665
1939	2,724	N.A.	2,724	521	N.A.	521	3,245	N.A.	3,245
1937	3,508	N.A.	3,508	645	N.A.	645	4,153	N.A.	4,153
1935	2,867	N.A.	2,867	552	N.A.	552	3,419	N.A.	3,419
1933	1,526	N.A.	1,526	261	N.A.	261	1,787	N.A.	1,787
1931	1,903	N.A.	1,903	328	N.A.	328	2,231	N.A.	2,231

N.A.-Not available.
SOURCE: Ward's Communications.

U.S. Retail Sales
of Passenger Cars

U.S. PASSENGER CAR SALES

Model	2004	2003	2002	2001	2000
BMW 3-Series*	106,549	111,944	115,428	103,227	89,681
BMW 5-Series*	45,584	46,964	40,842	40,005	39,703
BMW 6-Series*	8,198	—	—	—	—
BMW 7-Series*	16,155	20,473	22,006	13,389	16,619
BMW 8-Series*	—	—	—	—	1
BMW Z3	—	155	6,786	14,914	16,382
BMW Z4	13,654	20,169	3,704	—	—
BMW Z8*	110	439	524	970	317
BMW Total	**190,250**	**200,144**	**189,290**	**172,505**	**162,703**
Mini Cooper*	36,032	36,010	24,590	—	—
Mini Total	**36,032**	**36,010**	**24,590**	**—**	**—**
BMW TOTAL	**226,282**	**236,154**	**213,880**	**172,505**	**162,703**
300M	5,110	24,910	32,375	36,583	50,682
300 Series	107,820	—	—	—	—
Cirrus	—	—	—	371	38,086
Concorde	4,223	28,519	31,611	32,331	50,206
Crossfire*	14,969	4,021	—	—	—
LHS	—	—	552	8,852	20,982
Prowler	—	516	1,328	1,134	—
PT Cruiser Convertible	15,996	—	—	—	—
Sebring Convertible	36,434	41,883	43,977	45,242	39,114
Sebring Coupe	10,410	10,878	11,784	16,601	12,870
Sebring Sedan	57,250	47,348	56,606	56,616	10,632
Chrysler Total	**252,212**	**158,075**	**178,233**	**197,730**	**222,572**
Avenger	—	—	—	143	5,512
Intrepid	7,880	76,473	111,356	109,098	143,840
Neon	113,476	120,101	126,118	107,299	113,381
Stratus Coupe	19,752	19,070	19,044	22,177	5,791
Stratus Sedan	79,017	80,854	90,189	88,948	97,906
Viper	1,782	2,103	1,511	1,388	1,470
Dodge Total	**221,907**	**298,601**	**348,218**	**329,053**	**367,900**
Breeze	—	—	—	127	6,319
Neon	—	—	439	30,054	49,951
Prowler	—	—	166	1,053	2,631
Plymouth Total	**—**	**—**	**605**	**31,234**	**58,901**
CHRYSLER GROUP TOTAL	**474,119**	**456,676**	**527,056**	**558,017**	**649,373**
Lanos*	—	—	13,274	15,619	22,061
Leganza*	—	—	9,619	18,347	24,826
Nubira*	—	—	14,958	14,330	21,473
DAEWOO TOTAL	**—**	**—**	**37,851**	**48,296**	**68,360**
Contour	—	—	—	—	45,109
Crown Victoria	70,816	78,541	79,716	95,261	92,047
Escort	1,210	25,473	51,857	90,503	110,736
Five Hundred	14,106	—	—	—	—
Focus	208,339	229,353	243,199	264,414	286,166
Ford GT	144	—	—	—	—
Mustang	129,858	140,350	138,356	169,198	173,676
Taurus	248,148	300,496	332,690	353,560	382,035
Thunderbird	11,998	18,100	19,085	5,177	—
Ford Total	**684,619**	**792,313**	**864,903**	**978,113**	**1,089,769**
S-Type*	10,975	14,876	15,965	19,548	24,507

U.S. Retail Sales of Passenger Cars

U.S. PASSENGER CAR SALES — continued

Model	2004	2003	2002	2001	2000
Vanden Plas*	2,445	2,225	2,424	3,162	3,944
X-Type*	21,542	26,772	33,018	9,765	—
XJ6/8*	6,990	6,249	4,738	5,850	7,155
XJR Sedan*	1,117	1,628	1,124	1,070	1,393
XK8*	2,806	2,905	3,935	5,137	6,729
Jaguar Total	**45,875**	**54,655**	**61,204**	**44,532**	**43,728**
Continental	—	280	15,435	20,392	22,648
Lincoln LS	27,066	33,581	39,775	39,787	51,039
Town Car	51,908	56,566	59,312	66,859	81,399
Lincoln Total	**78,974**	**90,427**	**114,522**	**127,038**	**155,086**
Cougar	—	2,024	19,345	29,487	40,343
Grand Marquis	79,329	86,986	80,271	112,034	122,572
Montego	2,974	—	—	—	—
Mystique	—	—	—	—	16,208
Sable	42,737	61,342	98,998	102,646	103,030
Mercury Total	**125,040**	**150,352**	**198,614**	**244,167**	**282,153**
Volvo 40*	25,540	15,718	18,112	25,848	35,635
Volvo 50*	2,509	—	—	—	—
Volvo 60*	27,835	35,295	38,546	35,855	2,994
Volvo 70*	14,551	16,036	14,456	19,261	48,660
Volvo 80*	13,390	14,637	15,359	20,425	29,000
Volvo Total	**83,825**	**81,686**	**86,473**	**101,389**	**116,289**
FORD TOTAL	**1,018,333**	**1,169,433**	**1,325,716**	**1,495,239**	**1,687,025**
Century	67,264	94,279	163,739	142,157	143,085
LaCrosse	10,995	—	—	—	—
LeSabre	114,157	114,572	135,916	145,304	148,633
Park Ave	17,138	26,820	30,140	36,454	47,669
Regal	13,775	23,677	40,754	49,992	65,167
Riviera	—	—	—	17	58
Buick Total	**223,329**	**259,348**	**370,549**	**373,924**	**404,612**
Catera*	—	15	244	9,764	17,290
CTS	57,211	49,392	37,976	—	—
Deville	68,195	82,076	84,729	95,354	105,694
Eldorado	7	193	5,661	9,859	13,289
Seville	3,386	18,747	21,494	25,290	29,535
STS	9,484	—	—	—	—
XLR	3,665	875	—	—	—
Cadillac Total	**141,948**	**151,298**	**150,104**	**140,267**	**165,808**
Aveo*	56,642	5,677	—	—	—
Camaro	127	1,124	28,404	35,453	42,131
Cavalier	195,275	256,550	238,225	233,298	236,803
Cobalt	4,959	—	—	—	—
Corvette	35,276	27,974	32,555	33,655	31,208
Impala	290,259	267,882	198,918	208,395	174,358
Lumina	—	15	35	17,649	46,573
Malibu	268,017	173,263	169,377	176,583	207,376
Metro	—	1	13	6,515	33,878
Monte Carlo	57,679	66,976	64,771	72,596	66,364
Prizm	5	17	14,297	45,894	52,116
Chevrolet Total	**908,239**	**799,479**	**746,595**	**830,038**	**890,807**
Alero	20,156	99,123	94,285	109,302	122,722
Aurora	206	3,161	8,878	24,928	28,250
Cutlass	—	—	—	53	1,243

U.S. Retail Sales of Passenger Cars

U.S. PASSENGER CAR SALES — continued

Model	2004	2003	2002	2001	2000
Intrigue	55	789	15,015	39,395	64,109
Olds 88	–	–	–	16	477
Oldsmobile Total	**20,417**	**103,073**	**118,178**	**173,694**	**216,801**
Bonneville	29,852	25,250	37,599	48,598	65,606
Firebird	109	920	20,613	25,743	31,013
Grand Am	133,707	156,466	150,818	182,046	214,923
Grand Prix	131,551	125,441	130,141	128,935	148,521
GTO*	13,569	79	–	–	–
Pontiac G6	16,185	–	–	–	–
Sunfire	36,095	43,595	62,950	71,342	82,364
Vibe	58,894	56,922	39,082	–	–
Pontiac Total	**419,962**	**408,673**	**441,203**	**456,664**	**542,427**
Saab 9-2X*	1,788	–	–	–	–
Saab 9-3*	27,322	34,075	20,499	18,374	19,406
Saab 9-5*	9,049	13,839	17,306	19,182	19,993
Saab 900*	–	–	–	–	62
Saab 9000*	–	–	–	–	18
Saab Total	**38,159**	**47,914**	**37,805**	**37,556**	**39,479**
Ion	104,044	117,230	6,066	–	–
Saturn EV1	–	–	–	–	411
Saturn L	19,453	64,957	81,172	98,227	94,034
Saturn S	–	7,046	117,533	162,110	177,355
Saturn Total	**123,497**	**189,233**	**204,771**	**260,337**	**271,800**
GM TOTAL	**1,875,551**	**1,959,018**	**2,069,205**	**2,272,480**	**2,531,734**
Acura CL	283	6,593	12,072	18,993	24,677
Acura NSX*	178	221	233	182	221
Acura RL*	8,753	6,829	9,392	10,723	14,827
Acura RSX*	21,940	24,292	30,117	16,401	–
Acura TL	77,895	56,770	60,764	69,484	67,033
Acura TSX*	30,365	18,932	–	–	–
Integra*	–	–	19	13,736	25,975
Acura Total	**139,414**	**113,637**	**112,597**	**129,519**	**132,733**
Accord	352,925	325,465	330,692	350,090	317,483
Accord*	33,845	72,285	68,288	64,628	87,032
Civic	274,540	260,632	283,173	311,314	306,748
Civic*	34,656	39,040	29,986	20,466	17,780
Honda EV Plus*	–	–	–	–	2
Honda FCX*	6	4	1	–	–
Honda S2000*	7,320	7,888	9,684	9,682	6,797
Insight*	583	1,168	2,216	4,726	3,788
Prelude*	–	10	1,966	9,462	9,692
Honda Total	**703,875**	**706,492**	**726,006**	**770,368**	**749,322**
HONDA TOTAL	**843,289**	**820,129**	**838,603**	**899,887**	**882,055**
Accent*	43,258	56,585	71,488	79,480	66,736
Elantra*	112,892	120,858	120,638	111,293	104,099
Hyundai XG300*	–	–	–	13,268	2,004
Hyundai XG350*	16,630	17,928	16,666	4,616	–
Sonata*	107,189	82,330	68,085	62,385	45,983
Tiburon*	20,125	21,242	19,963	19,176	15,237
HYUNDAI TOTAL	**300,094**	**298,943**	**296,840**	**290,218**	**234,059**
Amanti*	19,894	1,425	–	–	–
Optima*	53,492	34,681	26,793	25,910	97
Rio*	38,518	41,285	51,195	51,541	16,624

U.S. Retail Sales of Passenger Cars

U.S. PASSENGER CAR SALES — continued

Model	2004	2003	2002	2001	2000
Sephia*	—	—	—	49,016	67,893
Spectra*	44,004	63,049	72,382	29,817	13,642
KIA TOTAL	**155,908**	**140,440**	**150,370**	**156,284**	**98,256**
Mazda3*	76,080	2,081	—	—	—
Mazda6	72,148	66,118	2,042	—	—
Mazda 626	15	1,629	40,689	50,997	71,046
Mazda RX-8*	23,690	12,346	—	—	—
Miata*	9,356	10,920	14,392	16,486	18,299
Millenia*	18	1,812	18,066	19,849	16,558
Protege*	6,371	68,788	83,367	78,688	62,851
MAZDA TOTAL	**187,678**	**163,694**	**158,556**	**166,020**	**168,754**
Mercedes C-Class*	69,251	65,982	64,025	51,210	34,600
Mercedes CL*	2,683	3,377	3,938	3,748	2,204
Mercedes CLK*	22,556	19,230	17,251	19,423	17,796
Mercedes E-Class*	58,954	55,683	42,598	44,445	49,592
Mercedes S-Class*	20,460	22,940	21,118	25,998	30,319
Mercedes SL Class*	12,885	13,318	13,717	4,217	5,409
Mercedes SLK*	7,360	6,023	7,784	11,268	12,930
MERCEDES TOTAL	**194,149**	**186,553**	**170,431**	**160,309**	**152,850**
3000 GT*	—	—	1	1	117
Diamante*	4,379	9,174	14,352	17,227	9,219
Eclipse	19,361	38,875	72,040	70,351	71,307
Galant	43,491	65,141	97,343	93,878	96,452
Lancer*	41,706	48,159	69,007	25,052	—
Mirage*	—	174	6,919	29,989	49,369
MITSUBISHI TOTAL	108,937	161,523	259,662	236,498	226,464
Infiniti G20*	1	11	5,758	11,512	13,095
Infiniti G35*	71,177	64,730	34,775	—	—
Infiniti I30*	—	—	—	25,534	39,532
Infiniti I35*	11,637	14,091	25,712	9,858	—
Infiniti J30*	—	—	1	—	1
Infiniti M45*	2,090	4,755	1,010	—	—
Infiniti Q45*	1,972	2,440	3,717	5,726	4,178
Infiniti Total	**86,877**	**86,027**	**70,973**	**52,630**	**56,806**
Altima	235,889	201,240	201,822	148,345	136,971
Altra EV*	—	139	72	38	50
Maxima	76,340	60,591	—	—	—
Maxima*	27	26,167	98,502	102,535	129,235
Nissan 200SX	—	—	1	2	8
Nissan 240SX*	—	—	—	—	18
Nissan 300ZX*	—	—	3	3	3
Nissan 350Z*	30,690	36,728	13,250	—	—
Sentra	106,934	94,500	106,060	111,082	98,803
Nissan Total	**449,880**	**419,365**	**419,710**	**362,005**	**365,088**
NISSAN TOTAL	**536,757**	**505,392**	**490,683**	**414,635**	**421,894**
Boxster*	3,513	6,088	9,875	12,278	13,312
Carrera GT*	189	—	—	—	—
Porsche 911*	9,654	9,408	11,443	10,763	9,098
PORSCHE TOTAL	**13,356**	**15,496**	**21,318**	**23,041**	**22,410**
Impreza*	32,209	36,525	38,226	35,612	19,220
Legacy	89,453	79,839	85,359	95,291	96,393
SUBARU TOTAL	**121,662**	**116,364**	**123,585**	**130,903**	**115,613**
Aerio*	9,439	19,828	18,441	—	—
Esteem*	—	113	3,849	13,061	16,877

U.S. Retail Sales of Passenger Cars

U.S. PASSENGER CAR SALES — continued

Model	2004	2003	2002	2001	2000
Forenza*	24,796	633	—	—	—
Swift	—	—	177	2,547	3,379
Verona*	12,874	1,967	—	—	—
SUZUKI TOTAL	**47,109**	**22,541**	**22,467**	**15,608**	**20,256**
Lexus ES300*	—	42,325	71,450	44,847	41,320
Lexus ES330*	75,916	23,437	—	—	—
Lexus GS300*	6,914	11,228	14,788	19,848	21,921
Lexus GS400*	—	—	—	—	5,111
Lexus GS430*	1,348	2,078	2,458	4,613	1,047
Lexus IS300*	9,972	13,559	20,306	22,486	15,540
Lexus LS400*	—	—	—	—	7,653
Lexus LS430*	32,272	23,895	26,261	31,110	8,218
Lexus SC300*	—	—	—	7	450
Lexus SC400*	—	—	—	11	181
Lexus SC430*	9,708	10,298	14,462	14,315	—
Lexus Total	**136,130**	**126,820**	**149,725**	**137,237**	**101,441**
Scion tC*	28,062	—	—	—	—
Scion xA*	24,184	3,962	—	—	—
Scion xB*	47,013	6,936	—	—	—
Scion Total	**99,259**	**10,898**	**—**	**—**	**—**
Avalon	36,460	50,911	69,029	83,005	104,078
Camry	402,063	367,394	343,796	303,436	298,123
Camry*	24,927	45,902	90,349	87,013	124,838
Celica*	8,710	14,856	22,893	35,720	52,406
Corolla	248,105	202,185	155,181	245,023	230,156
Corolla*	26,651	60,028	32,343	—	—
Echo*	3,899	26,167	30,859	42,464	48,876
Matrix	58,405	63,264	66,836	—	—
MR2 Spyder*	2,621	2,934	4,705	6,254	7,233
Prius*	53,991	24,627	20,119	15,556	5,562
Supra*	—	—	—	3	2
Toyota Total	**865,832**	**858,268**	**836,110**	**818,474**	**871,274**
TOYOTA TOTAL	**1,101,221**	**995,986**	**985,835**	**955,711**	**972,715**
Audi A4*	33,438	41,087	42,852	35,739	34,460
Audi A4 Cabrio*	7,394	8,447	1,467	—	—
Audi A6*	14,455	16,599	24,372	26,364	30,487
Audi A8*	5,943	4,090	1,515	2,300	2,362
Audi Cabrio*	—	—	—	—	3
Audi RS6*	450	986	—	—	—
Audi S4*	6,336	1,509	—	—	—
Audi TT*	5,275	7,880	9,513	12,523	12,027
Audi Total	**73,291**	**80,598**	**79,719**	**76,926**	**79,339**
Beetle	21,025	32,716	48,696	65,201	81,134
Beetle Cabrio	21,132	24,255	853	—	—
Golf*	24,669	29,342	31,482	31,271	28,124
Jetta	91,790	117,867	145,604	145,221	144,853
Passat*	67,640	76,977	96,142	95,028	84,521
Phaeton*	1,939	343	—	—	—
VW Cabriolet	1	41	8,675	13,327	14,133
Volkswagen Total	**228,196**	**281,541**	**331,452**	**350,048**	**352,765**
VOLKSWAGEN TOTAL	**301,487**	**362,139**	**411,171**	**426,974**	**432,104**
TOTAL CARS	**7,505,932**	**7,610,481**	**8,103,229**	**8,422,625**	**8,846,625**

*Units imported from outside North America.
SOURCE: Ward's AutoInfoBank.

U.S. Retail Sales of Passenger Cars by Country of Origin, Market Class and Purchasing Sector

U.S. RETAIL SALES OF PASSENGER CARS

Year	Domestic	Imports From Japan	Imports From Germany	Imports From Other Countries	Total Imports	U.S. Total	Import Percent Total	Import Percent Japan	Import Percent Germany
2004	5,356,873	798,222	541,940	808,897	2,149,059	7,505,932	28.6	10.6	7.2
2003	5,527,430	817,038	543,823	722,190	2,083,051	7,610,481	27.4	10.7	7.1
2002	5,877,645	923,182	546,654	755,748	2,225,584	8,103,229	27.5	11.4	6.7
2001	6,324,996	836,685	522,659	738,285	2,097,629	8,422,625	24.9	9.9	6.2
2000	6,830,505	862,780	516,614	636,726	2,016,120	8,846,625	22.8	9.8	5.8
1999	6,979,357	757,568	466,870	494,489	1,718,927	8,698,284	19.8	8.7	5.4
1998	6,761,940	691,162	366,724	321,895	1,379,781	8,141,721	16.9	8.5	4.5
1997	6,916,769	726,104	297,028	332,173	1,355,305	8,272,074	16.4	8.8	3.6
1996	7,254,557	725,941	237,009	308,247	1,271,197	8,525,754	14.9	8.5	2.8
1995	7,128,707	981,506	207,482	317,269	1,506,257	8,634,964	17.4	11.4	2.4
1994	7,255,303	1,239,450	192,275	303,489	1,735,214	8,990,517	19.3	13.8	2.1
1993	6,741,667	1,328,445	186,177	261,570	1,776,192	8,517,859	20.9	15.6	2.2
1992	6,285,916	1,451,766	200,851	274,580	1,927,197	8,213,113	23.5	17.7	2.4
1991	6,161,573	1,504,690	192,713	330,454	2,027,857	8,189,430	24.8	18.4	2.4
1990	6,918,869	1,719,384	263,263	401,699	2,384,346	9,303,215	25.6	18.5	2.8
1989	7,098,098	1,897,957	246,206	536,256	2,680,419	9,778,517	27.4	19.4	2.5
1988	7,543,116	2,022,602	280,097	700,993	3,003,692	10,546,808	28.5	19.2	2.7
1987	7,085,279	2,114,224	337,232	655,142	3,106,598	10,191,877	30.5	20.7	3.3
1986	8,215,017	2,339,503	431,433	418,286	3,189,222	11,404,239	28.0	20.5	3.8
1985	8,204,670	2,170,898	407,684	195,935	2,774,517	10,979,187	25.3	19.8	3.7
1984	7,951,523	1,857,207	327,328	187,637	2,372,172	10,323,695	23.0	18.0	3.2
1983	6,795,299	1,896,835	265,079	190,825	2,352,739	9,148,038	25.7	20.7	2.9
1982	5,756,658	1,791,972	234,233	173,597	2,199,802	7,956,460	27.6	22.5	2.9
1981	6,180,784	1,851,324	272,001	185,093	2,308,418	8,489,202	27.2	21.8	3.2
1980	6,579,778	1,893,842	291,953	183,662	2,369,457	8,949,235	26.5	21.2	3.3

SOURCE: *Ward's AutoInfoBank.*

U.S. CAR SALES BY MARKET CLASS

Year	Small	Middle	Large	Luxury	Total
2004	30.6	45.0	7.3	17.1	100.0
2003	30.9	45.5	6.3	17.3	100.0
2002	30.4	46.1	6.1	17.4	100.0
2001	30.6	46.2	6.4	16.8	100.0
2000	29.7	46.1	7.0	17.1	100.0
1999	25.2	50.8	7.6	16.5	100.0
1998	24.1	51.7	8.2	16.0	100.0
1997	25.6	50.2	9.5	14.8	100.0
1996	26.4	50.3	9.9	13.5	100.0
1995	26.5	49.1	10.8	13.6	100.0
1990	33.3	43.7	9.4	13.6	100.0
1985	31.5	46.7	11.8	10.0	100.0

SOURCE: *Ward's AutoInfoBank.*

U.S. CAR SALES BY SECTOR

Year	Units by Consuming Sector (000) Consumer	Units by Consuming Sector (000) Business	Units by Consuming Sector (000) Government	Total	% of Total Sales Consumer	% of Total Sales Business
2004	4,186	3,112	208	7,506	55.8	41.5
2003	4,328	3,087	195	7,610	56.9	40.6
2002	4,486	3,434	183	8,103	55.4	42.4
2001	4,640	3,617	166	8,423	55.1	42.9
2000	4,694	3,989	169	8,852	53.0	45.1
1999	4,366	4,155	175	8,697	50.2	47.8
1998	3,988	3,992	161	8,142	49.0	49.0
1997	3,910	4,216	147	8,273	47.3	51.0
1996	4,079	4,273	176	8,527	47.8	50.1
1995	4,351	4,186	151	8,687	50.1	48.2
1994	4,600	4,268	124	8,991	51.2	47.5
1993	4,657	3,748	113	8,518	54.7	44.0
1992	4,566	3,529	119	8,214	55.6	43.0
1991	4,424	3,648	103	8,175	54.1	44.6
1990	5,677	3,477	147	9,301	61.0	37.4
1989	6,288	3,362	127	9,777	64.3	34.4
1985	7,092	3,754	132	10,978	64.6	34.2
1980	6,100	2,758	124	8,982	67.9	30.7
1975	5,907	2,508	123	8,538	69.2	29.4
1970	6,252	2,056	94	8,403	74.4	24.5

SOURCE: U.S. Department of Commerce, Bureau of Economic Analysis.

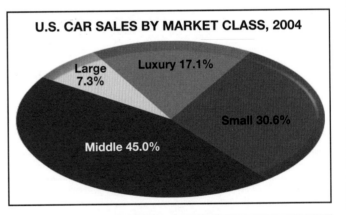

U.S. CAR SALES BY MARKET CLASS, 2004

Large 7.3%
Luxury 17.1%
Small 30.6%
Middle 45.0%

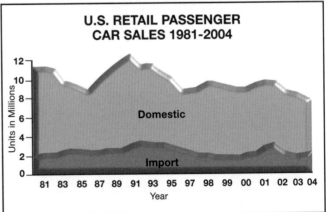

U.S. RETAIL PASSENGER CAR SALES 1981-2004

Units in Millions

Domestic

Import

81 83 85 87 89 91 93 95 97 98 99 00 01 02 03 04
Year

U.S. Light Truck Sales by Segment

U.S. LIGHT TRUCK SALES BY SEGMENT

	2004	2003	2002	2001	2000
BMW X3*	34,604	—	—	—	—
BMW X5	35,225	40,715	42,742	40,622	26,720
BMW Total	**69,829**	**40,715**	**42,742**	**40,622**	**26,720**
Chrysler Pacifica	92,363	56,656	—	—	—
Chrysler PT Cruiser	99,959	107,759	138,260	144,717	91,996
Dodge Magnum	39,217	—	—	—	—
Chrysler Group Total	**231,539**	**164,415**	**138,260**	**144,717**	**91,996**
Ford Escape	183,430	167,678	145,471	164,184	42,635
Ford Freestyle	8,509	—	—	—	—
Mercury Mariner	7,171	—	—	—	—
Volvo Cross Country*	16,059	17,177	19,818	24,321	6,890
Volvo XC90*	39,183	35,723	4,379	—	—
Ford Total	**254,352**	**220,578**	**169,668**	**188,505**	**49,525**
Buick Rendezvous	60,039	72,643	61,468	31,754	—
Cadillac SRX	30,019	5,049	—	—	—
Chevrolet Equinox	84,024	—	—	—	—
Pontiac Aztek	20,588	27,354	27,793	27,322	11,201
Saturn Vue	86,957	81,924	75,477	393	—
GM Total	**281,627**	**186,970**	**164,738**	**59,469**	**11,201**
Acura MDX	59,505	57,281	52,955	40,950	9,750
Honda CRV*	149,281	143,909	146,266	118,313	118,260
Honda Element	59,927	67,478	957	—	—
Honda Pilot	128,158	106,917	52,062	—	—
Honda Total	**396,871**	**375,585**	**252,240**	**159,263**	**128,010**
Hyundai Santa Fe*	111,447	101,278	78,279	56,017	10,332
Hyundai Tucson*	7,074	—	—	—	—
Hyundai Total	**118,521**	**101,278**	**78,279**	**56,017**	**10,332**
Isuzu Vehicross*	—	13	681	978	1,223
Isuzu Total	**—**	**13**	**681**	**978**	**1,223**
Mazda Tribute	41,078	49,512	44,989	45,270	21,048
Mazda Total	**41,078**	**49,512**	**44,989**	**45,270**	**21,048**
Mitsubishi Endeavor	22,433	32,054	—	—	—
Mitsubishi Outlander*	18,104	34,088	11,346	—	—
Mitsubishi Total	**40,537**	**66,142**	**11,346**	**—**	**—**
Infiniti FX*	30,964	27,637	—	—	—
Nissan Murano*	62,057	56,075	2,054	—	—
Nissan Total	**93,021**	**83,712**	**2,054**	**—**	**—**
Porsche Cayenne*	18,117	12,920	—	—	—
Porsche Total	**18,117**	**12,920**	**—**	**—**	**—**
Subaru Forester*	58,424	59,761	53,918	55,041	56,605
Subaru Total	**58,424**	**59,761**	**53,918**	**55,041**	**56,605**
Lexus RX300*	—	24,562	72,963	77,391	89,864
Lexus RX330	61,350	7,819	—	—	—
Lexus RX330*	45,181	59,985	—	—	—
Toyota Highlander*	133,077	120,174	113,134	86,699	—
Toyota RAV4*	70,314	73,204	86,601	86,368	53,777
Toyota Total	**309,922**	**285,744**	**272,698**	**250,458**	**143,641**
Audi Allroad*	4,626	5,823	6,007	6,357	1,033
Volkswagen Touareg*	27,706	16,410	—	—	—
Volkswagen Total	**32,332**	**22,233**	**6,007**	**6,357**	**1,033**
CROSS UTILITY TOTAL	**1,946,170**	**1,669,578**	**1,237,620**	**1,006,697**	**541,334**
Dodge Durango	137,148	108,010	106,925	130,799	173,567
Jeep Cherokee	—	—	—	74,490	141,457
Jeep Grand Cherokee	182,313	207,479	224,233	223,612	271,723
Jeep Liberty	167,376	162,987	171,212	88,485	—
Jeep Wrangler	77,550	70,093	64,351	68,830	82,254
Chrysler Group Total	**564,387**	**548,569**	**566,721**	**586,216**	**669,001**
Ford Excursion	20,010	26,259	29,042	34,710	50,786
Ford Expedition	159,846	181,547	163,454	178,045	213,483
Ford Explorer	339,333	373,118	433,847	415,921	445,157
Land Rover Discovery*	13,083	17,420	17,417	20,104	20,860
Land Rover Freelander*	5,430	9,529	15,021	1,329	—
Land Rover LR3*	3,447	—	—	—	—
Land Rover Range Rover*	13,546	12,086	8,549	5,771	6,287
Lincoln Aviator	23,644	29,517	1,856	—	—
Lincoln Navigator	36,398	38,742	30,613	31,759	37,923
Mercury Mountaineer	43,916	49,692	48,144	45,574	46,547
Ford Total	**658,653**	**737,910**	**747,943**	**733,213**	**821,043**
Buick Rainier	24,134	4,797	—	—	—
Cadillac Escalade	36,994	35,621	36,114	31,270	23,346
Cadillac Escalade ESV	15,618	12,866	36	—	—

U.S. Light Truck Sales by Segment

U.S. LIGHT TRUCK SALES BY SEGMENT — continued

	2004	2003	2002	2001	2000
Chevrolet S Blazer	32,950	53,426	95,937	149,195	225,948
Chevrolet Suburban	119,545	135,222	151,056	154,782	133,123
Chevrolet Tahoe	186,161	199,065	209,767	202,319	149,834
Chevrolet Tracker	14,898	35,123	42,212	52,368	48,020
Chevrolet TrailBlazer	283,484	261,334	249,568	115,103	—
GMC Envoy	134,897	127,782	110,720	51,208	—
GMC S Jimmy	—	52	964	30,825	79,489
GMC Suburban	—	—	—	94	4,776
GMC Yukon	86,571	86,238	76,488	77,254	56,297
GMC Yukon XL	65,917	70,887	67,556	70,706	47,016
Hummer H1	447	730	720	768	875
Hummer H2	25,558	34,529	18,861	—	—
Hummer H2 SUT	3,340	—	—	—	—
Oldsmobile Bravada	1,973	8,052	14,337	23,867	31,194
GM Total	**1,032,487**	**1,065,724**	**1,074,336**	**959,759**	**799,918**
Acura SLX*	—	—	—	—	198
Honda Passport	—	70	3,524	17,448	21,892
Honda Total	—	70	3,524	17,448	22,090
Isuzu Amigo	—	—	—	2,893	9,244
Isuzu Ascender	7,686	3,377	253	—	—
Isuzu Axiom	3,153	5,783	8,989	5,851	—
Isuzu Rodeo	16,331	19,681	32,056	56,904	59,570
Isuzu Trooper*	18	1,470	10,985	15,608	23,100
Isuzu Total	**27,188**	**30,311**	**52,283**	**81,256**	**91,914**
Kia Sorento*	52,878	40,787	8,451	—	—
Kia Sportage*	120	5,616	39,436	52,368	62,350
Kia Total	**52,998**	**46,403**	**47,887**	**52,368**	**62,350**
Mercedes G-Class*	1,491	1,980	3,114	674	—
Mercedes M-Class	25,681	30,018	39,680	45,655	52,764
Mercedes Total	**27,172**	**31,998**	**42,794**	**46,329**	**52,764**
Mitsubishi Montero*	5,181	8,839	19,181	24,802	21,578
Mitsubishi Montero Sport*	6,954	20,306	54,922	61,093	66,375
Mitsubishi Total	**12,135**	**29,145**	**74,103**	**85,895**	**87,953**
Infiniti QX4*	10	4,991	16,938	18,735	21,545
Infiniti QX56	13,136	—	—	—	—
Nissan Armada	37,275	6,673	—	—	—
Nissan Pathfinder	11,983	—	—	—	—
Nissan Pathfinder*	26,136	35,511	57,384	64,515	68,533
Nissan Xterra	66,690	67,799	79,779	86,757	88,578
Nissan Total	**155,230**	**114,974**	**154,101**	**170,007**	**178,656**
Suzuki Sidekick*	—	—	10	14	89
Suzuki Vitara	3,476	5,392	6,554	7,950	9,015
Suzuki Vitara*	4,860	7,945	11,529	16,030	31,482
Suzuki Vitara XL7*	18,501	22,560	27,295	25,096	—
Suzuki X90*	—	—	—	—	3
Suzuki Total	**26,837**	**35,897**	**45,388**	**49,090**	**40,589**
Lexus GX470*	35,420	31,376	2,190	—	—
Lexus LX470*	9,846	9,193	9,231	9,355	14,732
Toyota 4Runner*	114,212	109,308	77,026	90,250	111,797
Toyota Land Cruiser*	6,778	6,671	6,752	7,591	15,509
Toyota Sequoia	58,114	67,067	70,187	68,574	9,925
Toyota Total	**224,370**	**223,615**	**165,386**	**175,770**	**151,963**
SPORT UTILITY TOTAL	**2,781,457**	**2,864,616**	**2,974,466**	**2,957,351**	**2,978,241**
Chrysler Town & Country	142,523	120,767	126,378	142,902	99,252
Chrysler Voyager	1,834	20,333	37,392	45,105	70,477
Dodge Caravan	242,307	233,394	244,911	242,036	285,739
Dodge Ram Van	7,180	20,712	26,170	36,537	49,602
Dodge Ram Wagon	—	—	10,912	18,321	20,641
Dodge Sprinter Van*	9,209	1,572	—	—	—
Dodge Sprinter Wagon*	1,023	369	—	—	—
Plymouth Voyager	—	—	—	340	28,345
Chrysler Group Total	**404,076**	**397,147**	**445,763**	**485,241**	**554,056**
Ford Econoline	171,017	161,721	165,085	159,565	187,027
Ford Freestar	100,622	15,771	—	—	—
Ford Windstar	2,950	113,465	148,875	179,595	222,298
Mercury Monterey	17,407	2,213	—	—	—
Mercury Villager	—	—	16,442	22,046	30,443
Ford Total	**291,996**	**293,170**	**330,402**	**361,206**	**439,768**
Buick Terraza	2,137	—	—	—	—
Chevrolet Astro	34,564	40,123	50,616	59,395	92,585
Chevrolet Express	114,562	104,734	100,983	98,014	113,232
Chevrolet Uplander	3,948	—	—	—	—

U.S. Light Truck Sales by Segment

U.S. LIGHT TRUCK SALES BY SEGMENT — continued

	2004	2003	2002	2001	2000
Chevrolet Venture	66,522	94,521	94,056	88,788	97,450
GMC Safari	8,345	10,950	13,665	18,533	32,444
GMC Savana	41,702	34,370	32,335	36,674	42,391
Oldsmobile Silhouette	6,461	14,772	22,597	36,184	41,177
Pontiac Montana	31,411	39,588	47,836	49,416	59,849
Pontiac Montana SV6	2,218	—	—	—	—
Pontiac Trans Sport	—	—	—	—	71
Saturn Relay	1,563	—	—	—	—
GM Total	**313,433**	**339,058**	**362,088**	**387,004**	**479,199**
Honda Odyssey	154,238	154,063	153,467	131,036	126,686
Honda Odyssey*	—	—	—	5	19
Honda Total	**154,238**	**154,063**	**153,467**	**131,041**	**126,705**
Isuzu Oasis*	—	—	7	31	147
Isuzu Total	**—**	**—**	**7**	**31**	**147**
Kia Sedona*	61,149	50,628	39,088	15,069	—
Kia Total	**61,149**	**50,628**	**39,088**	**15,069**	**—**
Mazda MPV*	24,860	30,689	34,403	32,181	35,600
Mazda Total	**24,860**	**30,689**	**34,403**	**32,181**	**35,600**
Nissan Quest	46,430	23,170	17,480	29,232	42,800
Nissan Total	**46,430**	**23,170**	**17,480**	**29,232**	**42,800**
Toyota Previa*	—	—	—	—	1
Toyota Sienna	159,119	105,499	80,915	88,469	103,137
Toyota Total	**159,119**	**105,499**	**80,915**	**88,469**	**103,138**
Volkswagen Eurovan*	209	4,735	6,673	5,600	2,714
Volkswagen Total	**209**	**4,735**	**6,673**	**5,600**	**2,714**
VAN TOTAL	**1,455,510**	**1,398,159**	**1,470,286**	**1,535,074**	**1,784,127**
Dodge Dakota	105,614	111,273	130,712	154,479	177,395
Dodge Ram Pickup	426,289	449,371	396,934	344,538	380,874
Chrysler Group Total	**531,903**	**560,644**	**527,646**	**499,017**	**558,269**
Ford F-Series	891,482	806,887	774,037	865,152	820,248
Ford Ranger	156,322	209,117	226,094	272,460	330,125
Lincoln Blackwood	—	153	3,066	137	—
Ford Total	**1,047,804**	**1,016,157**	**1,003,197**	**1,137,749**	**1,150,373**
Cadillac Escalade EXT	9,638	11,256	13,494	546	—
Chevrolet Avalanche	80,566	93,482	89,372	52,955	—
Chevrolet C/K Pickup	—	—	292	6,687	84,928
Chevrolet Colorado	117,475	3,535	—	—	—
Chevrolet S10 Pickup	10,014	136,573	150,992	162,181	211,587
Chevrolet Silverado	680,663	683,889	647,748	701,699	549,190
Chevrolet SSR	9,648	1,664	—	—	—
GMC Canyon	27,193	1,471	—	—	—
GMC Sierra	213,736	196,429	200,146	206,930	185,187
GMC Sonoma	3,303	35,040	41,100	42,062	51,093
GM Total	**1,152,236**	**1,163,339**	**1,143,144**	**1,173,060**	**1,081,985**
Isuzu Hombre	—	4	21	115	4,782
Isuzu Total	**—**	**4**	**21**	**115**	**4,782**
Mazda Pickup	10,266	14,970	20,265	26,131	30,124
Mazda Total	**10,266**	**14,970**	**20,265**	**26,131**	**30,124**
Nissan Frontier	70,703	65,161	75,207	89,434	108,738
Nissan Titan	83,848	2,072	—	—	—
Nissan Total	**154,551**	**67,233**	**75,207**	**89,434**	**108,738**
Subaru Baja	7,316	10,694	2,513	—	—
Subaru Total	**7,316**	**10,694**	**2,513**	**—**	**—**
Toyota T100*	—	—	—	—	9
Toyota Tacoma	152,933	154,154	151,960	161,983	147,295
Toyota Tundra	112,484	101,316	99,333	108,863	100,445
Toyota Total	**265,417**	**255,470**	**251,293**	**270,846**	**247,749**
PICKUP TOTAL	**3,169,493**	**3,088,511**	**3,023,286**	**3,196,352**	**3,182,020**
General Motors	952	932	881	496	3,367
General Motors*	1,072	963	848	274	4,269
Isuzu	1,457	1,546	1,127	120	2,052
Isuzu*	3,535	2,890	3,335	1,633	4,367
Mercedes	270	370	146	80	576
Mitsubishi*	720	691	811	1,313	2,079
Nissan*	352	316	333	354	698
COMMERCIAL CHASSIS TOTAL	**8,358**	**7,708**	**7,481**	**4,270**	**17,408**
TOTAL LIGHT TRUCKS	**9,360,988**	**9,028,572**	**8,713,139**	**8,699,744**	**8,503,130**

*Units imported from outside North America.
SOURCE: *Ward's AutoInfoBank.*

U.S. Retail Sales of Trucks by Manufacturer and Gross Vehicle Weight Rating

U.S. RETAIL SALES OF TRUCKS BY MANUFACTURER AND GVWR, 2004

	Gross Vehicle Weight Rating (Pounds)								
	6,000 & Less	6,001- 10,000	10,000- 14,000	14,001- 16,000	16,001- 19,500	19,501- 26,000	26,001- 33,000	33,001 & Over	Total
DOMESTIC*									
BMW	35,225	—	—	—	—	—	—	—	35,225
Chrysler	1,151,056	540,758	29,859	—	—	—	—	—	1,721,673
Ford	883,304	1,210,138	68,615	18,840	21,330	16,091	4,277	—	2,222,595
Freightliner	—	—	270	4,491	556	23,709	23,058	73,731	125,815
General Motors	1,828,341	950,995	1,399	9,474	7,609	3,799	8,249	—	2,809,866
Hino	—	—	—	73	91	382	88	—	634
Honda	401,828	—	—	—	—	—	—	—	401,828
Isuzu	27,170	—	1,457	946	—	42	553	—	30,168
Kenworth	—	—	—	—	—	—	5,020	23,294	28,314
Mack	—	—	—	—	—	—	—	20,670	20,670
Mazda	51,344	—	—	—	—	—	—	—	51,344
Mercedes-Benz	25,681	—	—	—	—	—	—	—	25,681
Mitsubishi	22,433	—	—	—	—	—	—	—	22,433
Navistar	—	—	—	—	—	23,405	28,873	38,242	90,520
Nissan	246,217	83,848	—	—	—	—	—	—	330,065
Peterbilt	—	—	—	—	—	—	4,495	26,145	30,640
Subaru	7,316	—	—	—	—	—	—	—	7,316
Suzuki	3,476	—	—	—	—	—	—	—	3,476
Toyota	544,000	—	—	—	—	—	—	—	544,000
Volvo Truck	—	—	—	—	—	—	—	20,323	20,323
Other Domestic	—	—	—	—	—	—	—	792	792
Total Domestic	**5,227,391**	**2,785,739**	**101,600**	**33,824**	**29,586**	**67,428**	**74,613**	**203,197**	**8,523,378**
IMPORT									
BMW	34,604	—	—	—	—	—	—	—	34,604
Chrysler	—	10,232	—	—	—	—	—	—	10,232
General Motors	—	—	1,072	3,622	1,598	—	—	—	6,292
Hino	—	—	—	223	310	974	246	—	1,753
Honda	149,281	—	—	—	—	—	—	—	149,281
Hyundai	118,521	—	—	—	—	—	—	—	118,521
Isuzu	18	—	3,535	6,463	2,711	—	—	—	12,727
Kia	114,147	—	—	—	—	—	—	—	114,147
Land Rover	35,506	—	—	—	—	—	—	—	35,506
Mack	—	—	—	—	—	—	21	—	21
Mazda	24,860	—	—	—	—	—	—	—	24,860
Mercedes-Benz	1,491	—	—	—	—	—	—	—	1,491
Mitsubishi	30,239	—	—	—	—	—	—	—	30,239
Mitsubishi Fuso	—	—	720	2,336	1,226	709	113	—	5,104
Nissan	119,167	—	—	—	—	—	—	—	119,167
Nissan Diesel	—	—	352	619	828	909	97	—	2,805
Porsche	18,117	—	—	—	—	—	—	—	18,117
Subaru	58,424	—	—	—	—	—	—	—	58,424
Suzuki	23,361	—	—	—	—	—	—	—	23,361
Toyota	414,828	—	—	—	—	—	—	—	414,828
Volkswagen	32,541	—	—	—	—	—	—	—	32,541
Volvo (Car)	55,242	—	—	—	—	—	—	—	55,242
Total Import	**1,230,347**	**10,232**	**5,679**	**13,263**	**6,673**	**2,592**	**477**	**—**	**1,269,263**
Total Trucks	**6,457,738**	**2,795,971**	**107,279**	**47,087**	**36,259**	**70,020**	**75,090**	**203,197**	**9,792,641**

*Units produced in the United States, Canada and Mexico.
NOTE: Includes school bus chassis.
SOURCE: Ward's AutoInfoBank

U.S. Retail Sales of Trucks by Gross Vehicle Weight Rating and Body Type

U.S. RETAIL SALES OF LIGHT TRUCKS BY GROSS VEHICLE WEIGHT RATING AND BODY TYPE

GVWR/Body type	2004	2003	2002	2001
0-6,000 Lbs.				
Utility	3,859,330	3,622,877	3,321,454	3,052,310
Compact Pickup	670,787	743,652	798,864	908,845
Mini Van	20,406	21,337	26,669	31,180
Van	30,803	30,782	32,960	33,354
Conventional Pickup	781,606	792,103	777,867	919,959
Mini Passenger Carrier	1,090,411	1,053,344	1,101,459	1,137,922
Passenger Carrier	4,395	4,452	9,079	6,973
Total 0-6,000 lbs.	**6,457,738**	**6,268,547**	**6,068,352**	**6,090,543**
6,001-10,000 Lbs.				
Utility	692,026	710,011	671,264	686,156
Van	195,624	192,234	214,359	233,616
Van Cutaway	66,135	50,064	32,772	26,844
Conventional Pickup	1,608,988	1,464,813	1,374,750	1,281,918
Station Wagon	185,462	206,109	218,612	225,582
Passenger Carrier	47,736	45,946	52,988	62,045
Multi-Stop	0	0	0	262
Total 6,001-10,000 lbs.	**2,795,971**	**2,669,177**	**2,564,745**	**2,516,423**
10,001 - 14,000 lbs.				
Conventional Pickup	98,474	82,410	72,722	85,630
Other Body Types	8,805	8,438	7,320	7,148
Total 10,001 - 14,000 lbs.	107,279	90,848	80,042	92,778
Total Domestic Light Trucks	**9,360,988**	**9,028,572**	**8,713,139**	**8,699,744**

SOURCE: *Ward's Database Opers.*

U.S. RETAIL SALES OF DOMESTIC AND IMPORTED TRUCKS

	Domestic				Imports				
	Gross Vehicle Weight Rating								
Year	0-14,000 lbs.	14,001-33,000 lbs.	33,001 lbs. & Over	Total Domestic	From Japan	From Germany	From Other Countries	Total Imports	Total U.S. Sales
2004	8,114,730	205,451	203,197	8,523,378	774,203	60,890	434,170	1,269,263	9,792,641
2003	7,801,392	167,565	141,964	8,110,921	840,084	41,829	364,127	1,246,040	9,356,961
2002	7,646,764	159,128	146,031	7,951,923	812,433	12,680	258,387	1,083,500	9,035,423
2001	7,718,464	189,573	139,591	8,047,628	813,389	11,957	176,779	1,002,125	9,049,753
2000	7,650,805	229,836	211,502	8,092,143	759,836	3,747	109,322	872,905	8,965,048
1999	7,420,031	239,562	262,316	7,921,909	707,866	3,395	83,274	794,535	8,716,444
1998	6,745,284	196,321	209,483	7,151,088	621,187	1,742	51,549	674,478	7,825,566
1997	6,270,164	183,767	178,551	6,632,482	546,564	1,792	44,948	593,304	7,225,786
1996	6,131,673	176,140	170,009	6,477,822	415,959	995	34,583	451,537	6,929,359
1995	5,690,903	171,948	201,303	6,064,154	385,558	1,460	30,189	417,207	6,481,361
1994	5,658,302	151,897	185,696	5,995,895	406,014	4,675	14,273	424,962	6,420,857
1993	5,000,482	129,016	157,886	5,287,384	381,434	5,634	6,543	393,611	5,680,995
1992	4,247,097	115,643	119,029	4,481,769	413,926	2,681	5,955	422,562	4,904,331
1991	3,605,633	109,946	98,646	3,814,225	539,471	5,039	5,809	550,319	4,364,544
1990	3,956,756	138,771	121,117	4,216,644	610,402	6,368	12,749	629,519	4,846,163

SOURCE: *Ward's AutoInfoBank.*

Annual and Monthly Records for U.S. Production and Sales

RECORD U.S. PRODUCTION YEARS

Passenger Cars		Trucks	
Year	Units	Year	Units
1973	9,667,152	2004	7,730,729
1965	9,335,227	2003	7,576,559
1977	9,213,654	1999	7,387,029
1978	9,176,635	2002	7,260,805
1968	8,848,620	2000	7,231,497
1972	8,828,205	2001	6,545,570
1966	8,604,712	1998	6,448,290

RECORD U.S. RETAIL SALES YEARS

Passenger Cars		Trucks	
Year	Units	Year	Units
1973	11,423,851	2004	9,792,641
1986	11,404,239	2003	9,356,961
1978	11,314,079	2001	9,049,753
1977	11,183,412	2002	9,035,423
1985	10,979,187	2000	8,965,048
1972	10,940,482	1999	8,716,444
1979	10,672,768	1998	7,825,566

RECORD U.S. PRODUCTION BY MONTH

Month	Year	Units
Passenger Cars		
January	1973	917,273
February	1973	856,117
March	1965	963,101
April	1978	870,689
May	1973	941,019
June	1977	949,440
July	1965	740,576
August	1950	684,970
September	1972	758,578
October	1973	951,434
November	1965	913,146
December	1964	866,632
Trucks		
January	2003	632,322
February	2004	674,210
March	2004	783,795
April	2004	688,282
May	2000	707,996
June	2000	696,694
July	2003	425,176
August	1999	687,772
September	2003	703,425
October	2003	751,813
November	2004	619,700
December	2003	590,003

RECORD U.S. RETAIL SALES BY MONTH

Month	Year	Units
Passenger Cars		
January	1973	874,084
February	1973	918,681
March	1973	1,140,386
April	1978	1,043,341
May	1978	1,159,996
June	1978	1,138,504
July	1973	958,270
August	1986	1,000,658
September	1987	1,217,171
October	1972	1,068,400
November	1972	1,029,689
December	1987	995,415
Trucks		
January	2004	654,205
February	2000	770,225
March	2000	877,168
April	2004	811,617
May	2004	917,990
June	2001	841,067
July	2004	907,154
August	2003	918,029
September	2004	864,277
October	2001	939,731
November	2001	744,961
December	2004	931,450

U.S. FACTORY SALES MILESTONES

Passenger Cars		Trucks		Total Motor Vehicles	
Year	Units	Year	Units	Year	Units
2003	500 millionth	1998	150 millionth	2001	600 millionth
1994	400 millionth	1988	100 millionth	1992	500 millionth
1986	350 millionth	1979	75 millionth	1982	400 millionth
1979	300 millionth	1971	50 millionth	1972	300 millionth
1973	250 millionth	1965	40 millionth	1962	200 millionth
1967	200 millionth	1957	30 millionth	1955	150 millionth
1952	100 millionth	1949	20 millionth	1948	100 millionth
1935	50 millionth	1938	10 millionth	1931	50 millionth
1925	25 millionth	1929	5 millionth	1920	10 millionth
1920	10 millionth	1920	1 millionth	1912	1 millionth
1912	1 millionth	1915	100,000th	1906	100,000th

SOURCE: *Ward's Database Opers.*

Top Selling Vehicles and Automotive Color Popularity

TOP 20 SELLING PASSENGER CARS IN THE U.S.

2004		2003		2002	
Toyota Camry	426,990	Toyota Camry	413,296	Toyota Camry	434,145
Honda Accord	386,770	Honda Accord	397,750	Honda Accord	398,980
Toyota Corolla/Matrix	333,161	Toyota Corolla/Matrix	325,477	Ford Taurus	332,690
Honda Civic	309,196	Ford Taurus	300,496	Honda Civic	313,159
Chevrolet Impala	290,259	Honda Civic	299,672	Toyota Corolla/Matrix	254,360
Chevrolet Malibu	268,017	Chevrolet Impala	267,882	Ford Focus	243,199
Ford Taurus	248,148	Chevrolet Cavalier	256,550	Chevrolet Cavalier	238,225
Nissan Altima	235,889	Ford Focus	229,353	Nissan Altima	201,822
Ford Focus	208,339	Nissan Altima	201,240	Chevrolet Impala	198,918
Chevrolet Cavalier	195,275	Chevrolet Malibu	173,263	Chevrolet Malibu	169,377
Pontiac Grand Am	133,707	Pontiac Grand Am	156,466	Buick Century	163,739
Pontiac Grand Prix	131,551	Ford Mustang	140,350	Pontiac Grand Am	150,818
Ford Mustang	129,858	Pontiac Grand Prix	125,441	Volkswagen Jetta	145,604
Buick Lesabre	114,157	Hyundai Elantra	120,858	Ford Mustang	138,356
Dodge Neon	113,476	Dodge Neon	120,101	Buick Lesabre	135,916
Hyundai Elantra	112,892	Volkswagen Jetta	117,867	Pontiac Grand Prix	130,141
Chrysler 300 Series	107,820	Saturn Ion	117,230	Dodge Neon	126,118
Hyundai Sonata	107,189	Buick Lesabre	114,572	Hyundai Elantra	120,638
Nissan Sentra	106,934	BMW 3-Series	111,944	Saturn S	117,533
BMW 3-Series	106,549	Oldsmobile Alero	99,123	BMW 3-Series	115,428

TOP 20 SELLING LIGHT TRUCKS IN THE U.S.

2004		2003		2002	
Ford F-Series	891,482	Ford F-Series	806,887	Ford F-Series	774,037
Chevrolet Silverado	680,663	Chevrolet Silverado	683,889	Chevrolet Silverado	647,748
Dodge Ram Pickup	426,289	Dodge Ram Pickup	449,371	Ford Explorer	433,847
Ford Explorer	339,333	Ford Explorer	373,118	Dodge Ram Pickup	396,934
Chevrolet TrailBlazer	283,484	Chevrolet TrailBlazer	261,334	Chevrolet TrailBlazer	249,568
Dodge Caravan	242,307	Dodge Caravan	233,394	Dodge Caravan	244,911
GMC Sierra	213,736	Ford Ranger	209,117	Ford Ranger	226,094
Chevrolet Tahoe	186,161	Jeep Grand Cherokee	207,479	Jeep Grand Cherokee	224,233
Ford Escape	183,430	Chevrolet Tahoe	199,065	Chevrolet Tahoe	209,767
Jeep Grand Cherokee	182,313	GMC Sierra	196,429	GMC Sierra	200,146
Ford Econoline	171,017	Ford Expedition	181,547	Jeep Liberty	171,212
Jeep Liberty	167,376	Ford Escape	167,678	Ford Econoline	165,085
Ford Expedition	159,846	Jeep Liberty	162,987	Ford Expedition	163,454
Toyota Sienna	159,119	Ford Econoline	161,721	Honda Odyssey	153,467
Ford Ranger	156,322	Toyota Tacoma	154,154	Toyota Tacoma	151,960
Honda Odyssey	154,238	Honda Odyssey	154,063	Chevrolet Suburban	151,056
Toyota Tacoma	152,933	Honda CRV	143,909	Chevrolet S10 Pickup	150,992
Honda CRV	149,281	Chevrolet S10 Pickup	136,573	Ford Windstar	148,875
Chrysler Town & Country	142,523	Chevrolet Suburban	135,222	Honda CRV	146,266
Dodge Durango	137,148	GMC Envoy	127,782	Ford Escape	145,471

SOURCE: *Ward's AutoInfoBank*.

AUTOMOTIVE PAINT COLOR POPULARITY BY VEHICLE TYPE, 2004 MODEL YEAR

Luxury Cars		Full Size/Intermediate Cars		Compact/Sports Cars		Light Trucks	
Color	Percent	Color	Percent	Color	Percent	Color	Percent
Silver/Gray	26%	Silver	24%	Silver	20%	White/White Pearl	20%
White Pearl	17%	Light Brown	17%	Black	13%	Silver	16%
White	12%	Red	12%	Red	17%	Black	12%
Black	12%	White	13%	Blue	13%	Red	14%
Light Brown	11%	Black	9%	Medium/Dark Gray	8%	Blue	12%
Red	9%	Medium/Dark Gray	11%	White	9%	Medium/Dark Gray	10%
Blue	9%	Blue	6%	Light Brown	9%	Light Brown	9%
Yellow/Gold	4%	Green	5%	Green	4%	Green	5%
Other	1%	Yellow/Gold	1%	Yellow	4%	Yellow/Gold	1%
		Other	2%	Other	3%	Other	1%

SOURCE: Du Pont Automotive Products.

Motor Vehicle Sales and Registrations in Canada

VEHICLE SALES IN CANADA

Year	Passenger Cars Domestic[1]	Imports	Total	Commercial Vehicles Domestic[1]	Imports	Total	Total Vehicles
2004	543,630	275,783	819,413	651,662	103,728	755,390	1,574,803
2003	603,444	261,545	864,989	654,112	105,949	760,061	1,625,050
2002	651,703	282,354	934,057	700,427	97,339	797,766	1,731,823
2001	620,162	248,026	868,188	651,952	77,735	729,687	1,597,875
2000	640,916	208,216	849,132	673,631	63,320	736,951	1,586,083
1999	620,233	186,207	806,440	676,107	57,832	733,939	1,540,379
1998	590,041	150,775	740,816	629,720	56,056	685,776	1,426,592
1997	628,739	109,816	738,555	628,124	56,315	684,439	1,422,994
1996	572,001	88,803	660,804	516,288	25,302	541,590	1,202,394
1995	554,878	116,103	670,981	470,147	23,470	493,617	1,164,598
1994	584,985	165,343	750,328	478,826	27,828	506,654	1,256,982
1993	511,611	229,257	740,868	407,864	41,850	449,714	1,190,582
1992	511,220	289,107	800,327	369,896	54,155	424,051	1,224,378
1991	576,480	299,308	875,788	346,332	62,529	408,861	1,284,649
1990	588,944	299,037	887,981	358,098	68,132	426,230	1,314,211
1989	669,040	321,779	990,819	419,065	68,662	487,727	1,478,546
1988	738,388	314,649	1,053,037	456,016	52,419	508,435	1,561,472
1987	716,575	348,239	1,064,814	414,617	48,557	463,174	1,527,988
1986	756,265	331,314	1,087,579	370,148	54,361	424,509	1,512,088
1985	794,511	338,592	1,133,103	344,939	50,982	395,921	1,529,024
1984	724,932	246,278	971,210	273,604	38,688	312,292	1,283,502
1983	625,088	218,230	843,318	192,609	45,161	237,770	1,081,088
1982	489,435	224,046	713,481	166,986	40,435	207,421	920,902
1981	646,942	257,253	904,195	250,775	35,912	288,687	1,192,882
1980	740,767	191,293	932,060	310,273	21,474	331,747	1,263,807
1979	863,554	139,454	1,003,008	381,562	11,832	393,394	1,396,402
1978	815,994	172,896	988,890	364,241	13,413	377,654	1,366,544
1977	797,752	193,646	991,398	337,914	15,647	353,561	1,344,959

(1) Units produced in the United States, Canada and Mexico.
SOURCE: *Ward's AutoInfoBank*

TOTAL REGISTRATIONS BY PROVINCE, 2004

Province	Total Vehicle Registrations by Weight less than 9,000 lbs.	over 9,000 lbs.	Buses	Total
Alberta	2,148,694	166,218	12,789	2,327,701
British Columbia	2,273,461	92,820	8,201	2,374,482
Manitoba	616,014	24,791	3,701	644,506
New Brunswick	442,592	11,448	2,743	456,783
Newfoundland	253,182	6,853	1,348	261,383
Northwest Territories	19,939	1,518	99	21,556
Nova Scotia	518,429	7,789	1,818	528,036
Nunavut	2,927	343	14	3,284
Ontario	6,679,102	191,464	25,667	6,896,233
Prince Edward Island	75,162	4,333	49	79,544
Quebec	4,224,895	94,297	16,946	4,336,138
Saskatchewan	642,053	62,826	3,798	708,677
Yukon	23,904	2,624	268	26,796
Total	17,920,354	667,324	77,441	18,665,119

SOURCE: Statistics Canada.

TOTAL REGISTRATIONS IN CANADA

Year	Passenger Cars (000)	Commercial Vehicles (000)	Total (000)
2004	17,920	745	18,665
2003	17,755	741	18,496
2002	17,544	723	18,267
2001	17,055	728	17,783
2000	16,832	739	17,571
1999	16,538	2,679	19,217
1998	13,887	3,694	17,581
1997	13,487	3,591	17,078
1996	13,217	3,644	16,861
1994	13,122	3,466	16,588
1992	12,781	3,413	16,194
1990	12,622	3,931	16,553
1988	12,086	3,766	15,852
1986	11,586	3,213	14,799
1984	10,781	3,099	13,880
1982	10,530	3,293	13,823
1980	10,256	2,955	13,211
1978	9,745	2,771	12,516

NOTE: Beginning in 2000, data excludes farm tractors and off-road vehicles. SOURCE: Statistics Canada.

Motor Vehicle Sales in Canada

CANADA VEHICLE SALES

Model	2004	2003	2002	2001	2000
Lada Car*	—	—	—	—	25
AUTO VAZ TOTAL	**—**	**—**	**—**	**—**	**25**
3-Series*	7,727	8,461	8,175	6,784	6,047
5-Series*	2,002	1,744	1,742	1,802	2,000
6-Series*	478	—	—	—	—
7-Series*	605	760	1,002	466	551
Z3	—	1	349	790	547
Z4	521	822	74	—	—
Z8*	5	20	14	58	37
BMW Total	**11,338**	**11,808**	**11,356**	**9,900**	**9,182**
Mini Cooper*	2,800	2,708	2,102	—	—
BMW TOTAL	**14,138**	**14,516**	**13,458**	**9,900**	**9,182**
300M	407	3,463	3,753	3,731	4,255
300 Series	10,073	—	—	—	—
Avenger	—	—	—	—	65
Cirrus	—	—	—	579	10,851
Concorde	833	2,816	4,280	3,567	4,216
Crossfire*	763	85	—	—	—
Intrepid	2,648	11,546	15,489	15,873	22,935
LHS	—	—	17	517	1,246
Neon	—	566	12,954	22,096	31,222
Prowler	—	41	116	90	—
PT Cruiser Convertible	1,235	—	—	—	—
Sebring Convertible	1,591	2,085	2,129	1,845	1,339
Sebring Coupe	—	—	248	793	439
Sebring Sedan	15,444	16,920	19,750	18,927	3,860
Chrysler Total	**32,994**	**37,522**	**58,736**	**68,018**	**80,428**
Dodge SX 2.0	14,876	16,329	2,941	—	—
Neon	—	—	—	—	129
Viper	115	149	90	108	152
Dodge Total	**14,991**	**16,478**	**3,031**	**108**	**281**
Plymouth Prowler	—	—	—	14	144
CHRYSLER GROUP TOTAL	**47,985**	**54,000**	**61,767**	**68,140**	**80,853**
Lanos*	—	—	305	876	2,111
Leganza*	—	—	39	188	637
Nubira*	—	—	59	503	1,263
DAEWOO TOTAL	**—**	**—**	**403**	**1,567**	**4,011**
Contour	—	—	—	—	68
Crown Victoria	3,326	4,186	3,470	2,961	3,021
Escort	—	—	—	199	1,978
Five Hundred	730	—	—	—	—
Focus	28,391	35,705	40,228	41,752	48,598
Mustang	6,968	8,025	7,524	6,861	7,936
Taurus	12,724	16,319	23,389	22,810	27,291
Thunderbird	218	938	1,136	558	—
Ford Total	**52,357**	**65,173**	**75,747**	**75,141**	**88,892**
S-Type*	416	607	745	1,120	1,250
X-Type*	886	1,181	1,313	617	—
XJ6/8*	358	438	310	498	718
XK8*	91	140	188	226	355
Jaguar Total	**1,751**	**2,366**	**2,556**	**2,461**	**2,323**
Continental	—	13	658	508	435
Lincoln LS	1,100	1,335	1,852	2,145	2,498
Town Car	1,548	2,326	2,457	1,762	1,963
Lincoln Total	**2,648**	**3,674**	**4,967**	**4,415**	**4,896**
Cougar	—	168	509	1,263	2,799
Grand Marquis	1,375	1,476	1,603	1,771	2,806
Mystique	—	—	—	—	60
Sable	—	—	—	—	285
Mercury Total	**1,375**	**1,644**	**2,112**	**3,034**	**5,950**
40*	1,711	1,941	2,296	2,820	2,105
50*	456	—	—	—	—
60*	2,886	2,946	3,226	2,799	283
70*	1,180	1,134	1,281	1,325	4,210
80*	520	445	596	684	1,692
Volvo Total	**6,753**	**6,466**	**7,399**	**7,628**	**8,290**
FORD TOTAL	**64,884**	**79,323**	**92,781**	**92,679**	**110,351**
Allure	1,414	—	—	—	—
Century	7,151	12,252	15,023	12,154	10,964
Lesabre	2,583	3,469	4,564	4,947	7,283
Park Ave	150	277	319	561	932

Motor Vehicle Sales in Canada

CANADA VEHICLE SALES — continued

Model	2004	2003	2002	2001	2000
Regal	1,285	3,044	4,444	4,586	4,499
Riviera	—	—	—	2	10
Skylark	—	—	—	—	3
Buick Total	**12,583**	**19,042**	**24,350**	**22,250**	**23,691**
Catera*	—	3	62	484	669
CTS	2,079	2,406	1,977	—	—
Deville	1,363	1,878	2,261	2,318	3,013
Eldorado	—	3	50	74	136
Seville	263	636	1,131	1,223	1,603
STS	202	—	—	—	—
XLR	154	22	—	—	—
Cadillac Total	**4,061**	**4,948**	**5,481**	**4,099**	**5,421**
Aveo*	13,712	988	—	—	—
Camaro	7	83	803	398	507
Cavalier	29,229	41,254	53,614	49,094	45,966
Cobalt	178	—	—	—	—
Corvette	680	981	1,230	1,044	1,181
Epica*	6,089	243	—	—	—
Impala	20,876	25,028	20,018	18,352	14,771
Lumina	—	—	2	3	73
Malibu	15,062	18,174	17,880	17,714	24,389
Metro	—	—	—	3	534
Monte Carlo	2,216	2,854	2,597	2,773	3,269
Optra*	16,853	546	—	—	—
Chevrolet Total	**104,902**	**90,151**	**96,144**	**89,381**	**90,690**
Alero	7,461	15,958	17,371	17,721	17,347
Aurora	52	442	1,024	2,018	2,052
Intrigue	2	22	6,494	5,744	6,991
Olds 88	—	—	—	3	40
Oldsmobile Total	**7,515**	**16,422**	**24,889**	**25,486**	**26,430**
Bonneville	705	684	1,511	1,783	2,996
Firebird	4	29	842	468	651
Firefly	—	—	—	—	164
G6	2,556	—	—	—	—
Grand Am	17,082	24,322	23,774	26,203	26,876
Grand Prix	12,289	12,490	16,598	13,125	14,771
Pursuit	215	—	—	—	—
Sunfire	33,724	35,766	46,036	41,398	41,098
Vibe	10,025	7,462	6,631	—	—
Wave*	1,440	—	—	—	—
Pontiac Total	**78,040**	**80,753**	**95,392**	**82,977**	**86,556**
9-2X*	168	—	—	—	—
9-3*	1,308	1,114	986	940	871
9-5*	388	596	778	770	684
Saab Total	**1,864**	**1,710**	**1,764**	**1,710**	**1,555**
Ion	12,323	11,250	564	—	—
Saturn L	1,091	2,818	4,246	3,803	5,374
Saturn S	69	1,182	15,823	16,012	17,075
Saturn Total	**13,483**	**15,250**	**20,633**	**19,815**	**22,449**
GM TOTAL	**222,448**	**228,276**	**268,653**	**245,718**	**256,792**
CL	73	355	740	950	1,217
EL	5,010	5,572	8,085	9,073	7,997
Integra*	—	—	631	5,597	3,781
NSX*	6	2	3	4	6
RL*	333	172	327	313	459
RSX*	3,342	5,024	5,653	—	—
TL	5,801	4,320	4,802	5,781	5,714
TSX*	3,797	3,046	—	—	—
Acura Total	**18,362**	**18,491**	**20,241**	**21,718**	**19,174**
Accord	25,814	29,609	30,060	28,383	24,635
Civic	60,889	63,427	68,754	66,299	60,407
Civic*	1,236	1,742	1,219	1	—
Insight*	9	20	76	109	155
Prelude*	2	3	642	2,531	2,031
S2000*	250	238	336	401	412
Honda Total	**88,200**	**95,039**	**101,087**	**97,724**	**87,640**
HONDA TOTAL	**106,562**	**113,530**	**121,328**	**119,442**	**106,814**
Accent*	19,172	24,409	26,538	25,322	21,948
Elantra*	15,375	17,513	18,290	15,788	8,045
Sonata*	6,974	6,940	7,626	7,415	5,154
Tiburon*	2,155	3,865	4,828	4,047	2,802
XG300*	—	—	—	857	284

Motor Vehicle Sales in Canada

CANADA VEHICLE SALES — continued

Model	2004	2003	2002	2001	2000
XG350*	625	626	947	251	—
HYUNDAI TOTAL	**44,301**	**53,353**	**58,229**	**53,680**	**38,233**
Amanti*	946	269	—	—	—
Magentis*	2,041	2,560	2,222	2,037	12
Rio*	8,311	11,967	11,148	9,900	2,444
Sephia*	—	—	16	4,807	5,914
Spectra*	5,826	4,317	4,963	1,589	—
KIA TOTAL	**17,124**	**19,113**	**18,349**	**18,333**	**8,370**
Mazda3*	42,680	3,245	—	—	—
Mazda6	10,213	6,398	—	—	—
Mazda 626	—	1	1,766	1,755	2,953
Miata*	1,146	1,079	1,230	1,271	1,328
Millenia*	—	3	307	551	894
Protégé*	4,292	38,059	48,872	46,323	30,701
RX-8*	2,118	791	—	—	—
MAZDA TOTAL	**60,449**	**49,576**	**52,175**	**49,900**	**35,876**
C-Class*	6,295	6,981	7,755	5,552	4,612
E-Class*	2,151	2,563	1,919	1,651	2,012
Maybach*	7	8	—	—	—
S-Class*	785	1,315	1,140	1,218	1,459
SL-Class*	599	708	640	130	227
SLR*	10	—	—	—	—
Mercedes Total	**9,847**	**11,575**	**11,454**	**8,551**	**8,310**
Smart Fortwo*	915	—	—	—	—
MERCEDES TOTAL	**10,762**	**11,575**	**11,454**	**8,551**	**8,310**
Diamante*	84	3	—	—	—
Eclipse	993	1,496	410	—	—
Galant	931	2,801	475	—	—
Lancer*	5,406	6,498	1,805	—	—
MITSUBISHI TOTAL	**7,414**	**10,798**	**2,690**	**—**	**—**
G20*	—	4	176	558	564
G35*	4,954	5,494	4,122	—	—
I30*	—	—	—	855	1,439
I35*	113	431	1,058	412	—
M45*	31	98	45	—	—
Q45*	44	66	106	190	41
Infiniti Total	**5,142**	**6,093**	**5,507**	**2,015**	**2,044**
200SX	—	—	—	—	2
240SX*	—	—	—	—	4
350Z*	983	1,559	741	—	—
Altima	18,508	17,158	15,041	8,620	7,579
Maxima	5,209	6,302	—	—	—
Maxima*	—	1,208	6,275	6,913	8,543
Sentra	12,744	16,418	21,706	25,616	11,998
Nissan Total	**37,444**	**42,645**	**43,763**	**41,149**	**28,126**
NISSAN TOTAL	**42,586**	**48,738**	**49,270**	**43,164**	**30,170**
Boxster*	215	344	469	598	734
Carrera GT*	11	—	—	—	—
Porsche 911*	573	527	724	504	558
PORSCHE TOTAL	**799**	**871**	**1,193**	**1,102**	**1,292**
Impreza*	5,533	5,679	6,134	4,570	2,521
Legacy	6,493	5,399	6,834	7,089	7,477
SUBARU TOTAL	**12,026**	**11,078**	**12,968**	**11,659**	**9,998**
Aerio*	3,172	4,699	4,987	—	—
Esteem*	—	—	996	3,060	3,483
Swift	—	—	—	1,135	1,302
Swift+*	3,068	148	—	—	—
Verona*	626	31	—	—	—
SUZUKI TOTAL	**6,866**	**4,878**	**5,983**	**4,195**	**4,785**
ES300*	—	1,202	2,152	1,049	910
ES330*	2,123	604	—	—	—
GS300*	24	84	106	116	233
GS400*	—	—	—	—	170
GS430*	37	85	120	126	12
IS300*	448	747	897	1,024	728
LS400*	—	—	—	—	104
LS430*	309	282	385	455	159
SC430*	246	338	592	554	—
Lexus Total	**3,187**	**3,342**	**4,252**	**3,324**	**2,316**
Avalon	187	287	567	887	1,771
Camry	21,965	4,522	1,249	1,842	2,046
Camry*	593	19,182	28,967	21,507	19,770

Motor Vehicle Sales in Canada

CANADA VEHICLE SALES — continued

Model	2004	2003	2002	2001	2000
Celica*	1,027	1,290	2,422	2,515	3,587
Corolla	44,563	48,676	44,790	39,161	40,692
Echo*	31,252	24,952	23,909	21,562	24,611
Matrix	20,017	17,459	7,327	—	—
Paseo*	—	—	—	—	1
Prius*	1,951	249	210	418	225
Tercel*	—	—	—	—	4
Toyota Total	**121,555**	**116,617**	**109,441**	**87,892**	**92,707**
TOYOTA TOTAL	**124,742**	**119,959**	**113,693**	**91,216**	**95,023**
A4*	5,650	5,911	5,028	3,506	3,371
A6*	843	869	1,117	1,304	1,722
A8*	290	204	114	163	121
TT*	321	442	564	658	778
Audi Total	**7,104**	**7,426**	**6,823**	**5,631**	**5,992**
Beetle	872	1,604	2,610	4,190	6,023
Beetle Cabrio	909	1,247	—	—	—
Golf*	6,875	10,447	10,498	9,554	9,061
Jetta	15,826	20,372	23,984	23,315	22,455
Passat*	4,648	4,281	5,088	5,230	4,574
Phaeton*	93	22	—	—	—
VW Cabriolet	—	6	660	1,022	942
Volkswagen Total	**29,223**	**37,979**	**42,840**	**43,311**	**43,055**
VOLKSWAGEN TOTAL	**36,327**	**45,405**	**49,663**	**48,942**	**49,047**
TOTAL CARS	**819,413**	**864,989**	**934,057**	**868,188**	**849,132**
Lada Niva*	—	—	—	—	76
AUTO VAZ TOTAL	**—**	**—**	**—**	**—**	**76**
X3*	2,304	—	—	—	—
X5	2,956	3,352	3,164	2,802	1,840
BMW TOTAL	**5,260**	**3,352**	**3,164**	**2,802**	**1,840**
Pacifica	5,159	3,009	—	—	—
PT Cruiser	8,005	8,107	10,572	14,588	11,091
Town & Country	850	997	1,601	1,872	2,635
Chrysler Total	**14,014**	**12,113**	**12,173**	**16,460**	**13,726**
Caravan	63,559	61,869	83,588	84,056	87,737
Dakota	12,466	14,126	17,152	15,665	18,124
Durango	6,394	4,046	6,036	6,362	8,015
Magnum	2,137	—	—	—	—
Ram Pickup	37,709	36,686	32,950	26,110	29,124
Ram Van	—	1,399	1,737	2,984	4,153
Ram Wagon	—	—	214	411	565
Sprinter Van*	1,081	—	—	—	—
Dodge Total	**123,346**	**118,126**	**141,677**	**135,588**	**147,718**
Cherokee	—	—	—	1,746	4,805
Grand Cherokee	7,454	8,636	10,320	11,882	15,842
Liberty	13,543	15,045	15,164	6,676	—
Wrangler	4,524	5,015	5,676	5,060	5,844
Jeep Total	**25,521**	**28,696**	**31,160**	**25,364**	**26,491**
CHRYSLER GROUP TOTAL	**162,881**	**158,935**	**185,010**	**177,412**	**187,935**
Econoline	14,047	13,144	12,547	12,334	14,534
Escape	20,360	18,482	15,945	15,232	2,908
Excursion	426	600	619	776	1,978
Expedition	2,992	4,283	4,250	3,569	5,368
Explorer	14,266	21,224	24,218	20,768	23,201
Ford F-Series	68,009	65,241	64,455	62,215	71,115
Freestar	22,078	1,990	—	—	—
Freestyle	487	—	—	—	—
Ranger	8,775	10,323	11,235	8,828	7,854
Windstar	—	30,509	37,428	40,125	49,636
Ford Total	**151,440**	**165,796**	**170,697**	**163,847**	**176,594**
Discovery*	368	449	586	696	839
Freelander*	508	841	1,227	113	—
LR3*	132	—	—	—	—
Range Rover*	338	313	361	217	176
Land Rover Total	**1,346**	**1,603**	**2,174**	**1,026**	**1,015**
Aviator	1,072	1,145	128	—	—
Navigator	1,102	1,604	1,470	1,540	1,521
Lincoln Total	**2,174**	**2,749**	**1,598**	**1,540**	**1,521**
Cross Country*	1,923	2,001	1,976	1,609	368
Volvo XC90*	2,459	2,283	67	—	—
Volvo Total	**4,382**	**4,284**	**2,043**	**1,609**	**368**
FORD TOTAL	**159,342**	**174,432**	**176,512**	**168,022**	**179,498**
Rainier	937	129	—	—	—

Motor Vehicle Sales in Canada

CANADA VEHICLE SALES — continued

Model	2004	2003	2002	2001	2000
Rendezvous	7,203	9,267	9,318	3,623	—
Terraza	80	—	—	—	—
Buick Total	**8,220**	**9,396**	**9,318**	**3,623**	**—**
Escalade	801	1,129	1,582	1,038	621
Escalade ESV	307	322	—	—	—
Escalade EXT	246	342	664	7	—
SRX	1,232	149	—	—	—
Cadillac Total	**2,586**	**1,942**	**2,246**	**1,045**	**621**
Astro	2,915	3,881	4,918	5,276	7,432
Avalanche	7,816	6,947	6,104	2,296	—
C/K Pickup	—	—	—	348	3,828
Colorado	5,848	23	—	—	—
Equinox	5,450	—	—	—	—
Express	6,626	6,813	6,112	5,791	6,674
P Model	—	—	—	2	19
S Blazer	3,004	2,982	4,256	6,554	10,423
S10 Pickup	71	6,055	6,968	5,275	6,573
Silverado	38,005	37,790	42,625	41,783	37,408
SSR	368	39	—	—	—
Suburban	1,650	2,306	2,620	2,710	3,291
Tahoe	1,855	2,923	2,933	3,461	3,452
Tracker	1,553	6,221	6,695	5,685	5,966
TrailBlazer	6,147	7,731	8,354	3,486	—
Uplander	1,193	—	—	—	—
Venture	21,376	23,129	26,824	24,996	24,759
Chevrolet Total	**103,877**	**106,840**	**118,409**	**107,663**	**109,825**
Canyon	4,642	21	—	—	—
Envoy	8,270	8,921	9,454	3,993	—
Forward*	292	248	217	149	87
P Model	—	—	—	—	4
S Jimmy	2,701	2,227	3,188	6,612	10,169
Safari Van	2,668	3,517	4,593	5,158	7,254
Savana	6,752	5,953	5,456	5,546	6,059
Sierra	39,391	36,030	38,770	36,915	35,159
Sonoma	63	4,625	5,382	4,074	5,221
Suburban	—	—	—	4	52
Yukon	2,353	3,068	3,968	4,035	4,353
Yukon XL	1,722	2,239	2,785	2,667	3,355
GMC Total	**68,854**	**66,849**	**73,813**	**69,153**	**71,713**
H1	4	10	20	14	28
H2	445	872	424	—	—
H2 SUT	53	—	—	—	—
Hummer Total	**502**	**882**	**444**	**14**	**28**
Bravada	144	561	1,296	648	—
Silhouette	584	1,624	2,926	3,138	3,726
Oldsmobile Total	**728**	**2,185**	**4,222**	**3,786**	**3,726**
Aztek	525	1,630	2,707	4,286	923
Montana	27,730	30,292	33,783	31,234	26,906
Montana SV6	1,343	—	—	—	—
Trans Sport	—	—	—	5	94
Pontiac Total	**29,598**	**31,922**	**36,490**	**35,525**	**27,923**
Relay	52	—	—	—	—
Vue	6,220	5,675	4,637	—	—
Saturn Total	**6,272**	**5,675**	**4,637**	**—**	**—**
GM TOTAL	**220,637**	**225,691**	**249,579**	**220,809**	**213,836**
CRV*	15,388	17,831	21,245	13,141	13,613
Element	3,035	3,444	—	—	—
Odyssey	10,559	10,785	14,370	13,674	13,512
Pilot	4,730	4,608	3,396	—	—
Honda Total	**33,712**	**36,668**	**39,011**	**26,815**	**27,125**
Acura MDX	4,181	4,432	4,992	3,964	980
HONDA TOTAL	**37,893**	**41,100**	**44,003**	**30,779**	**28,105**
Santa Fe*	13,192	12,025	8,688	5,486	833
Tucson*	1,173	—	—	—	—
HYUNDAI TOTAL	**14,365**	**12,025**	**8,688**	**5,486**	**833**
Hombre	—	—	—	9	131
Rodeo	5	13	690	1,355	979
Trooper*	1	7	42	125	143
ISUZU TOTAL	**6**	**20**	**732**	**1,489**	**1,253**
Sedona*	4,772	6,068	6,024	1,838	—
Sorento*	4,346	5,078	1,555	—	—
Sportage*	167	264	3,086	5,842	4,973

Motor Vehicle Sales in Canada

CANADA VEHICLE SALES — continued

Model	2004	2003	2002	2001	2000
KIA TOTAL	**9,285**	**11,410**	**10,665**	**7,680**	**4,973**
Mazda Pickup	3,098	3,460	3,670	3,882	3,851
MPV*	4,863	6,485	8,565	8,494	9,115
Tribute	5,478	6,029	6,730	6,740	3,228
MAZDA TOTAL	**13,439**	**15,974**	**18,965**	**19,116**	**16,194**
G-Class*	674	91	174	73	—
M-Class	1,823	2,210	2,892	3,257	4,147
Mercedes Total	**2,497**	**2,301**	**3,066**	**3,330**	**4,147**
Freightliner	—	—	—	2	—
MERCEDES TOTAL	**2,497**	**2,301**	**3,066**	**3,332**	**4,147**
Endeavor	1,008	104	—	—	—
Montero*	181	481	112	—	—
Montero Sport*	65	771	163	—	—
Outlander*	2,115	1,968	258	—	—
Mitsubishi Total	**3,369**	**3,324**	**533**	**—**	**—**
Mitsubishi Fuso*	41	61	55	27	7
MITSUBISHI TOTAL	**3,410**	**3,385**	**588**	**27**	**7**
FX*	2,319	2,554	—	—	—
QX4*	—	291	1,462	1,750	2,296
QX56	380	—	—	—	—
Infiniti Total	**2,699**	**2,845**	**1,462**	**1,750**	**2,296**
Armada	613	152	—	—	—
Frontier	1,094	1,402	1,632	1,230	1,295
Murano*	6,157	7,911	966	—	—
Pathfinder	353	—	—	—	—
Pathfinder*	3,520	4,060	7,186	6,764	9,481
Quest	2,944	1,670	29	168	444
Titan	1,484	42	—	—	—
X-Trail*	6,602	—	—	—	—
Xterra	1,407	2,714	4,116	3,588	3,718
Nissan Total	**24,174**	**17,951**	**13,929**	**11,750**	**14,938**
NISSAN TOTAL	**26,873**	**20,796**	**15,391**	**13,500**	**17,234**
Cayenne*	1,017	741	—	—	—
PORSCHE TOTAL	**1,017**	**741**	**—**	**—**	**—**
Baja	84	331	70	—	—
Forester*	4,201	4,353	4,198	3,731	4,611
SUBARU TOTAL	**4,285**	**4,684**	**4,268**	**3,731**	**4,611**
Vitara	744	1,006	1,649	2,405	2,130
Vitara*	1,065	1,361	1,480	2,254	3,660
Vitara XL7*	1,243	2,116	2,446	2,779	—
SUZUKI TOTAL	**3,052**	**4,483**	**5,575**	**7,438**	**5,790**
GX470*	730	—	—	—	—
LX470*	94	154	205	185	278
RX300*	—	1,057	2,057	2,066	2,663
RX330	3,513	665	—	—	—
RX330*	794	2,914	—	—	—
Lexus Total	**5,131**	**4,790**	**2,262**	**2,251**	**2,941**
4Runner*	3,497	4,371	2,135	2,262	4,965
Highlander*	5,334	6,810	9,713	7,550	—
Land Cruiser*	182	114	74	68	89
RAV4*	6,991	7,026	9,059	8,728	4,631
Sequoia	562	983	1,700	2,103	463
Sienna	17,043	16,077	9,366	9,456	11,042
Tacoma	2,836	2,444	2,591	2,275	2,117
Tundra	3,898	2,450	2,173	1,845	2,325
Toyota Total	**40,343**	**40,275**	**36,811**	**34,287**	**25,632**
TOYOTA TOTAL	**45,474**	**45,065**	**39,073**	**36,538**	**28,573**
Eurovan*	5	84	135	65	83
Touareg*	1,519	784	—	—	—
Volkswagen Total	**1,524**	**868**	**135**	**65**	**83**
Audi Allroad*	318	435	413	441	—
VOLKSWAGEN TOTAL	**1,842**	**1,303**	**548**	**506**	**83**
TOTAL LIGHT TRUCKS	**711,558**	**725,697**	**765,827**	**698,667**	**694,988**
TOTAL LIGHT VEHICLES	**1,530,971**	**1,590,686**	**1,699,884**	**1,566,855**	**1,544,120**
TOTAL MED./HVY. TRUCKS	**43,832**	**34,364**	**31,939**	**31,020**	**41,963**
TOTAL VEHICLES	**1,574,803**	**1,625,050**	**1,731,823**	**1,597,875**	**1,586,083**

SOURCE: Ward's AutoInfoBank.

Motor Vehicle Sales in Mexico

MEXICO VEHICLE SALES

Model	2004	2003	2002	2001	2000
1-Series*	215	—	—	—	—
3-Series	39	595	901	914	1,926
3-Series*	1,819	2,001	2,974	3,499	1,369
5-Series	—	—	2	33	294
5-Series*	785	699	569	936	100
6-Series*	78	—	—	—	—
7-Series*	89	116	114	62	73
Z4	233	286	69	—	—
Z8*	—	—	6	9	4
BMW Total	**3,258**	**3,697**	**4,635**	**5,453**	**3,766**
Mini Cooper*	1,750	1,801	1,545	—	58
BMW TOTAL	**5,008**	**5,498**	**6,180**	**5,453**	**3,824**
300M	629	—	—	—	—
300 Series	434	408	465	943	925
Cirrus	2,831	1,917	2,489	3,570	2,021
Cirrus Convertible	—	—	—	102	—
Cirrus Coupe	47	69	—	—	—
Concorde	1	22	545	1,091	1,194
Crossfire*	360	34	—	—	—
Neon	10,512	13,841	15,372	24,156	28,068
PT Cruiser Convertible	135				
Chrysler Total	**14,949**	**16,291**	**18,871**	**29,862**	**32,208**
Atoz*	15,033	16,811	27,707	23,344	11,170
Intrepid	—	600	6	179	1,237
Stratus Sedan	16,761	17,961	20,990	32,511	21,637
Verna*	17,126	248	—	—	—
Viper	10	2	—	1	—
Dodge Total	**48,930**	**35,622**	**48,703**	**56,035**	**34,044**
CHRYSLER GROUP TOTAL	**63,879**	**51,913**	**67,574**	**85,897**	**66,252**
Alfa Romeo 147*	220	25	—	—	—
Alfa Romeo 156*	230	44	—	—	—
Alfa Romeo Total	**450**	**69**	**—**	**—**	**—**
Fiat Palio Adventurer*	6,048	616	—	—	—
FIAT GROUP TOTAL	**6,498**	**685**	**—**	**—**	**—**
Contour	—	—	7	194	5,367
Crown Victoria	325	88	52	51	390
Escort	—	—	25	1,433	2,017
Fiesta*	25,706	27,616	8,339	6,899	15,899
Five Hundred	515	—	—	—	—
Focus	6,344	14,956	24,065	27,180	28,096
Ikon	13,028	9,824	19,376	20,358	—
Ka*	11,894	14,943	19,808	14,116	—
Mondeo*	5,118	5,903	7,486	5,909	—
Mustang	1,109	511	787	967	1,537
Thunderbird	337	168	—	—	—
Ford Total	**64,376**	**74,009**	**79,945**	**77,107**	**53,306**
S-Type*	180	236	283	360	306
X-Type*	444	500	1,091	782	—
XJ*	29	19	21	24	44
XK8*	6	9	5	9	13
Jaguar Total	**659**	**764**	**1,400**	**1,175**	**363**
Continental	—	—	—	1	—
Lincoln LS	535	474	605	—	—
Town Car	196	207	207	1,019	1,391
Lincoln Total	**731**	**681**	**812**	**1,020**	**1,391**
Grand Marquis	291	584	1,156	1,827	3,251
Mystique	—	—	5	41	2,687
Sable	356	1,049	1,786	3,022	4,729
Mercury Total	**647**	**1,633**	**2,947**	**4,890**	**10,667**
40*	1,528	1,056	1,371	1,048	1,074
60*	618	746	959	867	53
70*	14	41	130	227	180
80*	127	174	236	163	199
Volvo Total	**2,287**	**2,017**	**2,696**	**2,305**	**1,506**
FORD TOTAL	**68,700**	**79,104**	**87,800**	**86,497**	**67,233**
CTS	390	467	—	—	—
Deville	—	—	598	468	564
XLR	22	4	—	—	—
Cadillac Total	**412**	**471**	**598**	**468**	**564**
Astra*	16,591	14,030	17,545	15,861	7,695
Camaro	—	5	38	65	178
Cavalier	1,747	5,058	7,833	4,881	7,912
Corsa*	38,584	40,224	18,933	693	—
Corvette	35	79	98	115	67
Impala	60	373	1,817	1,226	2,053
Joy/Swing	58,036	49,532	63,138	61,704	63,452
Joy/Swing*	149	2,674	9,282	12,125	8,504
Malibu	8,149	3,685	6,162	7,474	12,740
Meriva*	7,330	4,653	—	—	—
Monza	20,103	17,787	19,431	18,717	22,205

Motor Vehicle Sales in Mexico

MEXICO VEHICLE SALES — continued

Model	2004	2003	2002	2001	2000
Tigra*	—	—	—	1	117
Vectra*	3,403	4,478	66	—	—
Chevrolet Total	**154,187**	**142,578**	**144,343**	**122,862**	**124,923**
Bonneville	—	—	—	—	1
Firebird	—	—	—	2	100
G6	116	—	—	—	—
Grand Am	244	968	3,134	2,566	3,804
Grand Prix	—	2	26	118	265
Matiz*	7,142	1,694	—	—	—
Sunfire	1,370	268	3,510	3,692	6,844
Pontiac Total	**8,872**	**2,932**	**6,670**	**6,378**	**11,014**
9-3*	726	759	141	134	—
9-5*	76	139	116	97	—
Saab Total	**802**	**898**	**257**	**231**	—
GM TOTAL	**164,273**	**146,879**	**151,868**	**129,939**	**136,501**
RL*	9	—	—	—	—
TL	37	—	—	—	—
Acura Total	**46**	—	—	—	—
Accord	8,303	9,040	10,506	10,493	12,050
Civic	8,042	9,237	11,573	15,367	11,184
Honda Total	**16,345**	**18,277**	**22,079**	**25,860**	**23,234**
HONDA TOTAL	**16,391**	**18,277**	**22,079**	**25,860**	**23,234**
A-Class*	370	474	388	812	950
C-Class*	1,917	1,347	1,411	1,495	585
CL*	79	161	189	195	19
CLK*	81	93	57	64	67
CLS*	19	—	—	—	—
E-Class*	611	535	387	280	311
S-Class*	84	88	70	87	117
SL*	43	26	28	4	5
SLK*	235	103	153	212	168
Mercedes Total	**3,439**	**2,827**	**2,683**	**3,149**	**2,222**
Forfour*	41	—	—	—	—
Fortwo*	222	65	—	—	—
Roadster*	140	76	—	—	—
Smart Total	**403**	**141**	—	—	—
MERCEDES TOTAL	**3,842**	**2,968**	**2,683**	**3,149**	**2,222**
TF*	185	265	—	—	—
ZR*	188	17	—	—	—
ZT*	34	101	—	—	—
MG Total	**407**	**383**	—	—	—
Rover 75*	368	414	—	—	538
MG ROVER TOTAL	**775**	**797**	—	—	**538**
Eclipse	349	286	—	—	—
Galant	913	244	—	—	—
Lancer*	2,562	519	—	—	—
Space Star*	500	417	—	—	—
MITSUBISHI TOTAL	**4,324**	**1,466**	—	—	—
I30*	—	—	—	115	1,220
Q45*	66	205	396	331	—
Infiniti Total	**66**	**205**	**396**	**446**	**1,220**
350Z*	170	379	319	—	—
Almera*	2,533	3,829	5,642	4,219	—
Altima	8,154	7,372	8,407	3,029	3,801
Lucino	—	—	3	—	683
Maxima*	1,004	411	410	935	2,148
Micra*	569	—	—	—	—
Platina	55,869	53,657	36,683	—	—
Sentra	29,952	29,818	33,069	43,972	35,540
Tsubame	222	608	1,010	1,467	1,643
Tsuru	68,381	63,094	79,227	100,127	83,500
Nissan Total	**166,854**	**159,168**	**164,770**	**153,749**	**127,315**
NISSAN TOTAL	**166,920**	**159,373**	**165,166**	**154,195**	**128,535**
Porsche 911*	186	221	282	187	9
PORSCHE TOTAL	**186**	**221**	**282**	**187**	**9**
206*	10,196	9,358	7,006	4,496	2,121
306*	—	15	1,118	963	685
307*	4,144	2,368	—	—	—
406*	589	909	894	956	648
607*	123	149	130	—	—
Partner*	1,256	554	—	—	—
PEUGEOT TOTAL	**16,308**	**13,353**	**9,148**	**6,415**	**3,454**
Clio	11,817	11,579	8,933	—	—
Clio*	675	983	1,212	123	—
Laguna*	344	730	801	—	—
Megane*	8,238	2,883	2,163	—	—
RENAULT TOTAL	**21,074**	**16,175**	**13,109**	**123**	—
Camry	2,241	1,831	1,865	—	—
Corolla	4,057	3,248	1,888	—	—

Motor Vehicle Sales in Mexico

MEXICO VEHICLE SALES — continued

Model	2004	2003	2002	2001	2000
Matrix	1,422	1,041	—	—	—
MR2 Spyder*	104	—	—	—	—
Yaris*	873	94	—	—	—
TOYOTA TOTAL	**8,697**	**6,214**	**3,753**	**—**	**—**
A4*	2,976	2,388	3,030	2,148	1,660
A6*	403	259	297	418	288
A8*	60	50	10	24	24
Cabrio*	—	—	—	—	—
TT*	157	143	260	369	485
Audi Total	**3,596**	**2,840**	**3,597**	**2,959**	**2,457**
Cordoba*	6,922	5,985	8,053	4,870	—
Ibiza*	13,389	12,692	12,847	6,241	—
Leon*	1,569	1,823	2,055	869	—
Toledo*	514	1,162	1,319	740	—
SEAT Total	**22,394**	**21,662**	**24,274**	**12,720**	**—**
Beetle	2,598	2,369	2,933	4,897	2,267
Beetle Cabrio	250	192	—	—	—
Derby*	15,490	13,683	10,562	13,729	10,161
Golf	—	33	287	380	355
Golf*	2,468	3,978	6,315	6,953	11,106
Jetta	57,086	46,702	39,923	41,720	40,886
Jetta*	63	243	560	737	—
Lupo*	10,868	—	—	—	—
Passat*	1,344	1,733	2,230	2,518	2,080
Pointer*	62,707	66,325	62,720	46,346	57,234
Polo*	10,331	12,418	52	—	—
Sedan	882	10,485	22,986	36,891	40,937
Volkswagen Total	**164,087**	**158,161**	**148,568**	**154,171**	**165,026**
VOLKSWAGEN TOTAL	**190,077**	**182,663**	**176,439**	**169,850**	**167,483**
TOTAL CARS	**736,952**	**685,586**	**706,081**	**667,565**	**599,285**
X3*	836	—	—	—	—
X5	965	764	871	943	265
BMW TOTAL	**1,801**	**764**	**871**	**943**	**265**
Pacifica	783	523	—	—	—
PT Cruiser	2,192	2,144	2,027	1,177	3,742
Voyager	13,449	13,738	13,322	18,331	16,329
Chrysler Total	**16,424**	**16,405**	**15,349**	**19,508**	**20,071**
Durango	3,593	871	1,119	1,025	1,558
Ramcharger	—	1	6	771	2,905
Ram Pickup	13,832	13,359	16,723	15,194	19,926
Ram Van	294	2,865	3,351	2,795	4,398
Dodge Total	**17,719**	**17,096**	**21,199**	**19,785**	**28,787**
Cherokee	2,343	2,230	2,030	2,917	5,526
Liberty	14,277	11,480	8,705	4,288	—
Wrangler	1,102	826	644	540	693
Jeep Total	**17,722**	**14,536**	**11,379**	**7,745**	**6,219**
CHRYSLER GROUP TOTAL	**51,865**	**48,037**	**47,927**	**47,038**	**55,077**
Courier*	6,709	6,225	7,390	7,095	3,506
Econoline	2,455	2,003	2,213	2,659	3,722
Ecosport*	22,785	10,514	—	—	—
Escape	9,664	6,620	7,181	7,724	861
Excursion	162	180	176	398	431
Expedition	3,841	3,497	3,382	2,684	3,523
Explorer	4,033	5,008	5,692	5,877	8,207
Ford F-Series	42,175	29,406	28,612	28,667	36,608
Freestar	5,893	—	—	—	—
Ranger	10,662	8,405	7,738	4,197	6,732
Windstar	1,027	8,041	10,185	12,724	13,669
Ford Total	**109,406**	**79,899**	**72,569**	**72,025**	**77,259**
Discovery*	90	127	162	156	86
Freelander*	583	553	743	634	167
LR3*	63	—	—	—	—
Range Rover*	64	80	40	61	23
Land Rover Total	**800**	**760**	**945**	**851**	**276**
Aviator	980	1,123	91	—	—
Blackwood	29	105	70	—	—
Navigator	673	640	777	660	725
Lincoln Total	**1,682**	**1,868**	**938**	**660**	**725**
Cross Country*	10	—	—	—	—
Volvo XC90*	1,056	704	4	—	—
Volvo Total	**1,066**	**704**	**4**	**—**	**—**
Mercury Mariner	333	—	—	—	—
FORD TOTAL	**113,287**	**83,231**	**74,456**	**73,536**	**78,260**
Escalade	273	314	452	99	—
Escalade ESV	263	194	—	—	—
Escalade EXT	157	159	120	—	—
SRX	120	16	—	—	—
Cadillac Total	**813**	**683**	**572**	**99**	**—**
Avalanche	447	656	1,551	776	—

Motor Vehicle Sales in Mexico

MEXICO VEHICLE SALES — continued

Model	2004	2003	2002	2001	2000
Chevy Pickup	—	—	—	2	15
Chevy Pickup*	47	4,808	5,282	4,043	5,410
C/K Pickup	—	—	—	—	26,894
Colorado	2,620	—	—	—	—
Equinox	2,985	—	—	—	—
Express	3,268	3,120	3,332	3,790	4,453
LUV*	4,238	4,416	6,369	6,689	6,108
P Model	122	1,217	955	1,751	988
S Blazer	—	—	12	923	2,053
S10 Pickup	6	284	1,056	1,438	2,473
Silverado	29,287	32,081	29,839	26,529	6,545
Sonora	692	834	1,348	2,457	2,880
Suburban	2,842	2,488	2,636	3,187	5,442
Tahoe	—	—	2,646	1,709	50
Tornado*	8,113	386	—	—	—
Tracker	3,638	4,053	3,805	4,208	5,051
TrailBlazer	4,777	5,827	4,807	2,604	—
Uplander	158	—	—	—	—
Venture	3,393	3,892	5,942	5,279	5,940
Zafira*	2,274	2,586	4,708	1,704	—
Chevrolet Total	**68,907**	**66,648**	**74,288**	**67,089**	**74,302**
Hummer H2	160	—	—	—	—
Pontiac Aztek	362	642	1,565	1,917	1,525
GM TOTAL	**70,242**	**67,973**	**76,425**	**69,105**	**75,827**
CRV*	10,059	7,429	5,677	—	—
Odyssey	1,921	2,089	2,674	3,018	2,302
Pilot	1,342	1,221	—	—	—
Honda Total	**13,322**	**10,739**	**8,351**	**3,018**	**2,302**
Acura MDX	17	—	—	—	—
HONDA TOTAL	**13,339**	**10,739**	**8,351**	**3,018**	**2,302**
G-Class*	8	6	9	68	3
M-Class	383	480	619	613	433
Mercedes Total	**391**	**486**	**628**	**681**	**436**
Freightliner Sprinter Van*	2,384	908	113	—	—
MERCEDES TOTAL	**2,775**	**1,394**	**741**	**681**	**436**
Endeavor	1,546	—	—	—	—
Montero*	532	480	—	—	—
Montero Sport*	989	1,003	—	—	—
Outlander*	3,256	973	—	—	—
MITSUBISHI TOTAL	**6,323**	**2,456**	**—**	**—**	**—**
Armada	1,263	—	—	—	—
Frontier	1,830	2,558	3,314	2,443	770
Murano*	2,228	1,463	—	—	—
Nissan Chassis	20,481	17,009	15,378	15,714	17,747
Nissan Pickup	13,726	13,288	12,819	13,302	20,101
Pathfinder*	199	571	794	1,220	2,616
Quest	806	18	101	130	416
Titan	1,527	2	—	—	—
Urvan*	7,156	4,281	3,781	2,756	2,470
X-Trail*	18,077	14,387	8,667	1,240	—
Xterra	640	1,061	1,628	2,198	3,145
NISSAN TOTAL	**67,933**	**54,638**	**46,482**	**39,003**	**47,265**
Cayenne*	266	126	—	—	—
PORSCHE TOTAL	**266**	**126**	**—**	**—**	**—**
Kangoo*	1,536	225	—	—	—
Scenic	1,236	2,031	2,252	1,404	—
Scenic*	245	—	25	2,089	—
RENAULT TOTAL	**3,017**	**2,256**	**2,277**	**3,493**	**—**
4Runner*	809	444	83	—	—
Hilux*	1,940	164	—	—	—
Land Cruiser*	57	39	—	—	—
RAV4*	7,085	1,286	—	—	—
Sienna	5,288	1,695	—	—	—
TOYOTA TOTAL	**15,179**	**3,628**	**83**	**—**	**—**
Eurovan*	2,191	6,648	5,637	3,073	562
Pointer Pickup*	2,252	2,271	2,629	2,847	3,814
Sharan*	1,279	1,959	2,918	319	—
Touareg*	640	196	—	—	—
Vanagon*	—	—	30	1,615	2,617
Volkswagen Total	**6,362**	**11,074**	**11,214**	**7,854**	**6,993**
Audi Allroad*	14	26	28	94	—
Seat Alhambra*	310	468	842	77	—
VOLKSWAGEN TOTAL	**6,686**	**11,568**	**12,084**	**8,025**	**6,993**
TOTAL LIGHT TRUCKS	**352,713**	**286,810**	**269,697**	**244,842**	**266,425**
TOTAL LIGHT VEHICLES	**1,089,665**	**972,396**	**975,778**	**912,407**	**865,710**
TOTAL MED./HVY. TRUCKS	**29,920**	**26,710**	**28,083**	**30,024**	**36,662**
TOTAL VEHICLES	**1,119,585**	**999,106**	**1,003,861**	**942,431**	**902,372**

SOURCE: *Ward's AutoInfoBank.*

Car, Truck and Bus Registrations by State

TOTAL MOTOR VEHICLE REGISTRATIONS BY STATE

State	Passenger Cars		Trucks and Buses		Total	
	2003	2002	2003	2002	2003	2002
Alabama	1,770,924	1,785,645	2,558,321	2,617,427	4,329,245	4,403,072
Alaska	260,999	253,498	375,784	362,948	636,783	616,446
Arizona	1,991,931	2,220,521	1,582,063	1,697,257	3,573,994	3,917,778
Arkansas	955,188	950,587	933,367	905,156	1,888,555	1,855,743
California	18,699,434	18,253,474	11,548,635	11,118,654	30,248,069	29,372,128
Colorado	2,357,867	2,339,154	1,139,750	2,340,778	3,497,617	4,679,932
Connecticut	2,041,237	2,015,263	2,398,059	877,657	4,439,296	2,892,920
Delaware	419,150	407,936	267,667	255,622	686,817	663,558
District of Columbia	184,199	188,211	44,152	42,248	228,351	230,459
Florida	8,564,237	8,367,010	5,961,888	5,446,008	14,526,125	13,813,018
Georgia	4,191,745	4,184,940	3,538,555	3,416,904	7,730,300	7,601,844
Hawaii	525,277	524,920	377,633	355,436	902,910	880,356
Idaho	554,102	592,095	747,018	783,903	1,301,120	1,375,998
Illinois	5,768,554	6,028,268	3,481,460	3,459,649	9,250,014	9,487,917
Indiana	3,251,509	3,192,526	2,487,839	2,419,269	5,739,348	5,611,795
Iowa	1,883,135	1,851,332	1,485,780	1,440,258	3,368,915	3,291,590
Kansas	834,052	835,284	1,480,408	1,489,616	2,314,460	2,324,900
Kentucky	1,959,127	2,062,805	1,429,752	1,499,169	3,388,879	3,561,974
Louisiana	1,997,248	1,945,352	1,716,313	1,651,569	3,713,561	3,596,921
Maine	618,647	578,365	433,010	381,294	1,051,657	959,659
Maryland	2,478,873	2,509,343	1,397,737	1,348,960	3,876,610	3,858,303
Massachusetts	3,614,519	3,617,904	1,864,875	1,759,115	5,479,394	5,377,019
Michigan	4,804,822	4,826,224	3,735,503	3,632,991	8,540,325	8,459,215
Minnesota	2,501,883	2,493,461	2,023,257	2,001,358	4,525,140	4,494,819
Mississippi	1,138,561	1,126,068	812,438	809,184	1,950,999	1,935,252
Missouri	2,600,169	2,474,334	1,859,703	1,741,530	4,459,872	4,215,864
Montana	436,686	460,268	573,801	587,259	1,010,487	1,047,527
Nebraska	855,407	827,981	821,796	807,717	1,677,203	1,635,698
Nevada	623,886	640,238	597,982	600,867	1,221,868	1,241,105
New Hampshire	655,831	677,606	489,132	459,593	1,144,963	1,137,199
New Jersey	4,448,660	4,456,531	2,262,941	2,162,626	6,711,601	6,619,157
New Mexico	693,542	700,974	815,808	819,265	1,509,350	1,520,239
New York	8,313,058	7,843,302	2,488,643	2,472,639	10,801,701	10,315,941
North Carolina	3,653,665	3,657,453	2,464,979	2,430,817	6,118,644	6,088,270
North Dakota	345,504	343,920	348,737	347,911	694,241	691,831
Ohio	6,518,579	6,501,194	4,017,793	3,877,151	10,536,372	10,378,345
Oklahoma	1,622,782	1,609,681	1,450,925	1,431,884	3,073,707	3,041,565
Oregon	1,545,076	1,533,634	1,515,710	1,495,721	3,060,786	3,029,355
Pennsylvania	6,120,710	6,025,558	3,603,743	3,416,234	9,724,453	9,441,792
Rhode Island	548,568	533,827	257,172	235,185	805,740	769,012
South Carolina	1,914,753	1,948,939	1,247,141	1,225,345	3,161,894	3,174,284
South Dakota	387,897	384,976	439,047	421,970	826,944	806,946
Tennessee	2,782,246	2,784,155	2,013,430	1,954,509	4,795,676	4,738,664
Texas	7,841,637	7,700,051	7,047,143	6,773,418	14,888,780	14,473,469
Utah	1,013,762	957,582	992,661	877,573	2,006,423	1,835,155
Vermont	271,819	295,447	244,252	236,613	516,071	532,060
Virginia	4,043,727	3,976,463	2,302,282	2,243,339	6,346,009	6,219,802
Washington	2,968,936	2,959,569	2,409,955	2,346,644	5,378,891	5,306,213
West Virginia	756,405	767,348	652,395	677,548	1,408,800	1,444,896
Wisconsin	2,577,697	2,570,717	2,069,453	1,956,042	4,647,150	4,526,759
Wyoming	231,895	215,193	387,969	379,658	619,864	594,851
Total	137,140,117	135,997,127	97,195,857	94,091,488	234,335,974	230,088,615

NOTE: Registrations include both privately and publicly owned motor vehicles, except those owned by the military. Colorado data have been estimated by Ward's to compensate for under-reporting by the state.
SOURCE: U.S. Department of Transportation, Federal Highway Administration.

Total Truck Registrations by State

TOTAL MOTOR TRUCK REGISTRATIONS BY STATE

State	Privately Owned[1]				Privately and Publicly Owned[2]			
	2003	2002	2001	2000	2003	2002	2001	2000
Alabama	2,522,137	2,590,390	2,434,282	1,962,825	2,549,357	2,617,427	2,461,175	1,989,567
Alaska	364,487	354,332	342,937	337,788	373,478	362,948	352,873	347,584
Arizona	1,557,945	1,677,996	1,679,263	1,607,753	1,577,374	1,697,257	1,698,422	1,626,803
Arkansas	914,212	893,639	871,859	870,843	925,794	905,156	883,331	882,266
California	11,203,411	10,831,359	10,531,853	10,057,920	11,496,248	11,118,654	10,812,255	10,329,198
Colorado	2,346,822	2,290,000	2,248,782	1,673,059	2,392,275	2,334,278	2,275,380	1,699,469
Connecticut	883,925	850,006	828,221	806,763	911,955	877,657	855,531	833,730
Delaware	262,629	252,674	237,653	225,241	265,594	255,622	240,559	228,098
Dist. of Columbia	34,502	35,444	35,734	32,427	41,363	42,248	42,500	39,164
Florida	5,758,960	5,292,656	5,206,271	4,235,309	5,915,175	5,446,008	5,356,918	4,383,294
Georgia	3,449,647	3,349,450	3,135,791	3,006,443	3,518,944	3,416,904	3,201,501	3,070,459
Hawaii	364,450	347,391	326,897	266,709	372,793	355,436	334,811	273,735
Idaho	728,478	767,117	725,418	640,772	743,322	783,903	742,376	658,747
Illinois	3,448,723	3,444,574	3,403,474	2,984,475	3,463,546	3,459,649	3,418,902	3,000,302
Indiana	2,413,593	2,376,215	2,325,326	2,257,308	2,457,523	2,419,269	2,367,552	2,298,720
Iowa	1,446,618	1,409,471	1,408,356	1,314,375	1,477,430	1,440,258	1,439,536	1,346,310
Kansas	1,457,330	1,470,286	1,465,223	1,446,787	1,476,534	1,489,616	1,484,509	1,465,830
Kentucky	1,407,003	1,490,538	1,480,989	1,131,204	1,415,766	1,499,169	1,489,478	1,139,543
Louisiana	1,670,760	1,627,487	1,569,722	1,547,644	1,695,352	1,651,569	1,593,341	1,570,804
Maine	418,119	369,746	385,872	390,983	430,025	381,294	396,922	402,779
Maryland	1,361,940	1,325,379	1,307,622	1,206,630	1,385,737	1,348,960	1,331,033	1,229,870
Massachusetts	1,811,687	1,718,963	1,616,401	1,541,572	1,852,874	1,759,115	1,655,593	1,579,827
Michigan	3,629,977	3,554,752	3,446,848	3,309,618	3,708,975	3,632,991	3,524,396	3,386,473
Minnesota	1,979,974	1,977,137	1,949,541	1,966,300	2,007,075	2,001,358	1,973,849	1,989,580
Mississippi	786,501	792,205	780,334	943,205	803,200	809,184	797,299	960,389
Missouri	1,830,978	1,724,433	1,687,809	1,833,935	1,848,487	1,741,530	1,704,693	1,851,429
Montana	553,612	569,038	552,478	539,205	571,140	587,259	570,246	556,772
Nebraska	794,996	787,043	773,338	741,062	815,431	807,717	793,262	760,420
Nevada	581,212	586,013	583,979	547,542	596,159	600,867	598,787	562,296
New Hampshire	474,562	447,596	401,814	368,731	487,296	459,593	413,352	379,624
New Jersey	2,135,527	2,059,205	1,938,233	1,816,771	2,240,093	2,162,626	2,039,712	1,917,774
New Mexico	789,023	796,249	731,230	772,960	812,407	819,265	753,926	795,343
New York	2,326,458	2,376,411	2,449,908	2,577,983	2,427,652	2,472,639	2,543,399	2,679,105
North Carolina	2,383,947	2,382,254	2,386,976	2,401,817	2,433,059	2,430,817	2,434,858	2,448,806
North Dakota	337,649	339,056	348,878	343,519	346,339	347,911	357,674	352,311
Ohio	3,897,640	3,799,367	3,774,506	3,645,863	3,977,279	3,877,151	3,850,539	3,720,187
Oklahoma	1,383,732	1,383,222	1,467,462	1,364,050	1,433,425	1,431,884	1,515,152	1,410,783
Oregon	1,469,864	1,464,549	1,435,257	1,435,947	1,501,181	1,495,721	1,466,595	1,467,016
Pennsylvania	3,499,622	3,350,355	3,296,582	3,128,139	3,566,835	3,416,234	3,362,986	3,192,210
Rhode Island	249,858	229,785	221,175	213,483	255,459	235,185	226,372	218,638
South Carolina	1,202,861	1,198,632	1,180,417	1,128,250	1,230,042	1,225,345	1,206,704	1,154,113
South Dakota	422,356	408,360	398,262	396,206	436,321	421,970	411,866	409,502
Tennessee	1,940,289	1,901,315	2,055,918	1,893,080	1,995,706	1,954,509	2,109,976	1,948,009
Texas	6,740,890	6,556,597	6,347,204	6,098,055	6,962,883	6,773,418	6,554,917	6,368,516
Utah	975,273	861,721	810,824	744,226	991,382	877,573	826,451	759,633
Vermont	235,544	230,372	223,591	210,576	242,122	236,613	229,947	217,239
Virginia	2,247,519	2,207,074	2,140,150	2,117,495	2,284,202	2,243,339	2,176,757	2,154,027
Washington	2,357,343	2,304,051	2,224,258	2,173,842	2,400,135	2,346,644	2,266,177	2,215,182
West Virginia	620,448	648,026	632,314	612,638	649,440	677,548	662,393	643,282
Wisconsin	2,007,484	1,909,725	1,834,326	1,780,276	2,054,623	1,956,042	1,879,870	1,825,056
Wyoming	371,819	366,714	345,983	355,395	385,053	379,658	358,658	367,814
Total	94,054,336	91,976,370	89,987,541	85,004,999	96,201,860	94,084,988	92,045,311	87,107,628

(1) Excludes farm trucks registered in certain states and restricted for use in vicinity of owner's farm.
(2) Includes federal, state, county and municipal vehicles; excludes vehicles owned by military.
SOURCE: U.S. Department of Transportation, Federal Highway Administration.

Truck Registrations by State and Type

TOTAL TRUCK REGISTRATIONS BY STATE AND TYPE, 2003

State	Truck Tractors	Farm Trucks	Pickups	Vans	Sport Utilities	Other Light	Total
Alabama	78,108	24,259	1,291,372	356,291	247,123	504,696	2,501,849
Alaska	3,284	569	183,861	48,528	119,573	4,075	359,890
Arizona	17,080	1,118	740,758	240,650	494,622	9,028	1,503,256
Arkansas	17,647	24,895	544,654	116,309	236,319	4,963	944,787
California	129,928	—	3,877,093	2,239,711	3,784,918	52,781	10,084,431
Colorado	18,619	95,569	912,423	321,285	938,241	4,941	2,291,078
Connecticut[1]	2,565	—	295,788	208,593	368,012	5,275	880,233
Delaware	4,197	2,908	96,661	61,164	94,676	1,429	261,035
District of Columbia	181	—	5,171	9,566	16,643	532	32,093
Florida	174,102	—	1,969,086	1,238,470	1,912,716	30,116	5,324,490
Georgia[2]	79,095	—	1,546,121	552,737	1,062,398	18,556	3,258,907
Hawaii	1,019	—	159,424	82,794	115,924	2,450	361,611
Idaho	12,904	—	389,975	81,849	175,421	4,680	664,829
Illinois	66,724	34,233	1,128,903	922,538	1,158,245	18,373	3,329,016
Indiana	55,831	48,243	1,071,471	530,474	609,558	12,592	2,328,169
Iowa	58,235	24,000	696,585	279,023	294,052	8,598	1,360,493
Kansas	28,222	83,600	605,100	314,166	361,007	8,139	1,400,234
Kentucky	27,322	111,149	762,719	221,539	342,663	7,365	1,472,757
Louisiana	35,568	109,261	962,132	214,580	414,803	7,544	1,743,888
Maine	3,701	5,432	211,775	68,031	117,191	2,106	408,236
Maryland	16,264	8,983	449,201	347,635	523,518	8,402	1,354,003
Massachusetts	12,691	9,399	571,055	445,671	757,346	11,865	1,808,027
Michigan	71,823	46,329	1,358,994	887,938	1,120,452	14,507	3,500,043
Minnesota	31,777	32,076	785,079	412,851	532,017	12,246	1,806,046
Mississippi[2]	9,128	—	474,381	94,232	185,871	4,693	768,305
Missouri	45,275	65,010	891,936	336,948	471,566	10,219	1,820,954
Montana	20,423	142,394	299,383	55,268	117,956	3,310	638,734
Nebraska	37,735	148,456	365,147	131,754	191,590	4,144	878,826
Nevada	7,698	—	232,619	76,865	186,541	2,525	506,248
New Hampshire[1]	6,201	1,953	200,451	95,156	158,888	3,143	465,792
New Jersey[1]	11,460	16,227	514,279	612,141	976,669	17,826	2,148,602
New Mexico	12,467	18,016	409,754	93,611	203,887	3,993	741,728
New York[1]	11,834	39,650	615,474	673,459	946,132	19,554	2,306,103
North Carolina	57,956	79,932	1,079,578	405,416	675,651	13,332	2,311,865
North Dakota	9,232	37,635	161,415	47,366	69,125	1,567	326,340
Ohio	43,294	31,296	1,561,224	1,009,193	1,086,341	19,534	3,750,882
Oklahoma	12,428	147,326	732,898	175,779	302,059	7,683	1,378,173
Oregon	20,758	17,613	700,538	247,521	406,273	10,578	1,403,281
Pennsylvania[1]	72,676	—	1,148,747	772,035	1,198,595	17,550	3,209,603
Rhode Island[1]	3,562	—	93,732	56,871	82,341	1,275	237,781
South Carolina	17,316	27,032	560,826	206,089	383,450	7,333	1,202,046
South Dakota	18,477	—	194,052	57,595	88,318	2,401	360,843
Tennessee	65,382	38,262	970,868	312,160	581,954	9,145	1,977,771
Texas	165,233	181,047	3,395,608	907,140	2,134,427	32,438	6,815,893
Utah	41,139	59,200	433,812	137,950	316,228	6,255	994,584
Vermont	3,249	2,711	102,489	37,704	69,379	1,109	216,641
Virginia	34,720	24,229	882,216	457,491	780,561	11,020	2,190,237
Washington	29,072	20,090	1,063,011	433,695	697,117	16,965	2,259,950
West Virginia	9,943	2,205	327,419	84,234	171,075	2,783	597,659
Wisconsin	39,745	91,352	809,658	478,356	527,282	9,452	1,955,845
Wyoming	3,998	4,673	218,042	34,282	95,493	2,520	359,008
Total	**1,757,288**	**1,858,332**	**39,054,958**	**18,232,704**	**28,902,207**	**997,606**	**90,803,095**

NOTE:The registrations given in this table are as reported by the States in most instances, but have been supplemented in some cases by estimates based on data from other sources.In this partial classification a vehicle may be included more than once; for instance, a truck-tractor in farm use could appear in both columns.
(1) Except for Georgia and Mississippi (Footnote 2), farm registrations are shown for all States that have a special "Farm" classification.The numbers of vehicles shown do not necessarily represent the total number or registered vehicles used on the farm.The following farm trucks, registered at a nominal fee and restricted to use in the vicinity of the owner's farm, are not included in this table:Connecticut, 6,162; New Hampshire,7,586; New Jersey, 7,600; New York, 21,921; Pennsylvania, 24,354; and Rhode Island, 1,447.
(2) Although Georgia and Mississippi have a special "Farm" classification, their registration reports do not show a complete segregation of farm trucks from private carriers.
SOURCE: U.S. Department of Transportation, Federal Highway Administration.

Private, Commercial and Publicly Owned Trailer Registrations by State

TRAILER REGISTRATIONS BY STATE, 2003

State	Private and Commercial Trailers[1]				Publicly Owned Trailers			Grand Total
	Commercial Trailers[2]	Car and Light Farm Trailers[3]	House Trailers[4]	Total	Federal Government	State, County and Municipal	Total	
Alabama	68,645	82,029	16,555	167,229	15	1,133	1,148	168,377
Alaska	10,466	99,110	—	109,576	136	1,444	1,580	111,156
Arizona	86,203	299,986	136,253	522,442	101	3,986	4,087	526,529
Arkansas	49,004	431,139	10,541	490,684	6	276	282	490,966
California	718,115	1,560,921	569,160	2,848,196	383	56,215	56,598	2,904,794
Colorado	57,189	134,440	56,607	248,236	83	2,139	2,222	250,458
Connecticut	72,787	124,173	—	196,960	13	2,835	2,848	199,808
Delaware	25,975	35,518	—	61,493	7	910	917	62,410
District of Columbia	72	819	—	891	156	351	507	1,398
Florida	54,668	1,374,408	—	1,429,076	189	29,573	29,762	1,458,838
Georgia	177,326	591,022	41,713	810,061	133	4,433	4,566	814,627
Hawaii	4,184	20,213	—	24,397	5	1,097	1,102	25,499
Idaho	27,227	61,611	57,122	145,960	61	2,648	2,709	148,669
Illinois	117,699	530,019	124,853	772,571	239	272	511	773,082
Indiana	61,738	407,725	106,079	575,542	40	2,256	2,296	577,838
Iowa	130,887	29,628	75,965	236,480	21	6,120	6,141	242,621
Kansas	71,771	20,731	16,308	108,810	24	915	939	109,749
Kentucky	4,310	31,833	36,787	72,930	65	139	204	73,134
Louisiana	213,883	334,647	9,745	558,275	27	3,015	3,042	561,317
Maine	734,199	116,486	—	850,685	8	2,387	2,395	853,080
Maryland	19,761	255,312	—	275,073	106	417	523	275,596
Massachusetts	25,383	279,727	—	305,110	75	209	284	305,394
Michigan	119,879	953,029	146,354	1,219,262	88	4,658	4,746	1,224,008
Minnesota	173,434	754,140	102,662	1,030,236	84	3,501	3,585	1,033,821
Mississippi	29,310	62,333	9,188	100,831	32	1,692	1,724	102,555
Missouri	92,904	479,639	—	572,543	128	456	584	573,127
Montana	29,634	133,922	59,663	223,219	54	2,629	2,683	225,902
Nebraska	100,824	201,414	—	302,238	13	1,158	1,171	303,409
Nevada	10,915	83,955	37,334	132,204	49	1,178	1,227	133,431
New Hampshire	12,070	135,368	—	147,438	3	1,292	1,295	148,733
New Jersey	21,962	383,141	—	405,103	165	114	279	405,382
New Mexico	42,378	26,484	24,031	92,893	143	3,414	3,557	96,450
New York	15,502	607,150	—	622,652	365	10,531	10,896	633,548
North Carolina	88,673	656,001	1,706	746,380	46	8,010	8,056	754,436
North Dakota	26,167	31,369	18,701	76,237	10	1,093	1,103	77,340
Ohio	108,914	530,091	109,638	748,643	128	11,657	11,785	760,428
Oklahoma	118,938	65,923	8,816	193,677	36	2,150	2,186	195,863
Oregon	52,632	94,105	117,420	264,157	102	7,493	7,595	271,752
Pennsylvania	148,947	509,562	249,779	908,288	211	4,423	4,634	912,922
Rhode Island	6,082	48,043	—	54,125	8	962	970	55,095
South Carolina	18,547	31,806	134	50,487	34	1,242	1,276	51,763
South Dakota	51,590	60,225	54,861	166,676	31	1,404	1,435	168,111
Tennessee	81,727	40,234	205	122,166	73	369	442	122,608
Texas	257,764	1,535,735	—	1,793,499	186	36,265	36,451	1,829,950
Utah	46,429	67,552	66,113	180,094	77	486	563	180,657
Vermont	86,548	75,068	—	161,616	2	1,159	1,161	162,777
Virginia	80,901	165,735	70,863	317,499	62	2,761	2,823	320,322
Washington	53,845	481,706	104,151	639,702	163	2,146	2,309	642,011
West Virginia	64,444	86,306	43,207	193,957	9	3,470	3,479	197,436
Wisconsin	232,321	19,658	51,500	303,479	29	1,675	1,704	305,183
Wyoming	17,927	244,990	29,799	292,716	91	1,166	1,257	293,973
Total	**4,922,700**	**15,386,181**	**2,563,813**	**22,872,694**	**4,315**	**241,324**	**245,639**	**23,118,333**

(1) The completeness of data on trailer registrations varies greatly. Data are reported to the extent available and in some cases are supplemented by estimates of the Federal Highway Administration.
(2) This column includes all commercial type vehicles and semitrailers that are in private or for-hire use.
(3) Several States do not require the registration of light farm or automobile trailers.
(4) Mobile homes and house trailers are shown in this column for States which require them to be registered and are able to segregate them from other trailers. In States where this classification is not available, house trailers are included with light car trailers.
SOURCE: U.S. Department of Transportation, Federal Highway Administration.

Bus Registrations by State

TOTAL MOTOR BUS REGISTRATIONS BY STATE, 2003

State	Private and Commercial		Publicly Owned		Total Privately and Publicly Owned		
	Commercial Buses[1]	School and Other[2]	Federal	School[3]	Commercial and Federal	School	Total Buses
Alabama	2,356	231	42	6,335	2,398	6,566	8,964
Alaska	1,523	554	80	149	1,603	703	2,306
Arizona	1,076	232	400	2,981	1,476	3,213	4,689
Arkansas	49	1,552	31	5,941	80	7,493	7,573
California	25,813	9,524	496	16,554	26,309	26,078	52,387
Colorado	787	930	45	4,022	832	4,952	5,784
Connecticut	2,988	6,496	13	851	3,001	7,347	10,348
Delaware	445	1,031	7	590	452	1,621	2,073
District of Columbia	2,244	142	291	112	2,535	254	2,789
Florida	4,114	1,234	220	41,145	4,334	42,379	46,713
Georgia	1,446	2,958	112	15,095	1,558	18,053	19,611
Hawaii	2,866	757	30	1,187	2,896	1,944	4,840
Idaho	714	580	158	2,244	872	2,824	3,696
Illinois	6,177	11,125	90	522	6,267	11,647	17,914
Indiana	4,117	5,108	58	21,033	4,175	26,141	30,316
Iowa	1,197	289	14	6,850	1,211	7,139	8,350
Kansas	365	1,058	13	2,438	378	3,496	3,874
Kentucky	778	781	167	12,260	945	13,041	13,986
Louisiana	1,016	13,826	26	6,093	1,042	19,919	20,961
Maine	176	371	13	2,425	189	2,796	2,985
Maryland	3,132	3,821	160	4,887	3,292	8,708	12,000
Massachusetts	3,720	7,691	88	502	3,808	8,193	12,001
Michigan	3,360	7,370	82	15,716	3,442	23,086	26,528
Minnesota	2,313	4,555	8	9,306	2,321	13,861	16,182
Mississippi	902	2,573	83	5,680	985	8,253	9,238
Missouri	880	3,042	38	7,256	918	10,298	11,216
Montana	426	645	20	1,570	446	2,215	2,661
Nebraska	504	721	11	5,129	515	5,850	6,365
Nevada	1,375	171	150	127	1,525	298	1,823
New Hampshire	369	1,086	2	379	371	1,465	1,836
New Jersey	4,771	14,410	61	3,606	4,832	18,016	22,848
New Mexico	492	1,826	327	756	819	2,582	3,401
New York	14,833	9,123	234	36,801	15,067	45,924	60,991
North Carolina	2,272	7,588	58	22,002	2,330	29,590	31,920
North Dakota	146	556	70	1,626	216	2,182	2,398
Ohio	14,526	2,738	89	23,161	14,615	25,899	40,514
Oklahoma	437	1,807	145	15,111	582	16,918	17,500
Oregon	1,690	2,636	74	10,129	1,764	12,765	14,529
Pennsylvania	9,110	19,560	131	8,107	9,241	27,667	36,908
Rhode Island	337	1,363	6	7	343	1,370	1,713
South Carolina	986	3,895	34	12,184	1,020	16,079	17,099
South Dakota	357	421	126	1,822	483	2,243	2,726
Tennessee	2,560	1,493	84	13,587	2,644	15,080	17,724
Texas	3,305	14,763	266	65,926	3,571	80,689	84,260
Utah	353	109	40	777	393	886	1,279
Vermont	92	549	5	1,484	97	2,033	2,130
Virginia	2,309	243	259	15,269	2,568	15,512	18,080
Washington	929	2,553	209	6,129	1,138	8,682	9,820
West Virginia	720	63	48	2,124	768	2,187	2,955
Wisconsin	1,575	8,531	25	4,699	1,600	13,230	14,830
Wyoming	867	118	12	1,919	879	2,037	2,916
Total	**139,895**	**184,799**	**5,251**	**446,605**	**145,146**	**631,404**	**776,550**

(1) Includes municipally owned transit buses.
(2) In some instances church, industrial and other private buses are included here; and in other instances privately-owned school buses could not be segregated from commercial buses, and are included with the latter.
(3) This column consists primarily of publicly owned school buses but includes a few privately owned school, institutional, and industrial buses registered free or at a reduced rate.
SOURCE: U.S. Department of Transportation, Federal Highway Administration.

School Bus Ownership and Usage by State

SCHOOL BUS OWNERSHIP AND USAGE BY STATE, 2002-2003 SCHOOL YEAR

	Pupils Transported at Public Expense	Bus Ownership			Total Miles of Service	Total Expenditures for Pupil Transportation
		Publicly Owned	Contractor	Total		
Alabama	366,138	6,799	222	7,021	58,750,038	$202,251,122
Alaska	N.A.	136	723	859	12,312,731	N.A.
Arizona	929,687	6,045	1,825	7,870	72,786,608	N.A.
Arkansas	316,662	6,290	245	6,535	43,628,580	N.A.
California	992,649	16,396	8,797	25,193	277,193,098	N.A.
Colorado	295,872	6,500	200	6,700	50,516,643	N.A.
Connecticut	444,780	700	6,300	7,000	N.A.	168,978,833
Delaware	102,974	495	1,105	1,600	22,755,184	52,446,474
Florida	1,025,921	19,424	1,390	20,814	273,407,956	753,526,972
Georgia	1,218,879	17,154	N.A.	17,154	158,359,464	466,301,514
Hawaii	59,000	0	782	782	4,140,000	21,288,000
Idaho	111,824	1,959	679	2,638	23,367,016	67,920,145
Illinois	997,099	9,000	9,000	18,000	234,084,022	687,534,358
Indiana	739,388	10,131	2,605	12,736	85,989,063	394,551,766
Iowa	234,630	N.A.	N.A.	7,200	43,309,063	89,389,876
Kansas	199,556	3,327	1,258	4,585	46,319,307	107,571,719
Kentucky	411,000	9,650	0	9,650	102,000,000	212,000,000
Louisiana	467,787	5,218	2,983	8,201	70,115,220	267,846,691
Maine	180,240	2,111	653	2,764	34,828,884	75,255,406
Maryland	605,154	3,620	3,163	6,783	117,678,648	358,027,476
Massachusetts	623,160	N.A.	N.A.	8,500	N.A.	298,883,209
Michigan	844,342	14,164	1,476	15,640	187,261,767	578,188,756
Minnesota	745,308	4,227	6,065	10,292	135,018,462	403,543,227
Mississippi	430,779	6,746	208	6,954	53,490,913	143,590,561
Missouri	555,283	6,864	4,542	11,406	123,254,065	323,189,777
Montana	68,118	1,467	1,358	2,825	18,049,284	40,776,196
Nebraska	35,758	1,990	647	2,637	27,318,746	66,842,640
Nevada	179,523	2,050	0	2,050	26,682,366	N.A.
New Hampshire	136,541	482	2,181	2,663	N.A.	65,475,948
New Jersey	374,965	4,461	16,767	21,228	N.A.	674,000,000
New Mexico	168,878	778	1,562	2,340	33,594,899	95,329,176
New York	1,733,005	22,497	23,000	45,497	204,829,897	1,523,426,952
North Carolina	714,975	13,416	30	13,446	165,096,715	250,444,455
North Dakota	43,249	2,002	457	2,459	23,614,851	31,288,390
Ohio	1,198,632	17,024	926	17,950	185,681,880	525,509,086
Oklahoma	341,514	7,493	123	7,616	56,097,653	144,696,137
Oregon	272,761	4,072	2,247	6,319	57,731,255	189,812,525
Pennsylvania	1,350,000	5,471	16,181	21,652	381,400,000	885,626,000
Rhode Island	156,454	335	1,356	1,691	N.A.	N.A.
South Carolina	345,390	5,125	20	5,145	79,531,500	168,347,753
South Dakota	38,051	1,146	554	1,700	13,239,151	30,313,109
Tennessee	465,419	6,772	1,334	8,106	92,606,760	N.A.
Texas	1,400,000	N.A.	N.A.	35,355	331,943,099	909,492,989
Utah	165,640	2,269	40	2,309	23,100,000	74,740,447
Vermont	N.A.	530	780	1,310	13,061,969	33,877,246
Virginia	963,248	14,739	0	14,739	175,188,494	432,316,955
Washington	482,469	8,054	1,311	9,365	86,000,000	282,000,000
West Virginia	220,325	3,692	0	3,692	41,843,021	160,816,281
Wisconsin	550,000	2,000	8,000	10,000	N.A.	N.A.
Wyoming	32,930	1,424	0	1,424	12,378,117	33,536,626
Total	**24,335,957**	**286,245**	**133,095**	**470,395**	**4,279,556,389**	**$12,290,954,793**

Note: N.A. Not available.
SOURCE: Bobit Publishing Company, School Bus Fleet Fact Book.

Government Ownership of Motor Vehicles by State

GOVERNMENT OWNERSHIP OF MOTOR VEHICLES BY STATE, 2003

State	Federal[1]				State, County and Municipal[2]				Total Publicly Owned Vehicles
	Passenger Cars	Trucks	Buses	Total	Passenger Cars	Trucks	Buses	Total	
Alabama	1,736	5,458	42	7,236	14,434	21,762	6,335	42,531	49,767
Alaska	525	3,518	80	4,123	1,290	5,473	149	6,912	11,035
Arizona	2,324	10,236	400	12,960	14,827	9,193	2,981	27,001	39,961
Arkansas	968	3,055	31	4,054	8,721	8,527	5,941	23,189	27,243
California	13,208	49,570	496	63,274	186,330	243,267	16,554	446,151	509,425
Colorado	1,816	9,737	45	11,598	8,478	17,289	4,022	29,789	41,387
Connecticut	920	4,857	13	5,790	10,633	23,173	851	34,657	40,447
Delaware	283	857	7	1,147	8,589	2,108	590	11,287	12,434
District of Columbia	2,647	4,157	291	7,095	1,672	2,704	112	4,488	11,583
Florida	4,925	16,597	220	21,742	101,357	139,618	41,145	282,120	303,862
Georgia	2,591	8,078	112	10,781	24,654	61,219	15,095	100,968	111,749
Hawaii	534	1,914	30	2,478	6,929	6,429	1,187	14,545	17,023
Idaho	690	5,450	158	6,298	4,996	9,394	2,244	16,634	22,932
Illinois	3,651	11,784	90	15,525	68,172	3,039	522	71,733	87,258
Indiana	1,436	4,918	58	6,412	22,864	39,012	21,033	82,909	89,321
Iowa	718	3,647	14	4,379	9,760	27,165	6,850	43,775	48,154
Kansas	828	3,511	13	4,352	6,994	15,693	2,438	25,125	29,477
Kentucky	1,647	4,841	167	6,655	23,903	3,922	12,260	40,085	46,740
Louisiana	1,687	5,357	26	7,070	43,550	19,235	6,093	68,878	75,948
Maine	445	1,340	13	1,798	4,691	10,566	2,425	17,682	19,480
Maryland	2,673	7,596	160	10,429	11,030	16,201	4,887	32,118	42,547
Massachusetts	2,761	7,583	88	10,432	16,050	33,604	502	50,156	60,588
Michigan	2,713	9,678	82	12,473	45,746	69,320	15,716	130,782	143,255
Minnesota	1,557	6,051	8	7,616	10,148	21,050	9,306	40,504	48,120
Mississippi	1,383	3,851	83	5,317	8,712	12,848	5,680	27,240	32,557
Missouri	3,159	5,218	38	8,415	4,364	12,291	7,256	23,911	32,326
Montana	912	5,464	20	6,396	4,656	12,064	1,570	18,290	24,686
Nebraska	1,112	3,027	11	4,150	12,120	17,408	5,129	34,657	38,807
Nevada	1,184	7,033	150	8,367	8,763	7,914	127	16,804	25,171
New Hampshire	612	1,205	2	1,819	3,848	11,529	379	15,756	17,575
New Jersey	2,275	11,216	61	13,552	44,070	93,350	3,606	141,026	154,578
New Mexico	1,401	7,399	327	9,127	13,317	15,985	756	30,058	39,185
New York	8,646	19,840	234	28,720	72,082	81,354	36,801	190,237	218,957
North Carolina	1,869	5,872	58	7,799	28,086	43,240	22,002	93,328	101,127
North Dakota	615	2,093	70	2,778	3,375	6,597	1,626	11,598	14,376
Ohio	3,191	9,829	89	13,109	51,230	69,810	23,161	144,201	157,310
Oklahoma	1,552	5,302	145	6,999	10,775	44,391	15,111	70,277	77,276
Oregon	1,412	9,831	74	11,317	23,418	21,486	10,129	55,033	66,350
Pennsylvania	5,204	13,833	131	19,168	42,300	53,380	8,107	103,787	122,955
Rhode Island	246	1,209	6	1,461	4,867	4,392	7	9,266	10,727
South Carolina	1,627	5,334	34	6,995	9,276	21,847	12,184	43,307	50,302
South Dakota	577	2,886	126	3,589	3,679	11,079	1,822	16,580	20,169
Tennessee	3,448	10,399	84	13,931	18,220	45,018	13,587	76,825	90,756
Texas	6,471	25,209	266	31,946	104,284	196,784	65,926	366,994	398,940
Utah	954	4,831	40	5,825	9,957	11,278	777	22,012	27,837
Vermont	341	522	5	868	2,460	6,056	1,484	10,000	10,868
Virginia	2,610	9,610	259	12,479	32,736	27,073	15,269	75,078	87,557
Washington	2,875	13,652	209	16,736	17,426	29,140	6,129	52,695	69,431
West Virginia	903	2,175	48	3,126	13,836	26,817	2,124	42,777	45,903
Wisconsin	1,135	5,181	25	6,341	15,041	41,958	4,699	61,698	68,039
Wyoming	398	3,153	12	3,563	4,935	10,081	1,919	16,935	20,498
Total	109,395	384,964	5,251	499,610	1,223,651	1,744,133	446,605	3,414,389	3,913,999

(1) Vehicles of the civilian branches of the Federal government are given in this table. Vehicles of the military services are not included. Distribution by State is estimated by the Federal Highway Administration.

(2) This information, compiled chiefly from reports of State authorities, is incomplete in many cases. Some States give State-owned vehicles only; others excludes from registration certain classes, such as fire apparatus and police vehicles. For the states not reporting state, county and municipal vehicles separately from private and commercial vehicles and those reporting unsegregated totals only, classification by vehicle type has been approximately on the basis of other available data.

SOURCE: U.S. Department of Transportation, Federal Highway Administration.

Motor Vehicles in Operation by Year

MOTOR VEHICLES IN OPERATION (as of July 1 of each year)

Year	Passenger Cars	Trucks	Total	% Change	Truck % of Total
2004[1]	132,822,614	98,575,667	231,398,281	2.4	42.6
2003[1]	130,785,738	95,096,365	225,882,103	2.2	42.1
2002	129,906,797	91,120,324	221,027,121	2.0	41.2
2001	128,714,022	87,968,915	216,682,937	1.6	40.6
2000	127,720,809	85,578,504	213,299,313	1.8	40.1
1999	126,868,744	82,640,417	209,509,161	2.2	39.4
1998	125,965,709	79,076,930	205,042,639	2.0	38.6
1997	124,672,920	76,397,477	201,070,397	1.4	38.0
1996	124,612,787	73,680,672	198,293,459	2.5	37.2
1995	123,241,881	70,198,512	193,440,393	2.5	36.3
1994	121,996,580	66,717,417	188,713,997	1.3	35.4
1993	121,055,398	65,260,066	186,315,464	2.6	35.0
1992	120,346,746	61,172,404	181,519,150	0.0	33.7
1991	123,327,046	58,178,883	181,505,929	1.2	32.1
1990	123,276,268	56,022,934	179,299,202	1.9	31.2
1989	122,758,378	53,201,657	175,960,035	2.5	30.2
1988	121,519,074	50,221,502	171,740,576	2.7	29.2
1987	119,848,769	47,344,319	167,193,088	3.1	28.3
1986	117,268,071	44,825,523	162,093,594	3.2	27.7
1985	114,662,333	42,386,882	157,049,215	3.2	27.0
1984	112,018,640	40,142,872	152,161,512	3.4	26.4
1983	108,961,215	38,143,304	147,104,519	2.3	25.9
1982	106,867,108	36,986,537	143,853,645	1.4	25.7
1981	105,838,582	36,069,197	141,907,779	1.5	25.4
1980	104,563,781	35,267,535	139,831,316	1.9	25.2
1979	104,676,507	32,582,991	137,259,498	2.8	23.7
1978	102,956,713	30,564,701	133,521,414	4.2	22.9
1977	99,903,594	28,221,661	128,125,255	3.0	22.0
1976	97,818,221	26,560,296	124,378,517	3.6	21.4
1975	95,240,602	24,812,843	120,053,445	3.6	20.7
1974	92,607,551	23,312,245	115,919,796	4.2	20.1
1973	89,805,159	21,411,931	111,217,090	4.7	19.3
1972	86,438,957	19,772,938	106,211,895	4.5	18.6
1971	83,137,324	18,462,287	101,599,611	3.5	18.2
1970	80,448,463	17,687,505	98,135,968	3.2	18.0
1969	78,494,938	16,586,368	95,081,306	4.4	17.4
1968	75,358,034	15,684,917	91,042,951	3.5	17.2
1967	72,967,686	14,988,491	87,956,177	2.7	17.0
1966	71,263,738	14,356,591	85,620,329	4.3	16.8
1965	68,939,770	13,126,579	82,066,349	4.5	16.0
1964	66,051,415	12,444,964	78,496,379	4.1	15.9
1963	63,493,277	11,902,039	75,395,316	4.2	15.8
1962	60,919,579	11,463,381	72,382,960	3.6	15.8
1961	58,854,380	11,042,770	69,897,150	2.9	15.8
1960	57,102,676	10,802,959	67,905,635	3.5	15.9
1959	55,086,761	10,532,145	65,618,906	4.9	16.1
1958	52,492,509	10,056,567	62,549,076	2.2	16.1
1957	51,432,460	9,775,950	61,208,410	3.1	16.0
1956	49,803,977	9,544,082	59,348,059	5.0	16.1
1955	47,377,970	9,162,444	56,540,414	6.3	16.2
1954	44,387,113	8,800,408	53,187,521	4.5	16.5
1953	42,202,349	8,692,574	50,894,923	5.6	17.1

(1) Estimated.
SOURCE: The Polk Company. Permission for further use must be obtained from the Polk Company.

Lease Penetration Rates and Used Vehicle Sales

LEASE PENETRATION RATES BY VEHICLE SEGMENT

Segment	2003	2002	2001	2000	1999	1998	1997	1995	1990	1985
PASSENGER CARS										
Budget	8.8	9.5	10.0	10.3	12.0	12.1	13.4	12.1	5.5	2.2
Small	8.9	9.7	12.1	14.2	14.4	14.8	15.4	18.9	5.3	1.8
Lower Middle	17.1	18.3	24.5	25.7	27.2	27.3	28.1	26.9	12.8	8.2
Core Middle	20.4	22.6	26.3	26.9	27.3	28.6	31.1	30.4	16.2	11.5
Upper Middle	30.6	30.8	30.0	29.2	29.4	29.1	28.1	26.2	14.7	11.5
Near Luxury	48.7	56.2	58.9	59.7	58.8	58.3	57.3	50.5	25.2	16.6
Luxury	45.2	51.4	55.5	51.3	57.8	65.2	65.9	62.0	52.6	39.6
Specialty	37.7	45.7	52.3	50.4	55.3	57.5	58.5	59.7	24.6	11.1
Sport	42.6	44.1	44.4	41.1	40.2	39.3	34.4	26.2	18.8	16.2
LIGHT TRUCKS										
Compact Pickup	10.1	15.1	15.8	15.7	15.6	15.7	16.3	14.6	4.4	1.3
Compact Sport Utility	29.7	38.8	42.2	40.7	41.2	39.7	38.4	34.3	9.6	5.2
Full Size Pickup	18.3	23.7	27.1	26.3	28.1	25.3	22.7	18.3	8.2	4.6
Full Size Sport Utility	37.8	42.1	45.9	46.5	44.4	42.7	42.1	36.9	9.3	4.2
Full Size Van	15.4	18.8	21.0	21.1	21.9	22.4	22.7	20.0	12.1	7.1
Minivan	28.1	34.5	36.6	32.3	35.7	33.5	32.8	25.8	8.4	4.2
Total	**24.7**	**27.9**	**29.2**	**28.7**	**29.1**	**31.5**	**29.3**	**24.2**	**7.3**	**3.5**

SOURCE: CNW Marketing Research, Inc.

USED VEHICLE SALES (in thousands)

Year	Franchised Dealers	Independent Dealers	Casual	Total
2004	15,953	14,751	11,841	42,545
2003	16,171	13,732	13,668	43,571
2002	16,470	13,078	13,478	43,026
2001	15,945	14,416	12,263	42,624
2000	16,178	13,559	11,883	41,620
1999	16,504	12,786	11,448	40,738
1998	15,684	13,182	11,976	40,842
1997	15,796	12,685	12,757	41,238
1996	15,713	13,247	11,871	40,831
1995	15,679	14,124	11,958	41,761
1994	15,047	14,548	10,541	40,136
1993	14,792	14,011	9,257	38,060
1992	14,619	11,681	10,646	36,946
1991	14,573	10,633	12,092	37,298
1990	14,222	10,678	12,632	37,532

Source: CNW Marketing Research, Inc.

AVERAGE USED VEHICLE TRANSACTION PRICES

Year	Franchised Dealers	Independent Dealers	Casual	Total
2004	$12,500	$7,750	$4,510	$8,629
2003	12,750	7,585	4,100	8,409
2002	12,537	7,157	3,688	8,130
2001	12,238	8,275	4,316	8,618
2000	12,748	7,613	4,539	8,896
1999	12,630	7,590	4,505	8,828
1998	12,165	7,172	4,190	8,341
1997	12,350	7,155	4,164	8,399
1996	12,256	7,076	4,283	8,257
1995	11,585	7,413	4,316	8,093
1994	11,150	7,209	3,762	7,781
1993	9,871	7,157	3,554	7,335
1992	8,895	6,934	3,405	6,693
1991	7,830	7,260	3,172	6,157
1990	7,410	7,125	2,956	6,830

Light Vehicle Fleet Registrations

LIGHT VEHICLE FLEET REGISTRATIONS BY MODEL YEAR, 2004

Make	Commercial	Rental	Government	Total Fleet	Total Sales	Fleet % of Total Sales
Audi	1,623	477	26	2,126	77,361	2.7
BMW	3,294	413	50	3,757	222,577	1.7
Buick	3,709	75,111	2,243	81,063	234,718	34.5
Cadillac	4,891	21,467	43	26,401	139,537	18.9
Chevrolet	41,877	313,441	23,989	379,307	876,585	43.3
Chrysler	6,570	63,568	317	70,455	203,216	34.7
Daewoo	25	153	—	178	472	37.7
Dodge	9,154	99,596	3,957	112,707	244,675	46.1
Ford	48,828	185,093	51,839	285,760	679,514	42.1
Honda/Acura	5,325	4,487	1,302	11,114	820,569	1.4
Hyundai/Kia	1,267	70,493	113	71,873	443,722	16.2
Jaguar	831	4,773	11	5,615	45,329	12.4
Lincoln/Mercury	13,315	46,141	415	59,871	211,194	28.3
Mazda	1,159	25,318	38	26,515	189,413	14.0
Mercedes-Benz	4,108	2,903	62	7,073	180,696	3.9
Mitsubishi	480	34,377	21	34,878	117,700	29.6
Nissan/Infiniti	6,222	50,826	134	57,182	519,588	11.0
Oldsmobile	395	35,987	68	36,450	47,148	77.3
Pontiac	28,818	150,599	2,058	181,475	436,843	41.5
Porsche	312	13	1	326	13,862	2.4
Saab	2,739	690	12	3,441	39,004	8.8
Saturn	552	6,060	44	6,656	137,133	4.9
Subaru	1,086	6,868	35	7,989	112,293	7.1
Suzuki	128	5,496	9	5,633	40,749	13.8
Toyota/Lexus	16,949	59,417	598	76,964	911,956	8.4
Volkswagen	1,929	2,913	86	4,928	231,292	2.1
Volvo	2,000	9,398	45	11,443	95,907	11.9
Other	3,688	3,263	1,386	8,337	119,404	7.0
Total Cars	**211,274**	**1,279,341**	**88,902**	**1,579,517**	**7,392,457**	**21.4**
BMW	994	76	16	1,086	58,026	1.9
Buick	1,332	19,208	101	20,641	90,912	22.7
Cadillac	2,941	2,557	19	5,517	87,530	6.3
Chevrolet	139,961	160,785	46,975	347,721	1,828,123	19.0
Chrysler	9,597	50,732	395	60,724	323,152	18.8
Dodge	36,532	107,382	8,061	151,975	915,305	16.6
Ford	193,461	144,908	62,310	400,679	2,002,546	20.0
Freightliner	1,613	21	59	1,693	2,987	56.7
GMC	28,838	39,134	5,808	73,780	586,358	12.6
Honda/Acura	3,060	1,026	208	4,294	526,964	0.8
Hummer	1,277	54	25	1,356	27,329	5.0
Hyundai/Kia	1,197	12,094	89	13,380	213,052	6.3
Isuzu	148	2,359	8	2,515	26,791	9.4
Jeep	11,354	39,662	1,276	52,292	450,075	11.6
Land Rover	1,020	1,334	9	2,363	32,128	7.4
Lincoln/Mercury	3,338	7,664	55	11,057	123,729	8.9
Mazda	621	6,307	37	6,965	78,446	8.9
Mercedes-Benz	633	518	15	1,166	26,773	4.4
Mitsubishi	410	18,962	18	19,390	70,632	27.5
Nissan/Infiniti	3,621	9,946	157	13,724	396,497	3.5
Oldsmobile	137	2,981	2	3,120	12,143	25.7
Pontiac	3,834	20,047	114	23,995	60,438	39.7
Porsche	661	18	24	703	15,504	4.5
Saturn	1,022	1,355	15	2,392	87,531	2.7
Subaru	413	944	50	1,407	65,723	2.1
Suzuki	191	2,193	5	2,389	28,201	8.5
Toyota/Lexus	14,689	11,518	418	26,625	939,236	2.8
Volkswagen	554	21	19	594	31,087	1.9
Volvo Truck	599	45	15	659	37,413	1.8
Total Trucks	**464,048**	**663,851**	**126,303**	**1,254,202**	**9,144,631**	**13.7**
Total	**675,322**	**1,943,192**	**215,205**	**2,833,719**	**16,537,088**	**17.1**

NOTE: Total sales includes fleet plus retail. SOURCE: Bobit Business Media, Automotive Fleet Fact Book 2005.

Total Motor Vehicle Registrations by Country

MOTOR VEHICLE REGISTRATIONS BY COUNTRY

Country	2003					2002		
	Passenger Cars	Commercial Vehicles	Total	Population (000)	Persons Per Car	Passenger Car	Commercial Vehicle	Total
AFRICA								
Algeria	372,300	528,000	900,300	31,714	85.2	360,000	522,000	882,000
Angola	40,000	63,400	103,400	11,186	279.7	39,000	61,000	100,000
Benin	9,400	14,900	24,300	7,231	769.2	9,350	14,650	24,000
Botswana	52,120	75,400	127,520	1,636	31.4	52,000	75,000	127,000
Burkina Faso	49,800	28,650	78,450	12,706	255.1	48,500	28,000	76,500
Burundi	24,000	23,500	47,500	7,252	302.2	23,650	23,000	46,650
Cameroon	157,800	84,250	242,050	16,286	103.2	155,000	83,000	238,000
Central African Republic	1,850	1,650	3,500	4,112	2,222.8	1,800	1,600	3,400
Congo	40,585	17,540	58,125	3,413	84.1	40,000	17,100	57,100
Congo, Democratic Republic of	148,900	135,000	283,900	57,125	383.6	147,500	134,100	281,600
Egypt	2,282,760	688,300	2,971,060	74,719	32.7	2,123,500	650,000	2,773,500
Ethiopia	63,200	48,900	112,100	69,628	1,101.7	60,000	45,400	105,400
Ghana	104,550	53,450	158,000	21,020	201.0	103,000	52,000	155,000
Ivory Coast	19,450	94,000	113,450	16,596	853.3	19,000	93,950	112,950
Kenya	261,920	110,540	372,460	32,168	122.8	254,000	101,200	355,200
Liberia	12,000	35,950	47,950	2,810	234.1	11,850	35,700	47,550
Libya	368,600	354,000	722,600	5,499	14.9	360,000	351,200	711,200
Madagascar	70,705	43,000	113,705	16,980	240.1	69,250	40,650	109,900
Malawi	11,400	14,220	25,620	12,113	1,062.6	10,750	13,900	24,650
Mali	7,920	9,900	17,820	10,848	1,369.7	7,850	9,600	17,450
Mauritania	11,450	6,850	18,300	2,913	254.4	11,200	6,600	17,800
Mauritius	101,436	39,412	140,848	1,210	11.9	96,000	37,000	133,000
Morocco	1,360,000	400,000	1,760,000	31,689	23.3	1,350,000	395,000	1,745,000
Mozambique	29,530	28,580	58,110	18,801	636.7	28,400	28,600	57,000
Namibia	73,550	81,300	154,850	1,993	27.1	71,000	80,000	151,000
Niger	21,000	18,650	39,650	11,470	546.2	20,500	18,000	38,500
Nigeria	681,200	427,000	1,108,200	122,790	180.3	678,000	425,000	1,103,000
Reunion	228,700	94,100	322,800	755	3.3	225,000	92,000	317,000
Sierra Leone	20,300	9,350	29,650	5,564	274.1	20,000	9,000	29,000
South Africa	4,154,593	2,079,860	6,234,453	44,482	10.7	4,041,828	2,023,845	6,065,673
Sudan	37,100	47,465	84,565	38,114	1,027.3	36,300	46,500	82,800
Tanzania	20,100	50,200	70,300	35,355	1,758.9	18,000	48,000	66,000
Togo	97,800	43,200	141,000	5,115	52.3	96,000	41,400	137,400
Tunisia	585,194	288,285	873,479	9,873	16.9	575,000	270,000	845,000
Uganda	51,010	43,150	94,160	25,556	501.0	50,500	42,000	92,500
Zambia	114,300	68,500	182,800	10,799	94.5	113,000	67,800	180,800
Zimbabwe	347,007	54,000	401,007	12,005	34.6	330,100	52,800	382,900
Total Africa	**12,033,530**	**6,204,452**	**18,237,982**	**793,527**	**65.9**	**11,656,828**	**6,036,595**	**17,693,423**
AMERICA, Caribbean								
Bahamas	83,500	27,000	110,500	297	3.6	82,300	26,900	109,200

Total Motor Vehicle Registrations by Country

MOTOR VEHICLE REGISTRATIONS BY COUNTRY — continued

Country	2003 Passenger Cars	2003 Commercial Vehicles	2003 Total	Population (000)	Persons Per Car	2002 Passenger Car	2002 Commercial Vehicle	2002 Total
Barbados	66,900	13,200	80,100	277	4.1	65,500	12,500	78,000
Bermuda	29,000	6,750	35,750	64	2.2	28,550	6,350	34,900
Cuba	184,980	210,300	395,280	11,269	60.9	182,250	207,500	389,750
Dominican Republic	171,200	207,000	378,200	8,783	51.3	167,000	202,000	369,000
Haiti	34,800	34,325	69,125	7,771	223.3	33,850	34,900	68,750
Jamaica	115,260	30,100	145,360	2,689	23.3	112,750	29,000	141,750
Netherlands Antilles	76,780	31,250	108,030	216	2.8	76,000	26,950	102,950
Puerto Rico	991,510	378,000	1,369,510	3,878	3.9	925,000	370,000	1,295,000
Trinidad and Tobago	297,020	38,275	335,295	1,093	3.7	290,000	36,750	326,750
Virgin Islands (US)	32,400	16,800	49,200	109	3.4	31,650	16,000	47,650
Total Caribbean	**2,083,350**	**993,000**	**3,076,350**	**36,447**	**17.5**	**1,994,850**	**968,850**	**2,963,700**
AMERICA, Central & South								
Argentina	5,380,000	1,493,000	6,873,000	38,741	7.2	5,445,100	1,530,520	6,975,620
Belize	11,500	14,380	25,880	268	23.3	11,000	14,000	25,000
Bolivia	203,500	290,100	493,600	8,586	42.2	200,000	289,000	489,000
Brazil	16,650,000	4,200,000	20,850,000	182,033	10.9	17,004,000	4,332,000	21,336,000
Chile	1,373,121	749,914	2,123,035	15,663	11.4	1,350,000	750,000	2,100,000
Colombia	850,000	534,500	1,384,500	41,662	49.0	825,000	526,000	1,351,000
Costa Rica	367,832	230,048	597,880	3,896	10.6	359,500	227,200	586,700
Ecuador	529,359	269,248	798,607	13,074	24.7	510,000	280,000	790,000
El Salvador	67,500	98,250	165,750	6,470	95.9	65,500	97,000	162,500
Guatemala	127,800	145,900	273,700	11,456	89.6	125,500	145,500	271,000
Guyana	28,000	13,000	41,000	761	27.2	26,000	11,750	37,750
Honduras	25,000	87,300	112,300	6,843	273.7	24,000	86,400	110,400
Nicaragua	64,650	99,350	164,000	5,254	81.3	62,200	96,000	158,200
Panama	266,900	171,800	438,700	3,040	11.4	265,000	170,000	435,000
Paraguay	81,837	80,400	162,237	6,037	73.8	73,200	77,750	150,950
Peru	346,300	234,800	581,100	27,159	78.4	325,400	215,000	540,400
Suriname	65,400	27,000	92,400	435	6.7	67,500	29,200	96,700
Uruguay	547,800	121,900	669,700	3,382	6.2	546,000	121,300	667,300
Venezuela	1,480,000	1,157,138	2,637,138	24,655	16.7	1,357,000	1,095,000	2,452,000
Total Central & S. America	**28,466,499**	**10,018,028**	**38,484,527**	**399,414**	**14.0**	**28,641,900**	**10,093,620**	**38,735,520**
AMERICA, North								
Canada	17,755,075	740,456	18,495,531	32,207	1.8	17,543,666	723,669	18,267,335
Mexico	13,600,100	6,246,000	19,846,100	103,718	7.6	12,964,702	5,919,073	18,883,775
United States	130,800,000	95,262,300	226,062,300	290,343	2.2	129,906,797	91,120,324	221,027,121
Total North America	**162,155,175**	**102,248,756**	**264,403,931**	**426,268**	**2.6**	**160,415,165**	**97,763,066**	**258,178,231**
ASIA, Far East								
Afghanistan	29,300	22,500	51,800	27,060	923.6	29,150	22,400	51,550
Bangladesh	31,700	60,200	91,900	138,448	4,367.5	29,000	58,100	87,100
Brunei	73,500	15,550	89,050	358	4.9	72,000	15,000	87,000

Total Motor Vehicle Registrations by Country

MOTOR VEHICLE REGISTRATIONS BY COUNTRY — continued

Country	2003 Passenger Cars	Commercial Vehicles	Total	Population (000)	Persons Per Car	2002 Passenger Car	Commercial Vehicle	Total
Burma	6,800	14,000	20,800	46,030	6,769.2	6,450	13,100	19,550
Hong Kong	457,328	194,780	652,108	6,810	14.9	429,416	183,752	613,168
India	6,669,000	4,025,000	10,694,000	1,049,700	157.4	6,945,000	3,535,000	10,480,000
Indonesia	3,556,000	2,720,000	6,276,000	234,893	66.1	3,235,010	2,520,038	5,755,048
Japan	55,212,593	17,312,192	72,524,785	127,214	2.3	54,539,802	17,713,816	72,253,618
Korea, South	10,278,900	4,308,400	14,587,300	48,202	4.7	9,737,430	4,169,730	13,907,160
Malaysia	5,590,000	1,142,000	6,732,000	23,093	4.1	4,624,557	1,068,637	5,693,194
Pakistan	390,480	396,225	786,705	156,127	399.8	381,000	389,300	770,300
Peoples Republic of China	6,789,000	17,222,000	24,011,000	1,291,496	190.2	4,950,000	10,500,000	15,450,000
Philippines	796,385	1,774,300	2,570,685	84,620	106.3	787,915	1,757,000	2,544,915
Singapore	414,300	186,250	600,550	4,277	10.3	410,100	180,200	590,300
Sri Lanka	321,330	374,000	695,330	19,742	61.4	313,000	369,000	682,000
Taiwan	5,169,733	964,061	6,133,794	22,603	4.4	4,989,336	933,864	5,923,200
Thailand	3,115,000	4,580,000	7,695,000	63,271	20.3	2,985,000	4,365,000	7,350,000
Vietnam	101,100	144,600	245,700	81,791	809.0	93,000	140,500	233,500
Total Far East	**99,002,449**	**55,456,058**	**154,458,507**	**3,425,738**	**34.6**	**94,557,166**	**47,934,437**	**142,491,603**
ASIA, Middle East								
Azerbaijan	350,559	124,482	475,041	7,831	22.3	342,713	126,000	468,713
Bahrain	290,600	124,500	415,100	667	2.3	285,000	123,200	408,200
Cyprus	287,622	120,789	408,411	772	2.7	276,000	120,200	396,200
Iran	2,578,850	666,550	3,245,400	67,148	26.0	2,398,932	670,000	3,068,932
Iraq	747,530	130,275	877,805	24,683	33.0	732,873	128,987	861,860
Israel	1,522,112	358,980	1,881,092	6,117	4.0	1,461,154	345,000	1,806,154
Jordan	315,250	107,920	423,170	5,460	17.3	296,010	106,851	402,861
Kuwait	770,375	200,315	970,690	2,183	2.8	759,000	210,000	969,000
Lebanon	406,920	85,125	492,045	3,728	9.2	390,500	83,500	474,000
Oman	266,325	113,370	379,695	2,807	10.5	261,095	111,144	372,239
Qatar	145,280	75,000	220,280	817	5.6	131,065	72,500	203,565
Saudi Arabia	2,899,384	1,720,910	4,620,294	25,157	8.7	2,787,000	1,710,000	4,497,000
Syria	181,017	290,300	471,317	17,586	97.1	162,217	255,371	417,588
Turkey	4,700,343	1,747,385	6,447,728	68,109	14.5	4,600,140	1,636,203	6,236,343
United Arab Emirates	240,573	70,000	310,573	2,485	10.3	230,000	69,100	299,100
Yemen	290,208	331,410	621,618	19,350	66.7	287,500	329,500	617,000
Total Middle East	**15,992,948**	**6,267,311**	**22,260,259**	**254,899**	**15.9**	**15,401,199**	**6,097,556**	**21,498,755**
EUROPE, East								
Belarus	1,557,800	25,400	1,583,200	10,322	6.6	1,512,400	25,500	1,537,900
Bulgaria	2,309,300	337,200	2,646,500	7,588	3.3	2,174,112	323,145	2,497,257
Croatia	1,293,400	143,100	1,436,500	4,498	3.5	1,244,252	143,494	1,387,746
Czech Republic	3,706,012	445,000	4,151,012	10,251	2.8	3,648,905	434,874	4,083,779
Hungary	2,777,219	394,988	3,172,207	10,058	3.6	2,629,526	413,954	3,043,480
Poland	11,243,800	2,274,600	13,518,400	38,603	3.4	11,028,852	2,114,963	13,143,815
Romania	3,087,628	635,342	3,722,970	22,380	7.2	3,246,000	684,500	3,930,500

Total Motor Vehicle Registrations by Country

MOTOR VEHICLE REGISTRATIONS BY COUNTRY — continued

Country	2003 Passenger Cars	2003 Commercial Vehicles	2003 Total	Population (000)	Persons Per Car	2002 Passenger Car	2002 Commercial Vehicle	2002 Total
Russian Federation	23,383,000	5,400,000	28,783,000	144,586	6.2	22,100,000	5,215,000	27,315,000
Serbia & Montenegro	1,650,000	155,000	1,805,000	10,823	6.6	1,570,300	147,200	1,717,500
Slovak Republic	1,356,185	161,559	1,517,744	5,416	4.0	1,326,891	181,910	1,508,801
Slovenia	889,600	69,300	958,900	2,012	2.3	899,166	67,491	966,657
Ukraine	5,603,800	985,700	6,589,500	47,668	8.5	5,442,800	1,092,813	6,535,613
Total Eastern Europe	**58,857,744**	**11,027,189**	**69,884,933**	**314,206**	**5.3**	**56,823,204**	**10,844,844**	**67,668,048**
EUROPE, West								
Austria	4,054,308	335,318	4,389,626	8,163	2.0	3,987,093	347,973	4,335,066
Belgium	4,793,271	661,948	5,455,219	10,331	2.2	4,747,368	641,792	5,389,160
Denmark	1,894,649	428,949	2,323,598	5,394	2.8	1,892,900	410,585	2,303,485
Finland	2,259,383	334,009	2,593,392	5,204	2.3	2,180,025	326,284	2,506,309
France	29,560,000	6,068,000	35,628,000	60,181	2.0	29,160,000	5,984,000	35,144,000
Germany	45,022,926	3,541,193	48,564,119	82,398	1.8	44,657,303	3,567,530	48,224,833
Greece	3,885,908	1,138,692	5,024,600	10,626	2.7	3,647,834	1,108,857	4,756,691
Iceland	161,721	21,977	183,698	291	1.8	166,000	22,500	188,500
Ireland	1,520,000	272,000	1,792,000	3,924	2.6	1,425,210	257,015	1,682,225
Italy	34,310,446	4,166,033	38,476,479	57,998	1.7	33,706,153	3,976,037	37,682,190
Latvia	619,081	125,030	744,111	2,323	3.8	563,000	119,500	682,500
Luxembourg	287,245	35,904	323,149	457	1.6	282,433	35,073	317,506
Malta	200,509	44,586	245,095	395	2.0	193,175	44,893	238,068
Netherlands	7,151,000	1,080,000	8,231,000	16,223	2.3	6,854,700	1,038,635	7,893,335
Norway	1,932,663	468,500	2,401,163	4,555	2.4	1,899,815	464,810	2,364,625
Portugal	3,966,000	1,275,100	5,241,100	10,480	2.6	3,885,000	1,386,300	5,271,300
Spain	19,293,263	4,255,275	23,548,538	40,217	2.1	18,732,632	4,315,842	23,048,474
Sweden	4,078,000	435,561	4,513,561	8,970	2.2	4,044,928	422,977	4,467,905
Switzerland	3,753,890	335,958	4,089,848	7,408	2.0	3,700,951	332,543	4,033,494
United Kingdom	29,007,820	3,569,071	32,576,891	60,095	2.1	28,483,961	3,486,961	31,970,922
Total Western Europe	**197,752,083**	**28,593,104**	**226,345,187**	**395,634**	**2.0**	**194,210,481**	**28,290,107**	**222,500,588**
PACIFIC								
Australia	10,100,000	2,205,000	12,305,000	19,732	2.0	9,965,000	2,195,000	12,160,000
Fiji	76,000	52,350	128,350	869	11.4	74,000	51,000	125,000
French Polynesia	38,390	20,505	58,895	262	6.8	37,900	21,850	59,750
Guam	130,400	49,000	179,400	164	1.3	129,600	47,100	176,700
New Caledonia	60,500	24,650	85,150	211	3.5	57,850	23,900	81,750
New Zealand	2,473,500	468,800	2,942,300	3,951	1.6	2,265,145	450,801	2,715,946
Papua New Guinea	34,468	89,215	123,683	5,296	153.6	33,792	89,000	122,792
Samoa (American)	6,400	6,700	13,100	178	27.8	6,250	6,000	12,250
Vanuatu	8,350	4,450	12,800	199	23.9	8,250	4,300	12,550
Total Pacific	**12,928,008**	**2,920,670**	**15,848,678**	**30,862**	**2.4**	**12,577,787**	**2,888,951**	**15,466,738**
WORLD TOTAL	**589,271,786**	**223,728,568**	**813,000,354**	**6,076,993**	**10.3**	**576,278,580**	**210,918,026**	**787,196,606**

SOURCE: International Road Federation, VDA, World Bank and Ward's estimates.

Material Usage by the Automotive Industry

AUTOMOTIVE CONSUMPTION OF MATERIALS BY TYPE

Material	U.S. Total Consumption	Automotive Consumption	Automotive Percentage	Material	U.S. Total Consumption	Automotive Consumption	Automotive Percentage
ALUMINUM(Thousands of Pounds)				**PLASTIC(Thousands of Pounds)**			
2004	23,560,000	7,303,000	31.0	2004	113,826,000	5,190,000	4.6
2003	23,280,000	6,780,000	29.1	2003	107,669,000	4,117,995	3.8
2002	23,592,000	6,599,000	28.0	2002	108,262,000	3,984,000	3.7
2001	24,976,000	6,050,000	24.2	2001	101,958,000	3,981,460	3.9
2000	24,486,000	6,871,000	28.1	2000	105,940,000	4,137,957	3.9
COPPER AND COPPER ALLOY(Thousands of Pounds)				**RUBBER(Tire & Tire Products in Metric Tons)**			
2004	7,822,200	841,000	10.8	2004	NA	NA	NA
2003	7,440,900	749,200	10.1	2003	2,982,000	1,967,000	65.9
2002	7,388,800	754,100	10.2	2002	2,997,000	2,050,000	68.4
2001	7,877,200	717,800	9.1	2001	2,860,000	1,945,000	68.0
2000	9,379,300	894,400	9.5	2000	3,338,000	2,150,000	64.4
GRAY IRON(Tons)				**RUBBER(Non-Tire Products in Metric Tons)**			
2004	4,900,000	1,100,000	22.4	2004	NA	NA	NA
2003	4,800,000	1,312,000	26.2	2003	2,982,000	1,018,000	34.1
2002	5,250,000	1,569,750	29.9	2002	2,997,000	947,000	31.6
2001	5,648,000	1,707,000	30.2	2001	2,860,000	915,000	32.0
2000	5,712,000	1,738,000	30.4	2000	3,338,000	1,188,000	35.6
DUCTILE IRON(Tons)				**ALLOY STEEL(Tons)**			
2004	4,271,000	1,077,000	25.2	2004	5,032,638	634,112	12.6
2003	4,100,000	1,100,000	26.8	2003	4,500,186	449,198	10.0
2002	4,265,000	1,390,000	32.6	2002	5,060,983	668,050	13.2
2001	3,992,000	1,286,000	32.2	2001	4,789,000	574,680	12.0
2000	3,845,000	1,277,000	33.2	2000	5,378,889	561,346	10.4
MALLEABLE IRON(Tons)				**STAINLESS STEEL(Tons)**			
2004	120,000	63,000	52.5	2004	2,521,850	484,195	19.2
2003	130,000	68,000	52.3	2003	1,954,304	332,164	17.0
2002	145,000	73,950	51.0	2002	2,326,957	432,814	18.6
2001	160,000	82,000	51.2	2001	1,837,000	369,237	20.1
2000	165,000	87,000	52.7	2000	2,102,962	494,531	23.5
TOTAL IRON(Tons)				**TOTAL STEEL(Tons)**			
2004	9,291,000	2,240,000	24.1	2004	111,385,462	13,857,470	12.4
2003	9,030,000	2,480,000	27.5	2003	105,890,000	15,882,831	15.0
2002	9,660,000	3,033,700	31.4	2002	100,000,000	13,987,858	13.4
2001	9,800,000	3,075,000	31.4	2001	98,940,000	14,059,000	14.2
2000	9,722,000	3,102,000	31.9	2000	109,050,451	16,063,000	13.7
LEAD(Metric Tons)				**ZINC(Tons)**			
2004	1,410,000	1,029,600	73.0	2004	1,160,000	226,800	23.0
2003	1,390,000	1,037,000	74.6	2003	1,050,000	210,000	20.0
2002	1,678,634	1,203,069	71.7	2002	1,150,000	264,500	23.0
2001	1,696,224	1,233,557	72.5	2001	1,140,000	262,200	23.0
2000	1,720,000	1,293,600	75.2	2000	1,320,000	303,600	23.0

NOTE: For most materials listed, automotive consumption includes materials used for cars, trucks, buses and replacement parts.
SOURCE: Ward's Communications from various sources.

Material Usage, Vehicles Retired From Use and Vehicle Recycling

POUNDS OF MATERIAL IN A TYPICAL FAMILY VEHICLE

Material	2004 Pounds	2004 Percent	2003 Pounds	2003 Percent	1990 Pounds	1990 Percent	1985 Pounds	1985 Percent
Regular Steel, Sheet, Strip, Bar and Rod	1,361.0	40.1	1,354.5	40.3	1,405.0	44.7	1,481.5	46.5
High and Medium Strength Steel	395.0	11.6	379.0	11.3	238.0	7.6	217.5	6.8
Stainless Steel	57.5	1.7	56.5	1.7	34.0	1.1	29.0	0.9
Other Steels	28.0	0.8	26.5	0.8	39.5	1.3	54.5	1.7
Iron	308.0	9.1	328.0	9.8	454.0	14.5	468.0	14.7
Plastics and Plastic Composites	257.5	7.6	255.5	7.6	229.0	7.3	211.5	6.6
Aluminum	289.5	8.5	277.5	8.3	158.5	5.0	138.0	4.3
Copper and Brass	51.5	1.5	50.0	1.5	48.5	1.5	44.0	1.4
Powder Metal Parts	41.5	1.2	40.0	1.2	24.0	0.8	19.0	0.6
Zinc Die Castings	8.5	0.3	8.5	0.3	18.5	0.6	18.0	0.6
Magnesium Castings	10.0	0.3	9.5	0.3	3.0	0.1	2.5	0.1
Fluids and Lubricants	198.5	5.9	198.0	5.9	182.0	5.8	184.0	5.8
Rubber	152.0	4.5	149.0	4.4	136.5	4.3	136.0	4.3
Glass	99.5	2.9	98.5	2.9	86.5	2.8	85.0	2.7
Other Materials	133.0	3.9	127.5	3.8	83.5	2.7	99.0	3.1
Total	3,391.0	100.0	3,358.5	100.0	3,140.5	100.0	3,187.5	100.0

SOURCE: American Metal Market from Industry Reports. Copywrite 2004 American Metal Market.

MOTOR VEHICLES RETIRED FROM USE
(In Thousands)

Year Ending June 30	Passenger Cars	Trucks & Buses	Total
2004	5,524	6,379	11,903
2003	6,864	5,226	12,090
2002	7,310	5,986	13,296
2001	7,650	6,472	14,122
2000	8,085	6,214	14,299
1999	7,216	4,447	11,663
1998	6,819	4,846	11,665
1997	8,244	4,265	12,509
1996	7,527	3,284	10,811
1995	7,414	2,918	10,332
1994	7,824	4,545	12,369
1993	7,366	1,048	8,414
1992	11,194	1,587	12,781
1991	8,565	2,284	10,849
1989	8,981	2,189	11,170
1987	8,103	2,364	10,467
1985	7,729	2,100	9,829
1983	6,243	1,491	7,734
1981	7,542	1,519	9,061
1979	9,312	1,916	11,228
1977	8,234	1,668	9,902
1975	5,669	908	6,577
1973	7,987	1,208	9,195
1971	6,021	1,044	7,065
1969	6,348	966	7,314
1967	6,984	947	7,931
1965	5,704	736	6,440
1963	4,741	720	5,461
1961	4,294	647	4,941

NOTE: Figures represent vehicles which are not re-registered.
SOURCE: The Polk Company. Permission for further use mustbe obtained from The Polk Company.

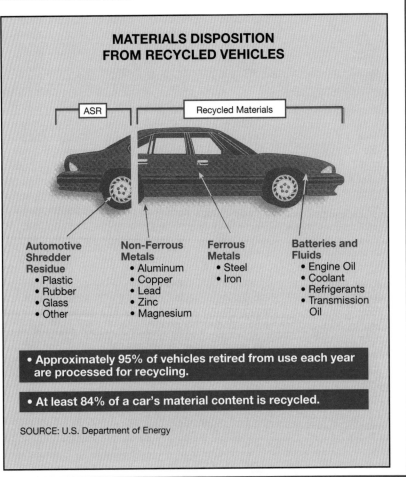

MATERIALS DISPOSITION FROM RECYCLED VEHICLES

ASR
Recycled Materials

Automotive Shredder Residue
- Plastic
- Rubber
- Glass
- Other

Non-Ferrous Metals
- Aluminum
- Copper
- Lead
- Zinc
- Magnesium

Ferrous Metals
- Steel
- Iron

Batteries and Fluids
- Engine Oil
- Coolant
- Refrigerants
- Transmission Oil

- **Approximately 95% of vehicles retired from use each year are processed for recycling.**

- **At least 84% of a car's material content is recycled.**

SOURCE: U.S. Department of Energy

U.S. Motor Vehicle Exports by Country of Destination and Vehicle Type

U.S. EXPORTS BY COUNTRY OF DESTINATION AND VEHICLE TYPE, 2004

COUNTRY	Passenger Cars Units	Passenger Cars Value ($000)	Trucks Units	Trucks Value ($000)	Buses Units	Buses Value ($000)	Total Units	Total Value ($000)
Afghanistan	266	1,569	1	23	2	308	269	1,900
Algeria	30	247	6	132	—	—	36	379
Andorra	61	1,056	—	—	—	—	61	1,056
Angola	455	6,218	25	736	7	372	487	7,326
Anguilla	94	1,145	1	5	2	50	97	1,200
Antigua Barbuda	132	1,862	9	185	5	103	146	2,150
Argentina	1,692	8,593	9	158	—	—	1,701	8,751
Armenia	288	3,686	—	—	—	—	288	3,686
Aruba	574	4,929	87	2,371	—	—	661	7,301
Australia	13,830	287,497	2,128	81,704	17	132	15,975	369,333
Austria	912	18,047	10	201	6	447	928	18,695
Azerbaijan	13	382	—	—	—	—	13	382
Bahamas	3,335	36,363	495	9,171	12	463	3,842	45,997
Bahrain	2,510	44,096	11	249	1	27	2,522	44,372
Bangladesh	—	—	—	—	—	—	—	—
Barbados	167	2,455	57	1,623	—	—	224	4,078
Belarus	379	2,150	—	—	—	—	379	2,150
Belgium	5,466	71,558	78	1,889	61	858	5,605	74,305
Belize	417	3,057	429	8,712	108	1,050	954	12,819
Benin	3,919	24,099	13	282	—	—	3,932	24,381
Bermuda	212	683	41	1,252	—	—	253	1,935
Bolivia	126	1,937	10	190	3	13	139	2,140
Bosnia-Hercegovina	36	295	—	—	—	—	36	295
Botswana	11	272	33	1,108	—	—	44	1,380
British Virgin Islands	230	3,090	12	265	1	23	243	3,377
Brazil	344	10,189	4	91	1	15	349	10,296
Brunei	188	651	1	3	—	—	189	654
Bulgaria	129	1,640	—	—	—	—	129	1,640
Cambodia	10,435	28,341	16	306	—	—	10,451	28,647
Cameroon	158	1,359	23	549	—	—	181	1,909
Canada	581,139	10,303,619	263,402	7,391,067	7,089	372,115	851,630	18,066,801
Cape Verde	73	623	—	—	—	—	73	623
Cayman Islands	2,951	38,623	83	2,032	14	292	3,048	40,947
Chile	3,404	50,385	1,158	18,281	6	49	4,568	68,716
China	9,099	130,618	146	4,885	77	657	9,322	136,160
Colombia	927	19,841	144	4,815	123	614	1,194	25,270
Congo (ROC)	42	450	2	41	—	—	44	491
Costa Rica	5,135	36,902	689	12,479	394	1,265	6,218	50,646
Cote d'Ivoire	472	5,879	90	2,942	—	—	562	8,820
Croatia	212	3,238	—	—	—	—	212	3,238
Cuba	10	163	1	5	—	—	11	168
Cyprus	94	1,798	—	—	—	—	94	1,798
Czech Republic	526	7,440	9	167	—	—	535	7,607
Denmark	702	18,604	6	104	—	—	708	18,708
Djibouti	20	210	—	—	—	—	20	210
Dominica Islands	34	446	132	3,327	—	—	166	3,773

U.S. Motor Vehicle Exports by Country of Destination and Vehicle Type

U.S. EXPORTS BY COUNTRY OF DESTINATION AND VEHICLE TYPE, 2004 — continued

COUNTRY	Passenger Cars Units	Passenger Cars Value ($000)	Trucks Units	Trucks Value ($000)	Buses Units	Buses Value ($000)	Total Units	Total Value ($000)
Dominican Republic	11,242	89,577	—	—	13	73	11,255	89,650
Ecuador	137	4,008	134	3,343	2	32	273	7,383
Egypt	838	11,791	72	1,765	—	—	910	13,556
El Salvador	2,740	16,586	1,729	49,427	517	2,125	4,986	68,137
Eq Guinea	134	2,017	6	108	14	364	154	2,488
Eritrea	22	141	2	31	—	—	24	172
Estonia	628	6,753	—	—	—	—	628	6,753
Ethiopia	21	456	—	—	1	10	22	466
F St Micronesia	6	87	—	—	1	64	7	151
Finland	17,506	224,209	1,572	44,681	2	32	19,080	268,922
French Polynesia	153	2,540	85	2,190	—	—	238	4,729
France	3,389	76,833	54	1,510	13	230	3,456	78,573
Gabon	35	451	2	24	—	—	37	475
Gambia	296	2,090	25	589	11	35	332	2,713
Georgia	887	9,175	—	—	—	—	887	9,175
Germany	129,664	3,993,061	187	6,308	80	6,519	129,931	4,005,888
Ghana	2,792	21,717	78	1,796	13	82	2,883	23,595
Gibraltar	—	—	—	—	—	—	—	—
Greece	5,188	91,034	2	24	7	35	5,197	91,093
Grenada	35	448	25	611	—	—	60	1,059
Guadeloupe	229	607	—	—	—	—	229	607
Guatemala	4,680	34,250	4,137	154,070	804	4,112	9,621	192,432
Guinea	659	3,704	—	—	28	227	687	3,931
Guyana	79	655	6	122	4	13	89	789
Haiti	2,992	14,006	1,103	17,772	101	494	4,196	32,272
Honduras	4,570	19,502	492	9,039	405	1,687	5,467	30,227
Hong Kong	13,262	97,928	14	287	1	65	13,277	98,280
Hungary	709	6,063	—	—	—	—	709	6,063
Iceland	1,572	33,481	9	177	1	8	1,582	33,666
India	17	679	4	85	—	—	21	764
Indonesia	3	19	15	288	—	—	18	307
Iraq	834	43,245	142	3,941	167	67,936	1,143	115,122
Ireland	165	2,860	22	500	1	15	188	3,374
Israel	2,509	47,172	508	10,530	18	881	3,035	58,583
Italy	3,756	66,292	776	13,407	2	14	4,534	79,713
Jamaica	959	9,988	307	7,674	62	532	1,328	18,193
Japan	26,929	476,620	88	2,887	27	428	27,044	479,935
Jordan	4,655	38,783	321	8,255	10	247	4,986	47,285
Kazakhstan	506	8,552	6	124	46	3,400	558	12,076
Kenya	25	537	—	—	—	—	25	537
Korea	2,864	50,436	281	6,386	34	395	3,179	57,216
Kuwait	24,814	429,600	1,477	35,409	81	5,527	26,372	470,535
Laos	16	230	—	—	—	—	16	230
Latvia	2,233	15,822	1	6	3	6	2,237	15,833
Lebanon	12,675	111,659	265	6,374	29	196	12,969	118,229
Liberia	515	3,058	22	458	7	35	544	3,551

EXPORTS

U.S. Motor Vehicle Exports by Country of Destination and Vehicle Type

U.S. EXPORTS BY COUNTRY OF DESTINATION AND VEHICLE TYPE, 2004 — continued

COUNTRY	Passenger Cars Units	Passenger Cars Value ($000)	Trucks Units	Trucks Value ($000)	Buses Units	Buses Value ($000)	Total Units	Total Value ($000)
Lithuania	14,528	82,308	3	49	—	—	14,531	82,357
Luxembourg	46	2,939	1	7	—	—	47	2,946
Macao	1	67	—	—	—	—	1	67
Macedonia	24	251	—	—	—	—	24	251
Malawi	—	—	9	171	—	—	9	171
Malaysia	42	1,002	2	28	—	—	44	1,030
Mali	21	305	4	85	—	—	25	391
Malta & Gozo	15	235	4	83	—	—	19	318
Marshall Islands	33	391	9	174	—	—	42	565
Mexico	247,218	3,092,723	63,817	1,000,610	3,273	38,569	314,308	4,131,902
Moldova	49	500	1	8	—	—	50	507
Monaco	26	414	—	—	—	—	26	414
Mongolia	99	911	—	—	9	84	108	995
Montserrat	4	30	1	18	—	—	5	48
Morocco	149	2,646	87	2,273	—	—	236	4,919
Mozambique	1	4	178	5,249	—	—	179	5,253
Namibia	89	685	19	334	1	22	109	1,041
Netherlands	7,515	189,518	43	1,334	40	421	7,598	191,273
Netherlands Antilles	1,733	18,469	39	1,200	11	134	1,783	19,803
New Zealand	2,355	46,780	187	6,174	10	101	2,552	53,055
Nicaragua	440	3,494	295	6,480	123	532	858	10,506
Niger	498	3,573	3	42	—	—	501	3,615
Nigeria	6,685	56,558	803	13,457	62	1,296	7,550	71,311
Norway	2,159	52,952	306	7,311	1	44	2,466	60,308
Oman	2,133	40,923	42	1,316	2	36	2,177	42,275
Pakistan	95	638	22	393	—	—	117	1,031
Palau	3	20	—	—	1	55	4	75
Panama	1,706	26,139	326	8,563	87	751	2,119	35,453
Paraguay	241	3,874	1	19	—	—	242	3,893
Peru	370	5,522	58	1,655	3	62	431	7,240
Philippines	1,257	23,381	29	935	—	—	1,286	24,316
Poland	2,879	32,160	1	20	3	8	2,883	32,188
Portugal	154	1,681	3	45	—	—	157	1,726
Qatar	3,277	63,667	80	1,960	1	14	3,358	65,641
Romania	163	3,129	2	40	1	3	166	3,172
Russia	13,728	196,813	989	17,641	5	54	14,722	214,507
Samoa	151	1,265	1	22	—	—	152	1,286
San Marino	3	43	—	—	—	—	3	43
Saudi Arabia	77,876	1,019,641	1,745	63,945	307	2,273	79,928	1,085,859
Senegal	255	2,820	46	1,430	2	18	303	4,267
Sierra Leone	495	2,766	5	103	—	—	500	2,869
Singapore	193	2,992	28	904	4	34	225	3,930
Slovakia	98	955	—	—	—	—	98	955
Slovenia	1,034	18,951	10	185	—	—	1,044	19,136
South Africa	6,559	234,117	1,242	26,056	8	129	7,809	260,302
Spain	2,806	52,049	69	1,758	5	41	2,880	53,849
St Kitts-Nevis	66	1,234	2	32	—	—	68	1,266

U.S. Motor Vehicle Exports by Country of Destination and Vehicle Type

U.S. EXPORTS BY COUNTRY OF DESTINATION AND VEHICLE TYPE, 2004 — continued

COUNTRY	Passenger Cars Units	Passenger Cars Value ($000)	Trucks Units	Trucks Value ($000)	Buses Units	Buses Value ($000)	Total Units	Total Value ($000)
St Lucia Islands	37	456	—	—	—	—	37	456
St Vinc & Gren	26	445	4	60	1	8	31	513
Suriname	189	1,874	2	33	3	23	194	1,930
Sweden	6,746	116,176	54	1,461	14	130	6,814	117,767
Switzerland	2,920	66,441	28	753	4	89	2,952	67,283
Syria	545	4,914	8	150	—	—	553	5,063
Taiwan	3,568	78,132	166	4,886	—	—	3,734	83,018
Tajikistan	11	65	—	—	—	—	11	65
Tanzania	18	176	—	—	—	—	18	176
Thailand	858	10,100	4	75	1	13	863	10,188
Togo	753	4,908	2	34	1	6	756	4,947
Trinidad & Tobago	98	1,864	21	392	—	—	119	2,256
Tunisia	56	938	8	149	—	—	64	1,087
Turkey	1,509	41,949	17	310	—	—	1,526	42,259
Turks & Caicos Islands	515	5,548	5	93	7	168	527	5,809
Uganda	9	234	6	125	—	—	15	359
Ukraine	1,856	23,783	8	150	1	44	1,865	23,977
United Arab Emirates	29,779	412,651	1,529	38,727	11	161	31,319	451,539
United Kingdom	30,324	882,729	138	3,364	56	807	30,518	886,899
Uruguay	22	618	7	136	—	—	29	754
Uzbekistan	5	182	—	—	—	—	5	182
Venezuela	1,101	20,271	598	11,693	31	1,621	1,730	33,585
Vietnam	1,499	11,879	629	12,204	—	—	2,128	24,082
Yemen	107	1,796	11	248	—	—	118	2,044
Yugoslavia	421	4,807	1	23	—	—	422	4,830
Zambia	2	50	38	1,128	—	—	40	1,178
Zimbabwe	7	122	100	3,311	—	—	107	3,433
Other	373	4,704	39	631	42	114	454	5,449
Total	**1,421,815**	**24,244,374**	**357,265**	**9,193,783**	**14,565**	**522,536**	**1,793,645**	**33,960,692**

SOURCE: Compiled from official statistics of the U.S. Department of Commerce.

U.S. EXPORTS OF PASSENGER CARS BY COUNTRY OF DESTINATION

Year	Canada	France	Germany	Japan	Kuwait	Mexico	Saudi Arabia	Taiwan	Other Countries	Total Exports
2004	581,139	3,389	129,664	26,929	24,814	247,218	77,876	3,568	327,218	1,421,815
2003	605,246	2,107	130,867	25,608	20,887	209,163	48,027	2,978	232,964	1,277,847
2002	612,070	5,815	77,054	27,265	6,957	227,131	31,271	4,720	187,946	1,180,229
2001	612,070	5,815	77,054	27,265	6,957	227,131	31,271	4,720	187,946	1,180,229
2000	611,696	3,834	55,812	40,441	4,307	191,885	23,138	10,932	188,050	1,130,095
1999	583,999	2,782	42,415	36,602	1,650	117,018	5,076	8,054	107,814	905,410
1998	566,481	2,675	44,611	43,580	2,519	70,130	11,956	9,604	147,080	898,636
1997	626,629	2,514	57,426	71,789	2,565	62,911	10,146	24,697	216,626	1,075,303
1996	502,652	3,802	59,462	109,917	7,708	46,562	18,253	35,141	190,137	973,634
1995	492,107	2,538	26,690	130,524	6,661	18,649	12,523	61,002	238,673	989,367
1994	559,513	6,083	39,568	100,400	9,246	36,569	18,587	72,491	176,801	1,019,258
1993	480,909	2,942	44,038	56,741	7,923	4,036	32,827	71,332	163,490	864,238
1992	459,910	8,704	56,615	40,598	15,208	4,261	35,502	90,231	140,045	851,074
1991	495,373	5,563	38,285	28,160	16,312	10,592	28,270	44,934	87,461	754,950
1990	505,352	10,475	34,485	39,188	2,919	12,827	23,288	66,609	98,614	793,757

SOURCE: Compiled from official statistics of the U.S. Department of Commerce.

U.S. Motor Vehicle Imports by Country of Origin and Vehicle Type

U.S. IMPORTS BY COUNTRY OF ORIGIN AND VEHICLE TYPE, 2004

Country of Origin	Passenger Cars Units	Passenger Cars Value ($000)	Trucks Units	Trucks Value ($000)	Buses Units	Buses Value ($000)	Total Units	Total Value ($000)
Australia	18,423	400,849	5	128	3	22	18,431	401,000
Austria	33,635	1,256,838	13	62	53	369	33,701	1,257,268
Belgium	64,639	1,252,709	1	41	302	90,426	64,942	1,343,176
Brazil	15,542	225,152	10	144	—	—	15,552	225,296
Canada	2,004,890	35,611,615	415,908	9,991,878	7,188	681,239	2,427,986	46,284,732
Finland	2,339	94,764	9	727	—	—	2,348	95,491
France	2,154	26,446	16	4,435	3	1,995	2,173	32,875
Germany	545,634	20,307,822	238	13,209	1,815	88,423	547,687	20,409,454
Hungary	4,889	140,569	—	—	538	56,918	5,427	197,486
Italy	3,184	397,055	11	793	6	507	3,201	398,356
Japan	1,538,805	31,609,457	32,383	662,277	—	—	1,571,188	32,271,734
Korea	860,057	10,039,869	—	—	—	—	860,057	10,039,869
Mexico	650,400	11,141,629	305,234	7,900,137	1	70	955,635	19,041,836
Netherlands	1,936	33,646	7	165	—	—	1,943	33,811
Slovakia	27,018	856,629	—	—	—	—	27,018	856,629
South Africa	15,224	423,433	—	—	—	—	15,224	423,433
Spain	7	93	2	14	—	—	9	107
Sweden	97,992	2,436,789	7	373	2	88	98,001	2,437,250
Switzerland	—	—	12	417	23	114	35	531
Taiwan	161	426	2	32	—	—	163	458
United Kingdom	185,059	4,824,124	218	1,736	17	321	185,294	4,826,181
Other	963	4,650	2,564	3,267	19	5,807	3,546	13,724
Total	**6,072,951**	**121,084,564**	**756,640**	**18,579,835**	**9,970**	**926,298**	**6,839,561**	**140,590,697**

SOURCE: Compiled from official statistics of the U.S. Department of Commerce.

U.S. IMPORTS OF NEW ASSEMBLED PASSENGER CARS BY COUNTRY OF ORIGIN*

Year	Canada	Germany	Japan	South Korea	Mexico	Sweden	United Kingdom	Other	Total Imports
2004	2,004,890	545,634	1,538,805	860,057	650,400	97,992	185,059	190,114	6,072,951
2003	1,751,958	560,381	1,575,599	690,885	677,771	119,833	205,937	174,990	5,757,354
2002	1,815,323	571,164	1,827,434	623,810	838,829	89,347	156,258	157,992	6,080,157
2001	1,809,236	492,177	1,616,950	631,945	853,264	89,412	81,261	178,380	5,752,625
2000	2,076,181	489,086	1,661,906	560,728	927,574	85,713	79,639	125,007	6,005,834
1999	2,125,876	456,246	1,560,857	369,264	637,486	82,808	67,689	99,590	5,399,816
1998	1,817,836	372,632	1,317,702	207,165	586,973	84,404	49,037	65,690	4,501,439
1997	1,722,199	298,032	1,383,519	222,535	539,384	79,725	43,726	68,100	4,357,220
1996	1,688,123	234,480	1,190,581	225,613	550,622	86,595	43,616	44,817	4,064,447
1995	1,678,276	206,892	1,387,193	216,618	463,305	82,634	42,176	36,823	4,113,917
1994	1,591,326	187,999	1,593,169	217,962	360,370	63,867	28,239	54,082	4,097,014
1993	1,468,272	184,356	1,597,391	126,576	299,634	58,742	20,048	53,441	3,808,460
1990	1,220,221	245,286	1,867,794	201,475	215,986	93,084	27,271	73,485	3,944,602
1985	1,144,805	473,110	2,527,467	N.A.	13,647	142,640	24,474	71,536	4,397,679
1980	594,770	338,711	1,991,502	N.A.	1	61,496	32,517	97,451	3,116,448
1975	733,766	370,012	695,573	N.A.	—	51,993	67,106	156,203	2,074,653
1970	692,783	674,945	381,338	N.A.	N.A.	57,844	76,257	130,253	2,013,420
1965	33,378	376,950	25,538	N.A.	N.A.	26,010	66,565	35,232	563,673

N.A.-Not available.
*Data include imports into Puerto Rico; data do not include automobiles assembled in U.S. foreign trade zones.
SOURCE: Compiled from official statistics of the U.S. Department of Commerce.

World Trade in Motor Vehicles

EXPORTS AND IMPORTS OF MOTOR VEHICLES FOR SELECTED COUNTRIES, 2004

Country	Exports			Imports		
	Passenger Cars	Commercial Vehicles	Total	Passenger Cars	Commercial Vehicles	Total
Argentina	91,391	54,845	146,236	NA	NA	NA
Austria	222,783	21,162	243,945	346,423	37,356	383,779
Belgium	830,061	40,740	870,801	1,154,167	101,643	1,255,810
Brazil	496,568	151,398	647,966	32,011	29,711	61,722
Czech Republic	386,143	3,825	389,968	68,486	33,953	102,439
Finland	10,051	81	10,132	29,132	3,863	32,995
France	3,819,541	449,321	4,268,862	844,037	146,735	990,772
Germany	3,666,524	257,526	3,924,050	1,673,367	98,339	1,771,706
Italy	377,754	217,953	595,707	1,627,638	286,375	1,914,013
Japan	4,214,027	743,636	4,957,663	270,491	3,682	274,173
Korea, South	2,276,576	102,987	2,379,563	26,295	8,290	34,585
Mexico	903,313	667,183	1,570,496	NA	NA	NA
Netherlands	—	—	—	483,885	101,482	585,367
Portugal	149,774	69,426	219,200	176,986	9,495	186,481
Spain	1,967,973	511,955	2,479,928	1,158,936	202,589	1,361,525
Sweden	519,084	129,302	648,386	242,243	27,341	269,584
Switzerland	—	—	—	268,978	23,911	292,889
Turkey	305,072	203,337	508,409	314,697	121,534	436,231
United Kingdom	1,179,756	128,107	1,307,863	2,103,351	296,087	2,399,438
United States	1,421,815	371,830	1,793,645	6,072,951	766,610	6,839,561
Total	**22,838,206**	**4,124,614**	**26,962,820**	**16,894,074**	**2,298,996**	**19,193,070**

SOURCE: Compiled by Ward's Communications from various sources.

WORLD MOTOR VEHICLE EXPORTS

Year	World Total[1]	Motor Vehicle Exports by Country of Origin (In Thousands)								
		Belgium	Canada	France	Germany	Italy	Japan	Sweden	United Kingdom	United States
2004	26,962.8	870.8	N.A.	4,268.9	3,924.1	595.7	4,957.7	648.4	1,307.9	1,793.6
2003	24,999.7	871.9	N.A.	4,045.6	3,935.9	703.6	4,756.3	565.3	1,246.7	1,613.9
2002	26,765.7	1,014.6	2,373.0	3,916.7	3,875.1	733.7	4,698.2	546.3	1,161.0	1,658.5
2001	25,577.3	1,140.8	2,023.3	3,734.7	3,915.8	813.7	4,166.2	575.4	991.8	1,462.3
2000	25,886.6	993.7	2,323.0	3,619.0	3,722.8	911.6	4,454.9	453.5	1,127.9	1,298.2
1999	24,241.3	983.0	2,331.8	3,255.5	3,675.8	797.8	4,408.9	221.0	1,213.5	1,219.2
1998	24,145.6	1,026.3	2,220.5	3,122.8	3,510.9	812.4	4,528.9	425.9	1,123.6	1,247.8
1997	23,620.8	1,050.8	2,220.5	2,822.5	3,035.6	739.3	4,553.2	416.6	1,065.3	1,591.0
1996	21,691.1	1,192.7	2,134.8	2,272.0	2,841.8	799.2	3,711.7	194.5	1,073.3	1,289.6
1995	20,142.7	1,218.8	1,908.6	2,261.2	2,639.5	806.5	3,790.8	206.3	837.0	1,243.6
1994	19,795.6	1,215.7	1,852.0	2,428.5	2,410.3	669.6	4,460.3	192.8	718.2	1,293.2
1993	19,095.9	1,097.8	2,023.8	2,264.0	2,176.1	504.0	5,017.8	194.4	633.0	1,045.3
1992	20,250.5	1,130.6	1,765.4	2,295.8	2,729.9	697.6	5,667.7	210.8	708.4	1,012.5
1991	19,598.6	1,127.8	1,639.1	2,420.6	2,346.7	806.2	5,753.4	203.4	702.0	962.9
1990	18,315.8	1,225.9	1,699.4	2,315.9	2,765.6	900.9	5,831.2	205.2	510.3	953.1
1989	19,498.8	1,203.0	1,664.2	2,379.1	2,897.7	846.6	5,883.9	205.4	431.3	975.8
1988	19,322.6	1,188.7	1,643.3	2,279.2	2,676.9	827.3	6,104.2	214.6	331.9	1,016.7
1987	18,653.3	1,166.8	1,364.8	2,103.0	2,607.3	766.0	6,304.9	273.4	299.6	861.0
Percent of World Motor Vehicle Exports										
2004	100.0	3.2	N.A.	15.8	14.6	2.2	18.4	2.4	4.9	6.7
2003	100.0	3.5	N.A.	16.2	15.7	2.8	19.0	2.3	5.0	6.5
2002	100.0	3.8	8.9	14.6	14.5	2.7	17.6	2.0	4.3	6.2
2001	100.0	4.5	7.9	14.6	15.3	3.2	16.3	2.2	3.9	5.7
2000	100.0	3.8	9.0	14.0	14.4	3.5	17.2	1.8	4.4	5.0
1999	100.0	4.1	9.6	13.4	15.2	3.3	18.2	1.0	5.0	5.4
1998	100.0	4.3	9.2	12.9	14.5	3.4	18.8	1.8	4.7	5.2
1997	100.0	4.4	9.4	11.9	12.9	3.1	19.3	1.8	4.5	6.7
1996	100.0	5.5	9.8	10.5	13.1	3.7	17.1	0.9	4.9	5.9
1995	100.0	6.1	9.5	11.2	13.1	4.0	18.8	1.0	4.2	6.2
1994	100.0	6.1	9.4	12.3	12.2	3.4	22.5	1.0	3.6	6.5
1993	100.0	5.7	10.6	11.9	11.4	2.6	26.3	1.0	3.3	5.5
1992	100.0	5.6	8.7	11.3	13.5	3.4	28.0	1.0	3.5	5.0
1991	100.0	5.8	8.4	12.4	12.0	4.1	29.4	1.0	3.6	4.9
1990	100.0	6.7	9.3	12.6	15.1	4.9	31.8	1.1	2.8	5.2
1989	100.0	6.2	8.5	12.2	14.9	4.3	30.2	1.1	2.2	5.0
1988	100.0	6.2	8.5	11.8	13.9	4.3	31.6	1.1	1.7	5.3
1987	100.0	6.3	7.3	11.3	14.0	4.1	33.8	1.5	1.6	4.6

(1) World total includes countries with vehicle exports not shown separately. N.A. Not available.
SOURCE: Compiled by Ward's Communications from various sources.

Licensed Drivers by Age Group, Sex and State

LICENSED DRIVERS BY STATE, 2003

State	Male (000)	Female (000)	Total (000)
Alabama	1,774	1,824	3,598
Alaska	257	225	481
Arizona	1,934	1,886	3,819
Arkansas	995	1,003	1,998
California	11,715	10,942	22,657
Colorado	1,496	1,480	2,975
Connecticut	1,319	1,341	2,660
Delaware	286	299	585
Dist. of Columbia	155	158	313
Florida	6,486	6,420	12,906
Georgia	2,845	2,913	5,758
Hawaii	441	394	834
Idaho	464	457	921
Illinois	3,996	4,058	8,054
Indiana	2,255	2,281	4,536
Iowa	973	1,005	1,978
Kansas	992	996	1,987
Kentucky	1,389	1,410	2,800
Louisiana	1,544	1,575	3,120
Maine	461	471	932
Maryland	1,712	1,840	3,552
Massachusetts	2,327	2,319	4,646
Michigan	3,503	3,563	7,065
Minnesota	1,539	1,497	3,036
Mississippi	909	977	1,886
Missouri	1,950	2,016	3,966
Montana	358	346	705
Nebraska	661	650	1,311
Nevada	776	712	1,488
New Hampshire	487	481	968
New Jersey	2,835	2,894	5,729
New Mexico	611	626	1,236
New York	5,950	5,407	11,357
North Carolina	3,013	3,002	6,015
North Dakota	232	228	460
Ohio	3,710	3,946	7,656
Oklahoma	1,143	1,206	2,348
Oregon	1,310	1,280	2,590
Pennsylvania	4,181	4,189	8,370
Rhode Island	362	369	731
South Carolina	1,508	1,411	2,919
South Dakota	277	278	555
Tennessee	2,056	2,149	4,204
Texas	6,532	6,966	13,498
Utah	783	766	1,548
Vermont	274	269	543
Virginia	2,479	2,566	5,046
Washington	2,265	2,142	4,407
West Virginia	641	631	1,272
Wisconsin	1,876	1,890	3,766
Wyoming	193	185	378
Total	**98,228**	**97,937**	**196,166**

SOURCE: U.S. Department of Transportation, Federal Highway Administration.

DRIVERS BY AGE GROUP AND SEX, 2003

Age (In Years)	Male (000)	Female (000)	Total (000)
Under 16	19	18	37
16	643	620	1,263
17	1,112	1,066	2,178
18	1,424	1,342	2,766
19	1,549	1,470	3,019
20	1,625	1,553	3,178
21	1,679	1,627	3,306
22	1,706	1,664	3,370
23	1,741	1,700	3,441
24	1,742	1,700	3,442
25-29	8,670	8,394	17,064
30-34	9,623	9,303	18,925
35-39	9,960	9,724	19,684
40-44	10,654	10,606	21,260
45-49	10,136	10,206	20,342
50-54	8,917	9,002	17,918
55-59	7,483	7,502	14,985
60-64	5,680	5,702	11,382
65-69	4,370	4,407	8,777
70-74	3,613	3,749	7,363
75-79	2,894	3,173	6,068
80-84	1,857	2,103	3,960
85 AND OVER	1,133	1,304	2,437
Total	**98,228**	**97,937**	**196,166**

SOURCE: U.S. Department of Transportation, Federal Highway Administration.

DRIVERS BY SEX

Year	Male (000)	Percent Male	Female (000)	Percent Female	Total (000)
2003	98,228	50.07	97,937	49.93	196,165
2002	97,461	50.16	96,834	49.84	194,295
2001	95,792	50.08	95,483	49.92	191,275
2000	95,796	50.30	94,829	49.70	190,625
1999	94,166	50.31	93,004	49.69	187,170
1998	93,105	50.33	91,875	49.67	184,980
1997	91,905	50.30	90,804	49.70	182,709
1996	90,519	50.42	89,021	49.58	179,540
1995	89,214	50.51	87,414	49.49	176,628
1994	89,194	50.85	86,209	49.15	175,403
1993	87,993	50.82	85,156	49.18	173,149
1992	88,387	51.05	84,738	48.95	173,125
1991	86,665	51.28	82,330	48.72	168,995
1990	85,792	51.37	81,223	48.63	167,015
1989	85,378	51.57	80,177	48.43	165,555
1988	85,230	51.91	78,967	48.09	164,197
1987	84,084	51.91	77,891	48.09	161,975
1986	82,494	52.02	76,100	47.98	158,594
1985	81,592	52.01	75,276	47.99	156,868
1984	80,977	52.10	74,447	47.90	155,424
1983	80,894	52.40	73,495	47.60	154,389
1982	78,553	52.29	71,681	47.71	150,234
1981	77,888	52.96	69,187	47.04	147,075
1980	77,187	53.12	68,108	46.88	145,295
1979	76,531	53.41	66,753	46.59	143,284
1978	75,594	53.67	65,249	46.33	140,843
1977	74,467	53.91	63,654	46.09	138,121
1976	72,523	54.11	61,513	45.89	134,036
1975	70,505	54.32	59,286	45.68	129,791
1974	68,574	54.67	56,853	45.33	125,427
1973	67,115	55.22	54,431	44.78	121,546
1972	66,027	55.76	52,387	44.24	118,414

SOURCE: U.S. Department of Transportation, Federal Highway Administration.

Demographics of New Car Buyers and Initial Vehicle Quality

DEMOGRAPHICS OF NEW VEHICLE BUYERS AND INITIAL VEHICLE QUALITY, 2005 MODEL YEAR

NEW PASSENGER CAR BUYERS					NEW LIGHT TRUCK BUYERS				
Characteristic	Domestic[1]	European[2]	Asian[2]	Total	Characteristic	Domestic[1]	European[2]	Asian[2]	Total
Gender					**Gender**				
Male	55.9%	55.5%	49.2%	52.2%	Male	65.4%	56.4%	55.9%	61.8%
Female	39.5	39.5	45.7	42.8	Female	29.7	38.6	39.5	33.4
No Answer	4.6	5.0	5.1	5.0	No Answer	4.9	5.0	4.6	4.8
Total	100.0	100.0	100.0	100.0	Total	100.0	100.0	100.0	100.0
Age of Principal Purchaser (In Years)					**Age of Principal Purchaser (In Years)**				
Under 25	3.5%	2.8%	5.7%	4.5%	Under 25	1.8%	1.3%	1.3%	1.6%
25-29	3.9	6.9	7.4	6.2	25-29	3.9	3.3	4.4	4.0
30-34	3.9	7.6	6.2	5.7	30-34	6.2	8.6	7.9	6.8
35-39	4.9	8.7	5.7	5.9	35-39	7.9	13.1	10.2	8.8
40-44	6.6	9.8	7.1	7.3	40-44	10.3	13.2	10.7	10.5
45-49	8.9	11.1	9.4	9.5	45-49	10.2	12.5	11.3	10.6
50-54	9.6	11.1	10.9	10.5	50-54	11.4	11.0	11.2	11.3
55-59	11.2	11.4	11.2	11.2	55-59	11.8	11.1	11.5	11.7
60-64	9.2	7.8	8.3	8.5	60-64	9.5	5.6	7.8	8.8
65 and over	27.7	11.1	17.0	19.6	65 and over	16.4	7.7	13.1	15.0
No Answer	10.6	11.7	11.1	11.1	No Answer	10.6	12.6	10.6	10.9
Total	100.0	100.0	100.0	100.0	Total	100.0	100.0	100.0	100.0
Highest Education Level					**Highest Education Level**				
8th Grade or Less	0.8%	0.1%	0.4%	0.5%	8th Grade or Less	0.8%	0.2%	0.3%	0.6%
Some High School	2.6	0.4	1.4	1.6	Some High School	2.1	0.5	0.8	1.6
High School Graduate	21.3	6.2	12.5	14.3	High School Graduate	20.3	4.9	10.4	16.4
Technical/Trade School	8.4	2.7	5.8	6.1	Trade/Technical	9.7	2.1	5.5	8.0
Some College	26.3	18.4	23.5	23.6	Some College	25.6	17.2	21.4	23.9
College Graduate	16.9	28.0	23.1	21.9	College Graduate	18.5	29.7	25.7	21.3
Post Graduate	5.9	9.1	7.0	6.9	Post Graduate	5.3	8.1	7.7	6.2
Advanced Degree	12.7	29.7	20.7	19.5	Advanced Degree	12.2	32.0	22.9	16.5
No Answer	5.1	5.4	5.6	5.6	No Answer	5.5	5.3	5.3	5.5
Total	100.0	100.0	100.0	100.0	Total	100.0	100.0	100.0	100.0
Census Region					**Census Region**				
Northeast	19.7%	21.4%	21.4%	20.8%	Northeast	17.4%	23.7%	21.4%	19.0%
North Central	35.1	14.6	15.9	21.8	North Central	33.7	12.8	15.2	26.7
South	31.0	30.3	35.2	33.1	South	32.6	27.9	35.4	33.3
West	14.2	33.7	27.5	24.3	West	16.3	35.6	28.0	21.0
Total	100.0	100.0	100.0	100.0	Total	100.0	100.0	100.0	100.0
Median Household Income	$64,037	$127,836	$72,611	$75,381	**Median Household Income**	$78,898	$176,778	$92,552	$85,467
Initial Quality (Problems per 100 Passenger Cars)					**Initial Quality (Problems per 100 Light Trucks)**				
Study 2 Results	118.6	108.0	105.7	110.0	Study 2 Results	125.9	152.9	121.8	125.5

NOTE: Study conducted among personal use buyers of '05 model year vehicles.
(1) Domestic figures include captive import buyers.
(2) Import figures include buyers of North American assembled vehicles.
SOURCE: J.D. Power and Associates, 2005 Initial Quality Study (Wave 1).

Passenger Car Operating Costs

PASSENGER CAR OPERATING COSTS

| Model Year | Variable Cost in Cents Per Mile | | | | Cost Per 10,000 Miles | | | |
	Gas & Oil	Maintenance	Tires	Total	Variable Cost	Fixed Cost	Total Cost	Total Cost Per Mile
2005	8.20	5.30	0.60	14.10	$1,410	$5,412	$6,822	68.22¢
2004[1]	6.50	5.40	0.70	12.60	1,260	5,633	6,893	68.93
2003	7.20	4.10	1.80	13.10	1,310	4,884	6,194	61.94
2002	5.90	4.10	1.80	11.80	1,180	4,874	6,054	60.54
2001	7.90	3.90	1.80	13.60	1,360	4,621	5,981	59.81
2000	6.90	3.60	1.70	12.20	1,220	4,724	5,944	59.44
1999	5.60	3.30	1.70	10.60	1,060	4,660	5,720	57.20
1998	6.20	3.10	1.40	10.70	1,070	4,528	5,598	55.98
1997	6.60	2.80	1.40	10.80	1,080	4,348	5,428	54.28
1996	5.60	2.80	1.20	9.60	960	4,193	5,153	51.53
1995	5.80	2.60	1.20	9.60	960	4,005	4,965	49.65
1994	5.60	2.50	1.00	9.10	910	3,836	4,746	47.46
1993	5.90	2.40	0.90	9.20	920	3,722	4,642	46.42
1992	5.90	2.20	0.90	9.00	900	3,784	4,684	46.84
1991	6.60	2.20	0.90	9.70	970	3,566	4,536	45.36
1990	5.40	2.10	0.90	8.40	840	3,256	4,096	40.96
1989	5.30	1.90	0.80	8.00	800	2,920	3,720	37.20
1987	4.40	1.50	0.80	6.70	670	2,328	2,998	29.98
1985	5.57	1.20	0.65	7.42	742	2,061	2,803	28.03
1983	6.13	0.98	0.69	7.80	780	2,084	2,864	28.64
1981	6.27	1.18	0.72	8.17	817	2,375	3,192	31.92
1980	5.86	1.12	0.64	7.62	762	2,033	2,795	27.95
1979	4.11	1.10	0.65	5.86	586	1,811	2,397	23.97
1977	4.11	1.03	0.66	5.80	580	1,439	2,019	20.19
1975	4.82	0.97	0.66	6.45	645	1,186	1,831	18.31
1971	2.96	0.73	0.56	4.25	425	1,125	1,550	15.50
1969	2.76	0.68	0.51	3.95	395	1,053	1,448	14.48

ANNUAL FIXED COST OF OPERATING A PASSENGER CAR

| Model Year | Insurance | | | License, Registration & Taxes | Depreciation | Finance Charge | Total | Average Fixed Cost Per Day |
	Fire & Theft[2]	Collision[3]	Property Damage & Liability[4]					
2005[1]	N.A.	$1,288	N.A.	$389	$3,879	$739	$6,295	$17.25
2004[1]	N.A.	1,603	N.A.	415	3,782	741	6,541	17.92
2003	203	401	498	205	3,738	744	5,789	15.86
2002	173	357	484	201	3,721	828	5,764	15.79
2001	167	345	479	208	3,548	866	5,613	15.38
2000	163	326	481	223	3,492	849	5,534	15.16
1999	162	324	484	226	3,436	828	5,460	14.96
1998	134	287	479	226	3,364	813	5,303	14.53
1997	120	326	401	216	3,272	768	5,103	13.98
1996	144	275	426	215	3,170	718	4,948	13.56
1995	121	252	410	203	3,073	686	4,745	13.00
1994	123	246	400	194	2,940	648	4,551	12.47
1993	116	243	385	178	2,830	670	4,422	12.12
1992	128	286	373	174	2,717	796	4,474	12.26
1991	108	247	353	168	2,504	266	3,646	9.99
1990	110	245	318	165	2,357	680	3,875	10.62
1989	102	234	309	144	2,018	588	3,395	9.30
1987	87	196	252	128	1,494	526	2,683	7.35
1985	75	177	213	110	1,262	534	2,371	6.50
1983	67	181	222	97	1,298	529	2,394	6.56
1981	76	180	254	88	1,287	490	2,375	6.51
1980	70	172	248	82	1,038	423	2,033	5.57
1979	74	168	241	90	942	296	1,811	4.96
1977	80	188	250	74	847	—	1,439	3.94
1975	53	141	189	30	773	—	1,186	3.25
1971	62	125	175	25	738	—	1,125	3.08
1969	44	102	154	24	729	—	1,053	2.88

Note: Methodology has changed beginning in 2004, data is not comparable to prior years. (1) Individual component costs of insurance are no longer available, therefore, Insurance costs for 2004 forward reflect the total amount of a full coverage policy.
(2) No deductible prior to 1973; $50 deductible 1973-1977; $100 deductible 1978-1992; $250 deductible 1993-2003, $100 deductible 2004-2005.
(3) $100 deductible 1967-1977; $250 deductible 1978-1992; $500 deductible 1993-2005.
(4) Coverage: 1949 to 1955-$15,000/$30,000; 1957 to 1965-$25,000/$50,000; 1967 to 2005-$100,000/$300,000
NOTE: Beginning in 1985 ownership costs are based on a six year/60,000 mile retention cycle rather than four year/60,000 miles.
SOURCE: American Automobile Association.

Light Truck Operating Costs

LIGHT TRUCK OPERATING COSTS

| Model Year | Variable Cost in Cents Per Mile | | | | Cost Per 10,000 Miles | | | |
	Gas & Oil	Maintenance	Tires	Total	Variable Cost	Fixed Cost	Total Cost	Total Cost Per Mile
2005	10.80	5.30	0.90	17.00	$1,700	$6,074	$7,774	77.74¢
2004	8.40	4.30	1.00	13.70	1,370	5,903	7,273	72.73
2003	7.90	4.10	1.50	13.50	1,350	5,527	6,877	68.77
2002	5.80	4.10	1.70	11.60	1,160	4,332	5,492	54.92
2001	8.05	4.00	1.60	13.65	1,365	5,197	6,562	65.62
2000	7.55	3.90	1.55	13.00	1,300	4,379	5,679	56.79
1999	6.15	3.60	1.35	11.10	1,110	5,312	6,422	64.22
1998	7.00	3.30	1.35	11.65	1,165	5,208	6,373	63.73
1997	7.40	3.00	1.35	11.75	1,185	5,028	6,213	62.13
1996	6.30	3.00	1.35	10.65	1,065	4,831	5,896	58.96
1995	5.95	2.65	1.30	9.90	990	3,854	4,844	48.44
1994	6.00	2.60	1.00	9.60	688	3,676	4,364	43.64

ANNUAL FIXED COST OF OPERATING A LIGHT TRUCK

| Model Year | Insurance | | Property Damage & Liability | License, Registration & Taxes | Depreciation | Finance Charge | Total | Average Fixed Cost Per Day |
	Fire & Theft	Collision						
2005[1]	N.A	$1,398	N.A	$435	$4,300	$891	$7,024	$19.24
2004[1]	N.A	1,491	N.A	454	4,043	865	6,853	18.78
2003	159	402	389	289	4,286	867	6,392	17.51
2002	204	451	389	261	3,220	662	5,187	14.21
2001	182	423	389	285	3,720	980	5,979	16.38
2000	202	491	481	355	2,940	638	5,107	13.99
1999	205	455	484	401	3,558	924	6,027	16.51
1998	205	447	479	388	3,483	907	5,909	16.19
1997	209	435	401	357	3,426	890	5,718	15.67
1996	138	311	426	356	3,378	885	5,494	15.05
1995	104	241	410	277	2,857	671	4,560	12.49
1994	91	206	400	288	2,745	637	4,367	11.96

Note: Methodology has changed beginning in 2004, data is not comparable to prior years. (1) Individual component costs of insurance are no longer available, therefore, Insurance costs for 2004 forward reflect the total amount of a full coverage policy.
NOTE: Ownership costs are based on a six year /60,000 mile retention cycle rather than four year/60,000 miles.
SOURCE: American Automobile Association.

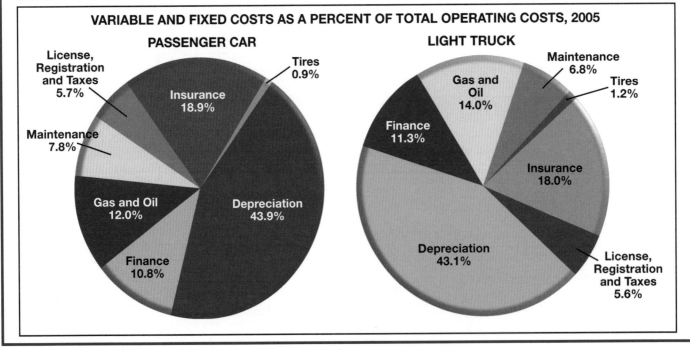

VARIABLE AND FIXED COSTS AS A PERCENT OF TOTAL OPERATING COSTS, 2005

PASSENGER CAR

- License, Registration and Taxes 5.7%
- Tires 0.9%
- Insurance 18.9%
- Maintenance 7.8%
- Gas and Oil 12.0%
- Depreciation 43.9%
- Finance 10.8%

LIGHT TRUCK

- Maintenance 6.8%
- Tires 1.2%
- Gas and Oil 14.0%
- Finance 11.3%
- Insurance 18.0%
- Depreciation 43.1%
- License, Registration and Taxes 5.6%

Automobile Financing

NEW AND USED CAR FINANCING WITH FINANCE COMPANIES

Year	Average Interest Rate	Average Maturity (Months)	Average Amount Financed	Average Monthly Payment
NEW CARS				
2004	4.4	60.5	$24,888	$459.44
2003	3.4	61.4	26,295	467.19
2002	4.3	56.8	24,747	482.31
2001	5.7	55.1	22,822	471.73
2000	6.6	54.9	20,923	442.58
1999	6.7	52.7	19,880	436.49
1998	6.3	52.1	19,083	419.60
1997	7.1	54.1	18,077	391.45
1996	9.8	51.6	16,987	404.75
1995	11.2	54.1	16,210	382.98
1994	9.8	54.0	15,375	353.25
1992	9.8	54.0	13,607	313.01
1990	12.6	54.6	12,071	291.31
1988	12.6	56.2	11,663	275.95
1986	9.4	50.0	10,665	258.74
USED CARS				
2004	8.9	57.0	$15,324	$330.64
2003	9.7	57.7	14,613	317.90
2002	10.7	57.6	14,532	323.70
2001	12.2	57.5	14,416	332.33
2000	13.6	57.0	14,058	336.16
1999	12.6	55.9	13,642	324.15
1998	12.6	53.5	12,691	311.51
1997	13.3	51.0	12,281	316.54
1996	13.5	51.4	12,182	313.39
1995	14.5	52.2	11,590	300.66
1994	13.5	50.2	10,709	280.37
1992	13.7	47.9	9,211	250.70
1990	16.0	46.1	8,289	249.35
1988	15.1	46.7	7,824	222.68
1986	16.0	42.6	6,555	202.52

SOURCE: Board of Governors of the Federal Reserve

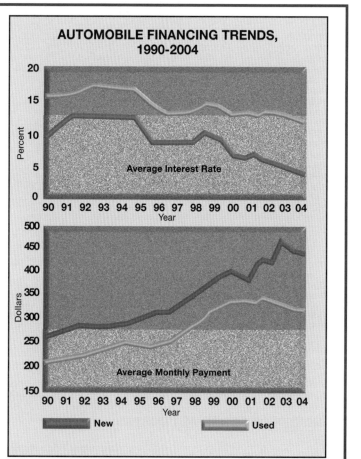

AUTOMOBILE FINANCING TRENDS, 1990-2004

CONSUMER CREDIT OUTSTANDING BY HOLDER, (In Billions of Dollars)

Year	Commercial Banks	Finance Companies	Credit Unions	Savings Institutions	Nonfinancial Business	Other	Total
2004	697.4	365.6	215.4	91.3	73.9	703.4	2,147.0
2003	661.0	295.4	205.9	77.9	70.3	739.6	2,050.1
2002	606.4	237.8	195.7	68.7	86.5	766.7	1,961.8
2001	571.8	238.1	189.6	71.1	88.8	719.2	1,878.6
2000	554.0	220.5	184.4	64.6	90.0	625.6	1,739.1
1999	499.8	201.5	167.9	61.5	78.7	448.6	1,458.0
1998	508.9	183.3	155.4	51.6	74.9	372.4	1,346.5
1997	511.2	161.1	147.8	46.8	70.2	281.9	1,219.0
1996	506.0	154.3	137.2	42.7	73.4	237.5	1,151.1
1995	475.3	142.1	125.6	38.9	80.1	172.4	1,034.4
1994	420.0	124.9	109.1	37.9	75.0	133.9	900.8
1992	358.5	118.0	89.9	38.4	62.3	109.9	777.0
1990	377.2	136.4	91.0	56.2	64.8	61.6	787.2
1985	278.1	100.4	71.1	51.2	57.4	—	558.2

SOURCE: Board of Governors of the Federal Reserve

Expenditures for Transportation

AVERAGE EXPENDITURE PER NEW CAR

Year	Average Expenditure Per New Car[1]			Estimated Average New Car Price for a 1967 "Comparable Car"		Annual Median Family Earnings[4]	Average New Car Expenditure[5]	Weeks of Median Family Earnings to Equal Cost of "Comparable Car"	
	Domestic*	Import	Average	With Added Safety & Emissions Equipment[2]	Without Added Safety & Emissions Equipment[3]			With Added Safety & Emissions Equipment[6]	Without Added Safety & Emissions Equipment[7]
2004	$19,604	$27,859	$21,967	$12,700	$8,784	$63,485	18.0	10.4	7.2
2003	18,859	27,920	21,343	12,763	8,838	60,135	18.5	11.0	7.6
2002	18,896	27,439	21,253	12,994	9,009	58,214	19.0	11.6	8.0
2001	18,757	27,563	20,962	13,134	9,116	56,628	19.5	12.1	8.4
2000	18,897	27,767	20,427	13,178	9,157	53,983	19.7	12.7	8.8
1999	18,630	28,931	20,658	13,163	9,157	50,784	21.2	13.5	9.4
1998	18,479	29,614	20,364	13,205	9,233	48,000	22.1	14.3	10.0
1997	17,907	27,722	19,531	13,240	9,297	45,326	22.4	15.2	10.7
1996	17,468	26,205	18,777	13,184	9,281	42,789	22.8	16.0	11.3
1995	16,864	23,202	17,959	12,857	9,115	40,572	23.0	16.5	11.7
1994	16,930	21,989	17,903	12,429	8,925	38,178	24.4	16.9	12.2
1993	15,976	20,261	16,871	11,808	8,631	36,764	23.9	16.7	12.2
1992	15,644	18,593	16,636	11,488	8,424	35,672	24.3	16.7	12.3
1991	15,192	16,327	15,475	11,187	8,224	34,775	23.1	16.7	12.3
1989	13,936	15,510	14,371	10,282	7,825	32,448	23.0	16.5	12.5
1987	12,922	14,470	13,386	9,775	7,518	29,744	23.4	17.1	13.1
1985	11,589	12,853	11,838	9,014	6,958	27,144	22.7	17.3	13.3
1983	10,516	10,868	10,606	8,415	6,544	24,580	22.4	17.8	13.8
1981	8,912	8,896	8,910	7,726	6,115	22,388	20.7	17.9	14.2
1979	6,889	6,704	6,847	6,198	5,337	19,661	18.1	16.4	14.1
1977	5,985	5,072	5,814	5,292	4,593	16,009	18.9	17.2	14.9
1975	5,084	4,384	4,950	4,689	4,103	13,719	18.8	17.8	15.6
1973	4,181	3,344	4,052	3,903	3,572	12,051	17.5	16.8	15.4
1971	3,919	2,769	3,742	3,777	3,601	10,285	18.9	19.1	18.2

*Includes transplants
(1) U.S. Departments of Commerce, Bureau of Economic Analysis (BEA) , "Average Transaction Price Per New Car." Includes purchases by business, government, and consumers.
(2) 1967 "Average Transaction Price" plus the value of added safety and emissions equipment as determined by the U.S. Bureau of Labor Statistics (BLS), all inflated to current dollars using the BLS, "New Car Consumer Price Index - All Urban Consumers." For example, 1969 is equal to the 1968 value plus the BLS stated value of added safety and emissions equipment for the 1969 model year multiplied by 1968-1969 monthly changes in the New Car Consumer Price Index. The cost to improve fuel economy, which prior to 1980 was included with "Other Quality Adjustments", has since been included by the BLS with the cost of emissions improvements.
(3) 1967 "Average Transaction Price" inflated to current dollars.
(4) BLS, "Median Family Earnings."
(5) "Average Expenditure," as reported by the BEA, divided by "Annual Median Family Earnings", multiplied by 52 weeks. This index is not a good reflection car prices because it includes upgrading — the purchase of more expensive types of vehicles with more options — and downgrading.
(6) "Estimated Average New Car Price of Comparable Cars With New Safety and Emissions Equipment Added", divided by "Annual Median Family Earnings", multiplied by 52 weeks. This index is a good reflection of price as seen by car purchasers who would not otherwise buy safety / emissions equipment.
(7) "Estimated Average New Car Price of Comparable Cars Without New Safety and Emissions Equipment" divided by "Annual Median Family Earnings", multiplied by 52 weeks. This index is a good reflection of price as seen by purchasers who place full value on new safety/emissions equipment.

INDICES OF CONSUMER COSTS

Year	Consumer Price Index - All Urban Consumers (1982-4 = 100)							Calculated New Car Index With Added Safety & Emissions*
	All Items	Housing	Medical Care	Public Transportation	Gasoline	Used Cars	New Cars	
2004	188.9	189.5	310.1	209.1	159.7	133.3	133.9	151.0
2003	184.0	184.8	297.1	209.3	135.1	142.9	134.7	151.7
2002	179.9	180.3	285.6	207.4	116.0	152.0	137.3	154.5
2001	177.1	176.4	272.8	210.6	124.0	158.7	138.9	156.2
2000	172.2	169.6	260.8	209.6	128.6	155.8	139.6	156.7
1999	166.6	163.9	250.6	197.7	100.1	152.0	139.6	156.5
1998	163.0	160.4	242.1	190.3	91.6	150.6	140.7	157.0
1997	160.5	156.8	234.6	186.7	105.8	151.1	141.7	157.4
1996	156.9	152.8	228.2	181.9	105.9	157.1	141.5	156.7
1995	152.4	148.5	220.5	175.9	99.8	156.5	139.0	152.9
1994	148.2	144.8	211.0	172.0	98.2	141.7	136.0	147.8
1993	144.5	141.2	201.4	167.0	97.7	133.9	131.5	140.4
1992	140.3	137.5	190.1	151.4	99.0	123.2	128.4	136.6
1990	130.7	128.5	162.8	142.6	101.0	117.6	121.0	126.2
1986	109.6	110.9	122.0	117.0	77.0	108.8	110.6	112.1
1984	103.9	103.6	106.8	105.7	97.8	112.5	102.8	103.6
1982	96.5	96.9	92.5	94.9	102.8	88.8	97.4	96.4

*Calculated by Ward's Communications.
SOURCE: U.S. Department of Labor, Bureau of Labor Statistics.

Personal Consumption Expenditures for Transportation

PERSONAL CONSUMPTION EXPENDITURES FOR TRANSPORTATION, (In Millions)

	2004	2003	2002	2001	2000	1998	1996	1994
User-Operated Transportation								
New Autos	$97,148	$97,508	$101,144	$103,287	$103,582	$87,727	$81,872	$86,478
Net Purchases of Used Autos	53,943	52,990	56,079	59,287	60,925	59,636	51,436	43,001
Other Motor Vehicles*	235,435	241,468	211,143	195,275	165,359	144,867	84,349	77,682
Tires, Tubes, Accessories and Parts	53,199	56,165	49,731	49,050	49,037	43,876	38,654	35,165
Repair, Greasing, Washing, Parking, Storage and Rental	188,969	186,198	187,081	181,610	173,422	153,119	134,175	109,980
Gasoline and Oil	224,627	191,335	165,768	173,066	175,656	122,389	124,160	108,955
Bridge, Tunnel, Ferry and Road Tolls	7,561	6,633	5,579	5,345	5,075	4,395	3,726	3,255
Insurance Premiums, Less Claims Paid	48,653	50,520	46,454	44,599	43,033	40,382	31,781	27,767
Total User-Operated Transportation	**$909,535**	**$882,817**	**$822,979**	**$811,519**	**$699,144**	**$599,376**	**$550,153**	**$492,283**
Purchased Local Transportation								
Transit Systems	8,830	9,079	9,561	8,466	$9,087	$8,280	$7,691	$7,091
Taxicabs	3,720	4,032	3,336	3,228	3,139	3,524	3,530	2,953
Total Purchased Local Transportation	**$12,550**	**$13,111**	**$12,897**	**$13,278**	**$12,965**	**$12,063**	**$11,221**	**$10,044**
Purchased Intercity Transportation								
Railway Excluding Commutation	554	563	573	559	$518	$438	$642	$603
Bus	2,128	2,251	2,336	2,366	2,376	2,241	1,769	1,518
Airline	32,150	30,347	30,535	32,149	36,725	31,772	26,183	23,665
Other	6,702	6,835	7,360	7,257	7,807	7,309	4,677	4,025
Total Purchased Intercity Transportation	**$41,534**	**$39,996**	**$40,804**	**$42,331**	**$44,031**	**$37,168**	**$33,271**	**$29,811**
Total Transportation Expenditures	**$963,619**	**$935,924**	**$876,680**	**$867,128**	**$756,140**	**$648,607**	**$594,645**	**$532,138**
Total Personal Consumption Expenditures	**$8,229,938**	**$7,760,880**	**$7,385,314**	**$7,045,362**	**$6,739,378**	**$5,879,483**	**$5,237,499**	**$4,716,394**

*New and used trucks, recreation vehicles, etc.
SOURCE: U.S. Department of Commerce, Bureau of Economic Analysis.

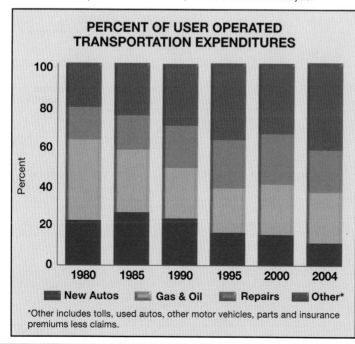

PERCENT OF USER OPERATED TRANSPORTATION EXPENDITURES

*Other includes tolls, used autos, other motor vehicles, parts and insurance premiums less claims.

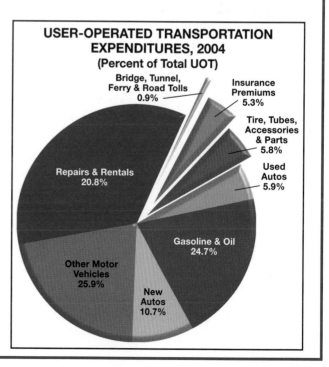

USER-OPERATED TRANSPORTATION EXPENDITURES, 2004
(Percent of Total UOT)

Bridge, Tunnel, Ferry & Road Tolls 0.9%
Insurance Premiums 5.3%
Tire, Tubes, Accessories & Parts 5.8%
Used Autos 5.9%
Repairs & Rentals 20.8%
Gasoline & Oil 24.7%
Other Motor Vehicles 25.9%
New Autos 10.7%

U.S. Motor Vehicle Thefts by State, Area and Year

MOTOR VEHICLE THEFTS BY STATE

State	2003	2002	Percent Change	State	2003	2002	Percent Change
Alabama	14,957	13,890	7.68	Montana	1,906	1,783	6.90
Alaska	2,448	2,471	-0.93	Nebraska	6,124	6,409	-4.45
Arizona	56,997	57,668	-1.16	Nevada	20,838	17,486	19.17
Arkansas	6,010	6,813	-11.79	New Hampshire	1,917	1,944	-1.39
California	241,326	222,364	8.53	New Jersey	34,568	35,739	-3.28
Colorado	22,699	23,183	-2.09	New Mexico	7,256	7,437	-2.43
Connecticut	11,026	11,572	-4.72	New York	45,217	47,366	-4.54
Delaware	2,880	3,057	-5.79	North Carolina	26,892	24,866	8.15
Dist. of Columbia	9,903	9,599	3.17	North Dakota	1,078	1,018	5.89
Florida	81,563	88,516	-7.86	Ohio	40,996	42,767	-4.14
Georgia	43,371	38,036	14.03	Oklahoma	12,958	12,772	1.46
Hawaii	9,651	9,910	-2.61	Oregon	18,989	16,524	14.92
Idaho	2,609	2,627	-0.69	Pennsylvania	33,442	32,817	1.90
Illinois	41,764	44,857	-6.90	Rhode Island	4,387	4,876	-10.03
Indiana	20,768	20,287	2.37	South Carolina	15,762	16,867	-6.55
Iowa	5,601	5,823	-3.81	South Dakota	874	819	6.72
Kansas	7,777	7,212	7.83	Tennessee	26,410	26,541	-0.49
Kentucky	9,366	8,750	7.04	Texas	98,204	102,680	-4.36
Louisiana	19,882	20,186	-1.51	Utah	7,764	7,722	0.54
Maine	1,456	1,429	1.89	Vermont	646	769	-15.99
Maryland	36,405	34,020	7.01	Virginia	17,914	18,478	-3.05
Massachusetts	25,506	26,588	-4.07	Washington	40,619	40,493	0.31
Michigan	53,736	49,723	8.07	West Virginia	3,524	3,898	-9.59
Minnesota	13,759	13,842	-0.60	Wisconsin	12,320	13,458	-8.46
Mississippi	8,949	9,523	-6.03	Wyoming	798	743	7.40
Missouri	28,659	27,878	2.80	**Total**	**1,260,471**	**1,246,096**	**1.15**

SOURCE: Federal Bureau of Investigation.

MOTOR VEHICLE THEFTS

Year	Thefts*	Motor Vehicle Registrations	Ratio of Vehicles Stolen/Registered
2003	1,260,471	225,882,103	1 in 179
2002	1,246,096	221,027,121	1 in 177
2001	1,226,457	216,682,937	1 in 177
2000	1,177,304	213,299,313	1 in 181
1999	1,148,305	209,509,161	1 in 182
1998	1,317,324	205,042,639	1 in 156
1997	1,353,707	201,070,397	1 in 149
1996	1,394,238	198,293,459	1 in 142
1995	1,472,441	193,440,393	1 in 131
1994	1,539,287	188,713,997	1 in 123
1993	1,563,060	186,315,464	1 in 119
1991	1,661,738	181,505,929	1 in 109
1990	1,635,907	179,299,202	1 in 109
1989	1,564,800	175,960,035	1 in 112
1988	1,432,916	171,740,576	1 in 120
1987	1,288,674	167,193,088	1 in 130
1986	1,224,137	162,093,594	1 in 132
1985	1,102,862	157,049,215	1 in 142

*Includes cars, motorcycles, trucks and buses.
SOURCE: Federal Bureau of Investigation

HIGHEST RANKING TOP TEN AUTO THEFT AREAS

2003	2002
1. Detroit, Michigan	1. Phoenix, Arizona
2. Phoenix, Arizona	2. Fresno, California
3. Las Vegas, Nevada	3. Stockton, California
4. Modesto, California	4. Tucson, Arizona
5. Fresno, California	5. Las Vegas, Nevada
6. Tucson, Arizona	6. Seattle, Washington
7. Seattle, Washington	7. Honolulu, Hawaii
8. Sacramento, California	8. Modesto, California
9. Miami, Florida	9. Miami, Florida
10. Memphis, Tennessee	10. Oakland, California

SOURCE: Federal Bureau of Investigation

Vehicle Miles of Travel and Fuel Consumption

VEHICLE MILES OF TRAVEL AND FUEL CONSUMPTION

	Passenger Vehicles				Trucks			All Motor Vehicles
	Passenger Cars	Light Trucks	Buses	Total	Single Unit Trucks	Combination Trucks	Total	
Vehicle Miles of Travel (in Millions)								
2003	1,660,828	998,004	2,658,832	77,562	138,322	6,638	9,539	2,890,893
2002	1,658,474	966,034	2,624,508	75,866	138,737	6,845	9,552	2,855,508
2001	1,628,332	943,207	2,571,539	72,448	136,584	7,077	9,639	2,797,287
2000	1,600,287	923,059	2,523,346	70,500	135,020	7,590	10,469	2,746,925
1999	1,569,100	901,022	2,470,122	70,304	132,384	7,662	10,584	2,691,056
1998	1,549,577	868,275	2,417,852	68,021	128,359	7,007	10,283	2,631,522
1997	1,502,556	850,739	2,353,295	66,893	124,584	6,842	10,076	2,561,690
1996	1,469,854	816,540	2,286,394	64,072	118,899	6,563	9,920	2,485,848
1994	1,416,329	764,634	2,180,963	61,284	108,932	6,409	(1)	2,357,588
1990	1,417,823	574,571	1,992,394	51,901	94,341	5,726	(1)	2,144,362
1985	1,255,884	390,961	1,646,845	45,441	78,063	4,478	(1)	1,774,827
1980	1,121,810	290,935	1,412,745	39,813	68,678	6,059	(1)	1,527,295
Average Annual Miles Traveled Per Vehicle								
2003	12,242	11,467	11,939	13,687	61,611	8,548	1,776	12,210
2002	12,202	11,364	11,879	13,426	60,939	8,998	1,909	12,171
2001	11,831	11,204	11,593	12,702	63,404	9,442	1,966	11,887
2000	11,976	11,672	11,863	11,897	64,399	10,173	2,409	12,164
1999	11,848	11,957	11,889	12,199	65,260	10,514	2,549	12,206
1998	11,754	12,173	11,901	11,861	64,265	9,793	2,651	12,211
1997	11,581	12,115	11,762	12,637	69,601	9,809	2,633	12,107
1996	11,330	11,811	11,497	12,167	68,075	9,446	2,562	11,813
1994	10,759	12,156	11,205	12,491	64,783	9,560	(1)	11,683
1990	10,277	11,902	10,693	11,567	55,206	9,133	(1)	11,107
1985	9,419	10,506	9,649	9,893	55,629	7,545	(1)	10,020
1980	8,813	10,437	9,112	9,103	48,472	11,458	(1)	9,458
Fuel Consumed (Millions of Gallons)								
2003	74,590	56,302	130,892	10,690	26,895	957	191	169,625
2002	75,471	55,220	130,691	10,321	26,480	1,000	191	168,683
2001	73,559	53,522	127,081	9,667	25,512	1,026	193	163,479
2000	73,065	52,939	126,004	9,563	25,666	1,112	209	162,554
1999	73,283	52,859	126,142	9,372	24,537	1,148	212	161,411
1998	71,695	50,462	122,157	6,817	25,157	1,040	206	155,379
1997	69,892	49,388	119,280	9,576	20,302	1,027	202	150,386
1996	69,221	47,354	116,575	9,408	20,193	990	198	147,365
1994	68,079	44,112	112,191	9,032	18,653	964	(1)	140,839
1990	69,759	35,611	105,370	8,357	16,133	895	(1)	130,755
1985	71,700	27,363	99,063	7,399	14,005	834	(1)	121,301
1980	70,186	23,796	93,982	6,923	13,037	1,018	(1)	114,960
Average Annual Fuel Consumption Per Vehicle (Gallons)								
2003	550	647	588	1,886	11,980	1,232	36	716
2002	555	650	592	1,826	11,631	1,314	38	719
2001	534	636	573	1,695	11,843	1,369	39	695
2000	547	669	592	1,614	12,241	1,490	48	720
1999	553	701	606	1,626	12,096	1,576	51	729
1998	544	707	601	1,189	12,596	1,454	53	721
1997	539	703	596	1,809	11,342	1,472	53	711
1996	534	685	586	1,787	11,561	1,425	51	700
1994	517	701	580	1,841	11,093	1,438	(1)	698
1990	506	738	569	1,862	9,441	1,428	(1)	677
1985	538	735	584	1,611	9,980	1,405	(1)	685
1980	551	854	610	1,583	9,201	1,926	(1)	712

Note: N.A. means not available. (1) Passenger cars include motorcycles through 1994.
SOURCE: U.S. Department of Transportation, Federal Highway Admin.

Annual Motor Vehicle Miles of Travel

VEHICLE MILES OF TRAVEL, 2003 (In Millions)

	Rural Interstate	Total Rural	Urban Interstate	Total Urban	Total
Alabama	6,453	30,158	6,094	28,479	58,637
Alaska	824	2,419	678	2,523	4,942
Arizona	7,014	16,556	5,517	37,340	53,896
Arkansas	4,458	19,473	3,130	11,166	30,639
California	19,631	65,501	67,083	258,091	323,592
Colorado	3,939	13,935	6,278	29,444	43,379
Connecticut	709	3,970	9,343	27,462	31,432
Delaware	—	3,841	1,390	5,203	9,044
Dist. of Columbia	—	—	436	4,150	4,150
Florida	13,427	49,501	18,894	136,010	185,511
Georgia	12,047	50,624	17,818	58,622	109,246
Hawaii	102	2,771	1,770	6,541	9,312
Idaho	2,186	8,899	1,129	5,391	14,290
Illinois	10,708	31,934	20,418	74,602	106,536
Indiana	8,692	37,034	7,388	35,477	72,511
Iowa	4,764	19,194	2,394	11,914	31,108
Kansas	3,505	15,209	3,268	13,463	28,672
Kentucky	6,464	26,853	5,989	19,895	46,748
Louisiana	6,325	24,262	5,931	19,894	44,156
Maine	2,422	11,070	645	3,842	14,912
Maryland	3,282	13,536	13,254	41,165	54,701
Massachusetts	1,258	4,202	14,471	49,507	53,709
Michigan	5,791	31,080	16,782	69,676	100,756
Minnesota	4,819	26,750	7,477	28,546	55,296
Mississippi	3,635	22,999	3,054	14,468	37,467
Missouri	7,180	31,469	10,776	36,694	68,163
Montana	2,390	8,304	346	2,570	10,874
Nebraska	2,811	11,501	1,105	7,515	19,016
Nevada	2,096	5,978	2,379	13,323	19,301
New Hampshire	2,025	7,955	1,017	5,225	13,180
New Jersey	1,331	6,778	12,742	63,000	69,778
New Mexico	4,647	13,379	2,053	9,465	22,844
New York	7,927	38,600	17,921	96,447	135,047
North Carolina	8,258	46,452	9,764	47,307	93,759
North Dakota	1,378	5,581	280	1,887	7,468
Ohio	9,068	37,017	22,189	71,921	108,938
Oklahoma	5,016	21,933	4,453	23,792	45,725
Oregon	4,672	17,531	4,047	17,567	35,098
Pennsylvania	11,049	40,550	13,903	65,797	106,347
Rhode Island	416	857	1,937	7,508	8,365
South Carolina	9,015	30,817	3,747	17,303	48,120
South Dakota	2,066	6,585	402	1,942	8,527
Tennessee	8,804	29,677	10,438	39,477	69,154
Texas	16,796	78,758	34,925	144,660	223,418
Utah	3,610	8,728	5,184	15,301	24,029
Vermont	1,291	6,034	377	2,275	8,309
Virginia	8,611	29,810	14,380	47,058	76,868
Washington	4,997	17,914	10,864	37,101	55,015
West Virginia	3,962	14,699	1,570	5,383	20,082
Wisconsin	5,621	29,931	4,838	29,684	59,615
Wyoming	2,453	6,776	365	2,435	9,211
U.S. Total	**269,945**	**1,085,385**	**432,633**	**1,805,508**	**2,890,893**

NOTE: Includes travel by motorcycle.
SOURCE: U.S. Department of Transportation, Federal Highway Administration.

TOTAL VEHICLE MILES TRAVELED (In Billions)

Year	Rural	Urban	Total	% Change
2003	1,085	1,806	2,891	1.2
2002	1,128	1,728	2,856	2.7
2001	1,105	1,676	2,781	1.1
2000	1,085	1,665	2,750	2.1
1999	1,063	1,628	2,691	2.5
1998	1,033	1,592	2,625	3.5
1997	985	1,547	2,532	2.0
1996	960	1,522	2,482	2.5
1995	933	1,489	2,422	2.7
1994	909	1,449	2,358	2.7
1993	887	1,410	2,297	2.2
1992	884	1,363	2,247	3.4
1991	884	1,289	2,173	1.2
1990	870	1,277	2,147	1.9
1989	849	1,258	2,107	4.0
1988	818	1,208	2,026	5.5
1987	780	1,141	1,921	4.7
1986	748	1,087	1,835	3.4
1985	730	1,044	1,774	3.1
1984	718	1,002	1,720	4.1
1983	701	952	1,653	3.6
1982	689	906	1,595	2.7
1981	686	867	1,553	1.7
1980	672	855	1,527	-0.2
1979	676	854	1,530	-0.9
1978	682	862	1,544	5.2
1977	651	816	1,467	4.6
1976	625	777	1,402	5.6
1975	602	726	1,328	3.8
1973	606	707	1,313	4.2
1972	590	670	1,260	6.9
1971	573	606	1,179	6.3
1970	539	570	1,109	4.5
1969	524	537	1,061	4.4
1968	506	510	1,016	5.4
1967	481	483	964	4.1
1966	476	450	926	4.3
1965	464	424	888	5.0
1964	441	405	846	5.1
1963	420	385	805	5.0
1962	399	368	767	3.9
1961	398	340	738	2.6
1960	387	332	719	2.6
1959	377	324	701	5.4
1958	358	307	665	2.8
1957	350	297	647	2.5
1956	344	287	631	4.1
1955	331	275	606	7.8
1954	314	248	562	3.3
1953	308	236	544	6.0
1952	289	224	513	4.5
1950	240	218	458	8.0
1949	219	205	424	6.5
1948	199	199	398	7.3
1946	171	170	341	36.4
1944	102	111	213	2.4
1942	130	138	268	-19.8
1940	152	150	302	6.0
1938	135	136	271	0.4

SOURCE: U.S. Department of Transportation, Federal Highway Administration.

Selected Travel Data by State

TRAVEL DATA BY STATE, 2003

| State | Resident Population in Thousands | Population Per Vehicle | Annual Miles Traveled | | Public Road and Street Mileage | | | State Gasoline Tax Rate |
			Per Vehicle	Per Licensed Driver	Rural	Urban	Total	
Alabama	4,501	1.02	13,242	16,297	73,476	20,958	94,434	18.0
Alaska	649	1.05	7,966	10,264	12,160	2,070	14,230	8.0
Arizona	5,581	1.42	13,681	14,111	35,629	21,900	57,529	18.0
Arkansas	2,726	1.46	16,360	15,334	87,733	10,808	98,541	21.7
California	35,484	1.20	10,925	14,282	83,927	85,622	169,549	18.0
Colorado	4,551	2.12	20,171	14,580	68,693	18,128	86,821	22.0
Connecticut	3,483	1.20	10,783	11,817	6,120	14,969	21,089	25.0
Delaware	817	1.21	13,416	15,456	3,865	2,029	5,894	23.0
District of Columbia	563	2.37	17,470	13,258	—	1,536	1,536	20.0
Florida	17,019	1.22	13,285	14,374	51,896	68,479	120,375	13.9
Georgia	8,685	1.14	14,285	18,973	87,977	28,557	116,534	7.5
Hawaii	1,258	1.41	10,433	11,163	2,181	2,128	4,309	16.0
Idaho	1,366	0.99	10,312	15,511	42,517	4,410	46,927	25.0
Illinois	12,654	1.32	11,124	13,227	101,519	37,007	138,526	19.0
Indiana	6,196	1.09	12,800	15,985	73,997	20,600	94,597	18.0
Iowa	2,944	0.89	9,397	15,728	102,811	10,705	113,516	20.3
Kansas	2,724	1.17	12,270	14,428	124,419	10,593	135,012	24.0
Kentucky	4,118	1.14	12,983	16,698	65,029	11,982	77,011	16.4
Louisiana	4,496	1.23	12,063	14,153	46,987	13,950	60,937	20.0
Maine	1,306	1.35	15,412	15,992	20,060	2,633	22,693	22.0
Maryland	5,509	1.42	14,084	15,399	13,908	16,780	30,688	23.5
Massachusetts	6,433	1.19	9,934	11,561	7,909	27,681	35,590	21.0
Michigan	10,080	1.18	11,807	14,260	87,134	35,088	122,222	19.0
Minnesota	5,059	1.12	12,233	18,216	115,684	16,209	131,893	20.0
Mississippi	2,881	1.47	19,167	19,866	63,444	10,661	74,105	18.4
Missouri	5,704	1.35	16,095	17,189	107,109	17,576	124,685	17.0
Montana	918	0.87	10,296	15,435	66,697	2,753	69,450	27.0
Nebraska	1,739	1.05	11,486	14,501	87,431	5,767	93,198	24.6
Nevada	2,241	1.79	15,405	12,972	28,250	5,727	33,977	25.7
New Hampshire	1,288	1.13	11,529	13,619	12,594	3,036	15,630	19.5
New Jersey	8,638	1.29	10,433	12,180	7,411	31,541	38,952	10.5
New Mexico	1,875	1.22	14,850	18,475	57,139	6,814	63,953	18.5
New York	19,190	1.84	12,916	11,891	71,979	41,145	113,124	22.7
North Carolina	8,407	1.37	15,247	15,588	77,750	24,410	102,160	24.2
North Dakota	634	0.91	10,693	16,242	84,948	1,834	86,782	21.0
Ohio	11,436	1.09	10,405	14,228	80,260	43,262	123,522	24.0
Oklahoma	3,512	1.14	14,890	19,470	97,587	14,991	112,578	17.0
Oregon	3,560	1.16	11,435	13,553	54,884	11,067	65,951	24.0
Pennsylvania	12,365	1.30	11,165	12,706	82,734	37,689	120,423	25.9
Rhode Island	1,076	1.39	10,783	11,438	1,222	5,193	6,415	30.0
South Carolina	4,147	1.30	15,028	16,485	55,545	10,685	66,230	16.0
South Dakota	764	0.94	10,477	15,376	81,424	2,264	83,688	22.0
Tennessee	5,842	1.22	14,478	16,449	68,100	20,418	88,518	21.4
Texas	22,119	1.51	15,235	16,552	218,700	83,287	301,987	20.0
Utah	2,351	1.27	13,009	15,518	34,527	8,189	42,716	24.5
Vermont	619	1.15	15,469	15,290	12,977	1,382	14,359	20.0
Virginia	7,386	1.18	12,254	15,234	50,231	21,011	71,242	17.5
Washington	6,131	1.15	10,310	12,483	62,806	19,458	82,264	28.0
West Virginia	1,810	1.24	13,727	15,786	33,803	3,190	36,993	25.4
Wisconsin	5,472	1.20	13,081	15,831	92,977	20,293	113,270	28.5
Wyoming	501	0.83	15,277	24,367	24,978	2,504	27,482	14.0
Total	**290,810**	**1.27**	**12,590**	**14,737**	**3,033,138**	**940,969**	**3,974,107**	

SOURCE: U.S. Department of Commerce, Bureau of the Census, and U.S. Department of Transportation.

State Highway Agency Capital Outlay and Maintenance

STATE HIGHWAY AGENCY CAPITAL OUTLAY AND MAINTENANCE (In Thousands)

	Capital Outlay		Maintenance		Total		'03 vs. '02 Percent Change
	2003	2002	2003	2002	2003	2002	
Alabama	$958,803	$988,036	$121,086	$90,810	$1,079,889	$1,078,846	0.1
Alaska	401,540	334,725	51,592	41,348	$453,132	376,073	20.5
Arizona	978,273	1,117,218	81,467	73,365	$1,059,740	1,190,583	-11.0
Arkansas	754,977	835,196	126,630	201,098	$881,607	1,036,294	-14.9
California	4,205,423	3,602,074	302,986	339,316	$4,508,409	3,941,390	14.4
Colorado	827,371	982,462	360,310	176,725	$1,187,681	1,159,187	2.5
Connecticut	615,411	637,593	79,457	95,238	$694,868	732,831	-5.2
Delaware	248,387	272,624	32,877	40,087	$281,264	312,711	-10.1
District of Columbia	251,054	242,088	70,548	51,652	$321,602	293,740	9.5
Florida	3,598,581	3,162,573	526,282	479,057	$4,124,863	3,641,630	13.3
Georgia	1,250,761	1,293,294	132,480	123,384	$1,383,241	1,416,678	-2.4
Hawaii	151,891	140,856	33,622	32,932	$185,513	173,788	6.7
Idaho	308,622	281,622	24,247	20,043	$332,869	301,665	10.3
Illinois	2,512,873	2,336,995	308,912	344,175	$2,821,785	2,681,170	5.2
Indiana	1,114,396	942,575	275,525	229,687	$1,389,921	1,172,262	18.6
Iowa	620,041	604,890	51,969	58,844	$672,010	663,734	1.2
Kansas	793,662	746,873	109,148	94,321	$902,810	841,194	7.3
Kentucky	1,136,577	1,205,841	410,865	199,514	$1,547,442	1,405,355	10.1
Louisiana	803,432	645,401	208,061	199,142	$1,011,493	844,543	19.8
Maine	265,511	291,427	99,657	124,002	$365,168	415,429	-12.1
Maryland	820,022	868,411	92,000	91,714	$912,022	960,125	-5.0
Massachusetts	1,533,756	1,802,172	61,594	60,547	$1,595,350	1,862,719	-14.4
Michigan	1,198,299	1,241,034	171,968	182,974	$1,370,267	1,424,008	-3.8
Minnesota	678,085	748,397	351,384	211,115	$1,029,469	959,512	7.3
Mississippi	671,637	718,806	64,942	63,169	$736,579	781,975	-5.8
Missouri	1,258,831	1,299,271	261,537	250,457	$1,520,368	1,549,728	-1.9
Montana	322,101	289,987	58,642	54,983	$380,743	344,970	10.4
Nebraska	356,638	338,416	121,395	165,449	$478,033	503,865	-5.1
Nevada	373,456	298,639	52,270	52,814	$425,726	351,453	21.1
New Hampshire	154,722	167,095	84,416	85,643	$239,138	252,738	-5.4
New Jersey	1,956,815	1,943,613	183,783	176,691	$2,140,598	2,120,304	1.0
New Mexico	443,472	472,144	94,569	96,313	$538,041	568,457	-5.4
New York	2,519,317	2,926,598	394,036	332,683	$2,913,353	3,259,281	-10.6
North Carolina	1,834,157	1,810,495	534,513	519,295	$2,368,670	2,329,790	1.7
North Dakota	223,620	212,959	34,294	23,991	$257,914	236,950	8.8
Ohio	1,616,101	1,669,288	162,169	190,875	$1,778,270	1,860,163	-4.4
Oklahoma	562,679	645,175	153,222	127,990	$715,901	773,165	-7.4
Oregon	502,389	344,626	197,861	183,794	$700,250	528,420	32.5
Pennsylvania	2,835,396	2,648,972	318,452	748,349	$3,153,848	3,397,321	-7.2
Rhode Island	132,586	149,757	40,616	45,010	$173,202	194,767	-11.1
South Carolina	628,619	684,436	202,605	187,436	$831,224	871,872	-4.7
South Dakota	286,728	299,779	23,112	20,777	$309,840	320,556	-3.3
Tennessee	850,205	855,614	288,998	262,797	$1,139,203	1,118,411	1.9
Texas	3,733,889	3,551,826	1,056,820	1,026,784	$4,790,709	4,578,610	4.6
Utah	451,097	540,237	83,216	72,872	$534,313	613,109	-12.9
Vermont	136,542	101,107	16,865	28,369	$153,407	129,476	18.5
Virginia	1,245,921	1,607,717	691,741	724,175	$1,937,662	2,331,892	-16.9
Washington	887,516	930,991	234,242	247,141	$1,121,758	1,178,132	-4.8
West Virginia	612,529	649,843	223,056	292,911	$835,585	942,754	-11.4
Wisconsin	1,000,167	1,032,474	93,503	83,444	$1,093,670	1,115,918	-2.0
Wyoming	281,580	259,322	65,026	70,467	$346,606	329,789	5.1
Total	$51,906,458	$51,773,564	$9,820,568	$9,695,769	$61,727,026	$61,469,333	0.4

SOURCE: U.S. Department of Transportation, Federal Highway Administration.

Motor Vehicle and Equipment Manufacturing Employment by State

MOTOR VEHICLE AND EQUIPMENT MANUFACTURING EMPLOYMENT BY STATE, 2002

State	Vehicle Manufacturing	Motor Vehicle Body & Trailer	Engine & Engine Parts	Electrical Components	Transmission, Brake & Suspension Parts	Other Motor Vehicle Parts Manufacturing
Alabama	2,750	2,841	—	2,844	751	3,188
Alaska	—	10	—	—	—	—
Arizona	300	901	344	200	162	1,822
Arkansas	150	1,439	970	480	1,525	2,943
California	6,000	10,392	3,274	4,957	3,254	13,650
Colorado	750	596	—	50	175	1,117
Connecticut	—	—	1,239	1,268	525	1,214
Delaware	5,500	—	—	—	—	—
District of Columbia	—	—	—	—	—	—
Florida	350	3,884	—	1,367	250	2,380
Georgia	7,559	2,763	1,491	914	779	4,169
Hawaii	—	—	—	—	—	—
Idaho	—	1,175	—	—	—	—
Illinois	7,333	3,500	2,120	7,237	4,884	8,989
Indiana	14,112	23,203	9,697	10,635	25,030	21,111
Iowa	—	7,800	1,404	1,067	750	2,596
Kansas	2,750	2,106	200	1,303	100	1,271
Kentucky	19,216	750	3,010	2,400	8,249	8,307
Louisiana	2,000	400	—	—	—	—
Maine	—	—	—	—	—	—
Maryland	2,500	549	—	619	—	441
Massachusetts	150	—	224	679	—	—
Michigan	40,000	2,802	20,903	7,372	40,176	44,869
Minnesota	1,250	1,859	1,798	845	573	591
Mississippi	—	900	—	2,445	—	1,459
Missouri	17,524	1,456	710	1,475	4,690	5,417
Montana	—	283	—	—	—	—
Nebraska	—	1,141	1,016	—	—	2,000
Nevada	—	—	353	—	—	—
New Hampshire	—	—	—	134	—	—
New Jersey	3,000	570	320	410	43	170
New Mexico	1,250	75	—	—	—	—
New York	625	1,196	4,516	8,394	7,220	7,393
North Carolina	5,100	3,187	1,853	2,049	7,260	5,429
North Dakota	750	303	—	—	—	—
Ohio	32,000	4,171	8,462	5,813	23,276	13,182
Oklahoma	3,500	4,353	221	2,207	247	2,071
Oregon	2,300	5,225	123	569	395	1,029
Pennsylvania	1,875	7,339	900	4,422	2,807	2,536
Rhode Island	—	—	—	—	—	—
South Carolina	6,048	—	3,615	1,700	5,543	4,164
South Dakota	100	867	—	—	—	—
Tennessee	13,386	1,923	2,604	1,056	6,931	14,531
Texas	3,000	5,908	1,843	4,586	622	5,034
Utah	—	—	—	—	—	4,800
Vermont	—	—	—	150	—	—
Virginia	1,250	2,417	1,500	742	2,504	1,909
Washington	32	1,337	447	650	25	1,187
West Virginia	—	289	—	375	—	—
Wisconsin	7,400	3,950	4,159	1,674	1,366	4,730
Wyoming	—	—	—	—	—	—
Total	**216,886**	**114,410**	**80,507**	**83,434**	**164,982**	**216,271**

Note: In some cases, an average was taken based on the Bureau of the Census employment range.
*Omission of data for individual state is due to either the absences of such business from the state or the necessity of withholding the data to avoid disclosure of individual firm's data.
SOURCE: U.S. Department of Commerce, Bureau of the Census.

Motor Vehicle and Equipment Manufacturing Employment by State

MOTOR VEHICLE AND EQUIPMENT MANUFACTURING EMPLOYMENT BY STATE, 2002 — continued

State	Vehicle Metal Stamping	Tires & Inner Tubes	Storage Batteries	Total Motor Vehicle & Equipment Manufacturing	Total State Manufacturing Employment	% of Total State Manufacturing Employment
Alabama	618	6,448	—	19,440	283,356	6.9
Alaska	—	—	—	10	10,625	0.1
Arizona	212	—	—	3,941	167,570	2.4
Arkansas	—	—	150	7,657	213,866	3.6
California	1,022	999	1,000	44,518	1,559,532	2.9
Colorado	—	—	365	3,053	149,468	2.0
Connecticut	361	—	258	4,865	211,442	2.3
Delaware	—	—	345	5,845	38,872	15.0
District of Columbia	—	—	—	—	2,128	0.0
Florida	799	407	275	9,712	372,256	2.6
Georgia	1,051	2,353	1,400	22,479	449,849	5.0
Hawaii	—	—	—	—	13,365	—
Idaho	—	—	—	1,175	59,984	2.0
Illinois	4,249	5,132	786	44,230	726,681	6.1
Indiana	10,531	1,890	345	116,554	551,560	21.1
Iowa	—	2,100	750	16,467	222,501	7.4
Kansas	—	—	1,252	8,982	178,669	5.0
Kentucky	4,366	—	750	47,048	260,299	18.1
Louisiana	—	147	300	2,847	149,173	1.9
Maine	—	253	—	253	65,440	0.4
Maryland	—	—	—	4,109	145,328	2.8
Massachusetts	352	46	—	1,451	330,380	0.4
Michigan	46,911	250	—	203,283	690,655	29.4
Minnesota	329	132	75	7,452	336,128	2.2
Mississippi	—	—	325	5,129	182,905	2.8
Missouri	1,104	524	1,700	34,600	307,578	11.2
Montana	—	—	—	283	18,777	1.5
Nebraska	—	—	—	4,157	102,447	4.1
Nevada	—	—	—	353	38,784	0.9
New Hampshire	—	—	—	134	86,981	0.2
New Jersey	—	260	750	5,523	346,707	1.6
New Mexico	—	—	—	1,325	34,169	3.9
New York	—	1,580	365	31,289	624,523	5.0
North Carolina	—	7,435	1,750	34,063	613,450	5.6
North Dakota	—	—	—	1,053	21,999	4.8
Ohio	25,573	4,456	760	117,693	829,456	14.2
Oklahoma	212	6,397	80	19,288	147,617	13.1
Oregon	—	—	165	9,806	178,440	5.5
Pennsylvania	1,697	1,524	2,500	25,600	710,581	3.6
Rhode Island	—	—	—	—	59,954	—
South Carolina	1,731	4,609	365	27,775	289,953	9.6
South Dakota	—	—	—	967	36,853	2.6
Tennessee	3,060	7,317	365	51,173	408,387	12.5
Texas	304	2,161	350	23,808	850,616	2.8
Utah	—	—	—	4,800	109,823	4.4
Vermont	—	—	—	150	43,736	0.3
Virginia	—	3,512	—	13,834	313,453	4.4
Washington	—	—	—	3,678	268,839	1.4
West Virginia	—	—	—	664	69,102	1.0
Wisconsin	1,473	—	350	25,102	499,518	5.0
Wyoming	—	—	—	—	9,834	—
Total	**111,908**	**68,862**	**18,337**	**1,075,597**	**14,393,609**	**7.5**

Note: In some cases, an average was taken based on the Bureau of the Census employment range.
*Omission of data for individual state is due to either the absences of such business from the state or the necessity of withholding the data to avoid disclosure of individual firm's data.
SOURCE: U.S. Department of Commerce, Bureau of the Census.

U.S. Motor Vehicle and Related Industries Employment

U.S. EMPLOYMENT IN MOTOR VEHICLE AND RELATED INDUSTRIES, 2002

Industry	Establishments	Employees	Payrolls(000)
Motor Vehicle and Equipment Manufacturing			
Light vehicle manufacturing	308	196,197	$12,991,526
Heavy truck manufacturing	87	20,689	918,950
Motor Vehicle body & trailer	2,001	114,410	3,864,490
Motor Vehicle engine and engine parts	971	80,507	4,106,306
Motor vehicle electrical & electrical equipment	922	83,434	3,169,695
Motor vehicle suspension, brake and power trains	987	164,982	8,536,188
Other motor vehicle parts manufacturing	1,506	168,340	6,670,678
Motor vehicle metal stamping	719	111,908	5,379,524
Tires and Inner Tubes	149	60,905	2,900,383
Storage Batteries	128	18,337	680,220
Sub-total	**7,778**	**1,019,709**	**$49,217,960**
Motor Freight Transportation and Related Services			
Trucking and courier services, except by air or by the U.S. Postal Service	124,481	1,886,592	62,256,709
Road transporation support activities	1,425	18,616	511,137
Arrangement of transportation of freight and cargo	15,476	164,374	6,809,918
Miscellaneous services incidental to transportation	1,325	24,911	957,234
Sub-total	**142,707**	**2,094,493**	**$70,534,998**
Petroleum Refining and Wholesale Distribution			
Petroleum Refining	349	62,132	4,569,613
Asphalt paving mixtures and blocks	1,303	12,664	653,327
Lubricating oils and greases	330	9,605	481,534
Petroleum bulk stations and terminals	6,532	87,956	3,485,137
Petroleum and petroleum products wholesalers, except bulk stations and terminals	3,274	34,028	1,728,871
Sub-total	**11,788**	**206,385**	**$10,918,482**
Passenger Transportation			
Local and suburban transportation	7,388	206,348	5,384,756
Taxi & Limousine service	7,146	65,575	1,269,235
Intercity and rural bus transportation	579	20,705	730,794
Bus charter service	1,473	32,162	666,966
School and Employee bus transportation	4,352	171,599	2,612,166
Arrangement of passenger transportation	27,587	258,084	8,469,891
Passenger car rental	4,871	122,256	3,229,373
Passenger car leasing	776	9,088	385,333
Truck,utility trailer and RV rental	6,297	50,608	1,752,181
Automobile parking	11,775	86,176	1,365,243
Recreational vehicle parks and campsites	4,063	18,073	371,121
Sub-total	**76,307**	**1,040,674**	**$26,237,059**
Automotive Sales and Servicing			
Retail automotive dealers (New and Used)	25,625	1,138,977	47,866,732
Retail automotive dealers (used only)	26,424	120,236	3,463,726
Auto parts, accessories and tire stores	58,371	491,407	12,143,035
Gasoline service stations *	117,100	895,983	13,471,484
Recreational vehicle dealers	3,145	35,662	1,274,148
Wholesale trade in motor vehicles	27,370	390,438	14,036,008
Automotive repair shops	140,703	655,473	18,703,793
Automotive services, except repair	31,159	256,709	4,313,882
Sub-total	**429,897**	**3,984,885**	**$115,272,808**
Total of Motor Vehicle and Related Industries	**668,477**	**8,346,146**	**$272,181,307**
U.S. Total*	**7,200,770**	**112,400,654**	**$3,943,179,606**
Motor Vehicle Percent of U.S. Total	**9.3%**	**7.4%**	**6.9%**

SOURCE: U.S. Department of Commerce, Bureau of the Census.
*Includes truck stops and stations with and without convienience stores
The U.S. Census Bureau is currently in the process of changing over from the SIC coding system to the new NAICS, it will not be fully converted and implemented until 2004. Please note figures may reflect these modifications and are subject to change.

New-Car Dealerships

FRANCHISED NEW-CAR DEALERSHIPS BY STATE, 2004

State	Establish-ments*	Sales (Millions)	Paid Employees	Payrolls (Millions)	State	Establish-ments*	Sales (Millions)	Paid Employees	Payrolls (Millions)
Alabama	355	$10,133	16,006	$636	Nebraska	219	4,026	7,170	275
Alaska	43	1,347	2,340	111	Nevada	114	6,915	9,837	518
Arizona	248	17,334	26,412	1,228	New Hampshire	173	3,927	6,846	318
Arkansas	276	5,660	8,789	323	New Jersey	623	25,466	33,673	1,762
California	1,676	91,341	135,462	6,921	New Mexico	137	4,016	7,323	290
Colorado	281	11,468	18,369	867	New York	1,214	35,055	51,994	2,427
Connecticut	337	9,721	15,380	776	North Carolina	703	19,910	32,449	1,382
Delaware	63	2,089	3,906	167	North Dakota	102	1,772	3,305	115
Florida	951	55,265	74,850	3,474	Ohio	987	25,399	44,375	1,793
Georgia	623	22,081	34,141	1,534	Oklahoma	305	9,205	14,412	542
Hawaii	74	3,063	4,843	222	Oregon	281	7,866	13,711	595
Idaho	122	3,261	5,539	217	Pennsylvania	1,230	31,385	54,417	2,157
Illinois	1,015	27,219	44,518	2,025	Rhode Island	70	2,245	3,574	159
Indiana	551	15,113	23,672	961	South Carolina	331	8,325	14,493	591
Iowa	399	6,546	12,549	469	South Dakota	124	2,013	3,681	137
Kansas	283	5,829	10,379	412	Tennessee	435	13,864	22,681	994
Kentucky	318	7,253	13,450	508	Texas	1,368	55,754	85,790	3,943
Louisiana	342	9,880	17,175	674	Utah	150	5,216	8,393	337
Maine	153	2,916	5,439	210	Vermont	98	1,636	2,964	115
Maryland	378	14,503	25,202	1,147	Virginia	554	20,384	34,507	1,497
Massachussetts	531	16,412	25,326	1,209	Washington	388	13,318	22,570	1039
Michigan	779	26,843	38,777	1,884	West Virginia	180	3,622	6,938	230
Minnesota	469	12,837	20,585	857	Wisconsin	628	12,306	23,184	863
Mississippi	242	5,037	8,828	345	Wyoming	70	1,278	2,372	88
Missouri	509	13,741	22,686	970	Dist. of Columbia	3	167	104	5
Montana	135	2,339	4,211	145	**Total**	**21,640**	**714,300**	**1,129,600**	**50,464**

*Establishment data are NADA estimates for January 1, 2005.
SOURCE: National Automobile Dealers Association.

DEALERSHIPS' TOTAL SERVICE AND PARTS SALES
(Billions of Dollars)

	Amount	% Change
2004	85.48	0.2
2003	85.35	2.7
2002	83.11	3.8
2001	80.10	8.5
2000	73.83	9.1
1999	67.66	6.5
1998	63.56	1.7
1997	62.93	3.6
1996	60.76	7.4
1995	56.57	2.6
1994	55.12	7.4

SOURCE: National Automobile Dealers Association.

DEALERSHIPS' SERVICE AND PARTS SALES
(Billions of Dollars)

Service Labor Sales	2004	2003	Percent Change	Parts Sales	2004	2003	Percent Change
Customer mechanical	$16.64	$17.20	-3.3	Customer mechanical	$13.28	$12.85	3.3
Customer body	6.49	5.28	23.0	Customer body	3.48	3.79	-8.2
Warranty	6.70	6.83	-1.9	Wholesale	13.44	13.9	-3.3
Sublet	2.45	2.66	-7.9	Counter	2.74	2.74	0.0
Internal	4.75	4.92	-3.5	Warranty	9.05	8.87	2.1
Other	0.27	0.36	-24.1	Internal	4.29	4.16	3.1
				Other	1.90	1.79	6.3
Total Service Labor	**$37.31**	**$37.25**	**0.2**	**Total Parts**	**$48.18**	**$48.10**	**0.2**

SOURCE: National Automobile Dealers Association.

SHARE OF TOTAL DEALERSHIP SALES DOLLARS BY DEPARTMENT, 2004

Used Vehicles 27.6%
Parts & Service 11.5%
New Vehicles 60.9%

PROFILE OF THE FRANCHISED DEALERSHIP'S SERVICE AND PARTS OPERATION, 2004

	Average Dealership	All Dealers
Total service and parts sales	$3,802,537	$83.1 Billion
Total gross profit as percent of service and parts sales	46.1%	—
Total net profit as percent of service and parts sales	5.7%	—
Total number of repair orders written	11,696	253 Million
Total service and parts sales per customer repair order	$195	—
Total service and parts sales per warranty repair order	$198	—
Number of technicians	13	279,150
Number of service bays (excluding body)	17	369,125
Total parts inventory	$258,482	$5.6 Billion
Average customer mechanical labor rate	$75	—

SOURCE: National Automobile Dealers Association.

Personal Income of Motor Vehicle and Equipment Manufacturing Employees by State

PERSONAL INCOME OF MOTOR VEHICLE AND EQUIPMENT MANUFACTURING EMPLOYEES

	Personal Income (In Millions)				2003 Motor Vehicle & Equipment Percent of Total Manufacturing	2002 Motor Vehicle & Equipment Percent of Total Manufacturing
	Motor Vehicle and Equipment Manufacturing Employees		All Manufacturing Employees			
	2003	2002	2003	2002		
Alabama	$1,979	$1,494	$15,527	$15,023	12.7%	9.9%
Alaska	—	1	681	613	—	0.2%
Arizona	—	—	12,238	11,955	—	—
Arkansas	—	434	8,924	8,710	—	5.0%
California	2,996	2,589	115,869	113,278	2.6%	2.3%
Colorado	186	156	10,916	10,835	1.7%	1.4%
Connecticut	—	—	16,712	16,573	—	—
Delaware	—	—	2,827	2,455	—	—
District of Columbia	—	—	251	259	—	—
Florida	813	657	22,406	22,005	3.6%	3.0%
Georgia	1,617	1,335	24,403	24,273	6.6%	5.5%
Hawaii	—	—	795	760	—	—
Idaho	—	—	3,426	3,383	—	—
Illinois	3,339	2,873	46,603	46,166	7.2%	6.2%
Indiana	11,576	9,412	38,030	35,347	30.4%	26.6%
Iowa	600	575	12,059	11,575	5.0%	5.0%
Kansas	475	450	10,268	10,213	4.6%	4.4%
Kentucky	4,728	3,883	16,128	15,019	29.3%	25.9%
Louisiana	—	—	10,373	9,790	—	—
Maine	40	32	3,626	3,578	1.1%	0.9%
Maryland	—	278	10,343	10,307	—	2.7%
Massachusetts	154	140	25,623	25,519	0.6%	0.5%
Michigan	32,024	26,178	61,980	55,617	51.7%	47.1%
Minnesota	635	525	21,821	20,925	2.9%	2.5%
Mississippi	—	360	7,863	7,531	—	4.8%
Missouri	3,491	2,776	18,733	17,907	18.6%	15.5%
Montana	—	—	1,018	985	—	—
Nebraska	—	189	4,954	4,821	—	3.9%
Nevada	—	—	2,598	2,371	—	—
New Hampshire	140	150	5,302	5,229	2.6%	2.9%
New Jersey	490	496	28,418	27,651	1.7%	1.8%
New Mexico	50	55	2,159	2,097	2.3%	2.6%
New York	3,264	2,774	42,634	41,949	7.7%	6.6%
North Carolina	2,058	1,726	32,805	32,810	6.3%	5.3%
North Dakota	70	78	1,202	1,124	5.8%	6.9%
Ohio	13,540	11,128	55,625	52,894	24.3%	21.0%
Oklahoma	954	811	10,354	9,894	9.2%	8.2%
Oregon	590	514	12,160	11,837	4.9%	4.3%
Pennsylvania	1,525	975	45,870	45,646	3.3%	2.1%
Rhode Island	—	—	3,205	3,253	—	—
South Carolina	—	1,008	15,091	14,699	—	6.9%
South Dakota	—	78	1,722	1,648	—	4.7%
Tennessee	—	2,980	24,093	23,016	—	12.9%
Texas	2,393	1,993	68,010	65,724	3.5%	3.0%
Utah	—	350	6,108	5,817	—	6.0%
Vermont	—	45	2,285	2,338	—	1.9%
Virginia	—	800	17,233	16,892	—	4.7%
Washington	—	300	19,260	19,943	—	1.5%
West Virginia	215	177	3,842	3,847	5.6%	4.6%
Wisconsin	—	1,750	29,567	28,705	—	6.1%
Wyoming	21	6	586	500	3.6%	1.2%
Total	$105,819	$86,704	$954,525	$925,308	11.1%	9.4%

(1) Personal Income is measured as the sum of wage and salary disbursements, other labor income, proprietors' income, rental income, personal dividend income and personal interest income.
Omission of data for individual state is due to either the absences of such business from the state or the necessity of withholding the data to avoid disclosure of individual firm's data. Total includes states not listed individually.
SOURCE: U.S. Department of Commerce, Bureau of Economic Analysis.

Automotive Employment and Compensation

HOURLY COMPENSATION OF AUTOMOTIVE PRODUCTION EMPLOYEES IN SELECTED COUNTRIES

Country	Exchange Rate National Currency	Exchange Rate National Currency Per U.S. Dollar	Hourly Compensation National Currency 2002	Hourly Compensation National Currency 2001	Hourly Compensation U.S. Currency 2002	Hourly Compensation U.S. Currency 2001	2002 Percent of U.S. Earnings
France[1]	Euro	1.06	19.56	18.94	18.49	16.95	58.4
Germany[1]	Euro	1.06	34.70	34.75	32.81	31.11	103.6
Ireland[1]	Euro	1.06	14.78	14.86	13.97	13.30	44.1
Italy[1]	Euro	1.06	17.18	16.67	16.24	14.92	51.3
Japan	Yen	125.24	3,052.00	3,012.00	24.37	24.77	76.9
Korea	Won	1,249.63	17,020.00	14,146.00	13.62	10.95	43.0
Mexico	Peso	9.67	49.51	47.07	5.12	5.04	16.2
Spain[1]	Euro	1.06	15.69	14.87	14.83	13.31	46.8
Taiwan	Dollar	34.52	225.40	230.80	6.53	6.82	20.6
United Kingdom	Pound	0.67	14.08	13.42	21.15	19.32	66.8
United States	Dollar	1.00	31.67	29.84	31.67	29.84	100.0

SOURCE: U.S. Department of Labor, Bureau of Labor Statistics.

U.S. MOTOR VEHICLE AND EQUIPMENT MANUFACTURING EMPLOYMENT

Year	All Employees (000)	Production Workers Number (000)	Production Workers Percent of Total Employees	Production Workers Average Hourly Earnings
2004	1,109.1	900.0	81.1%	$21.71
2003	1,125.3	906.3	80.5%	21.68
2002	1,151.2	931.0	80.9%	21.09
2001	1,212.8	986.7	81.4%	19.62
2000	1,313.6	1,073.0	81.7%	19.07
1999	1,312.6	1,075.7	82.0%	18.45
1998	1,271.5	1,050.3	82.6%	18.19
1997	1,253.9	1,062.5	84.7%	18.35
1996	1,240.3	1,052.3	84.8%	18.07
1995	1,241.5	1,048.9	84.5%	17.63
1994	1,168.5	978.4	83.7%	17.28
1993	1,077.8	896.4	83.2%	15.13
1992	1,047.1	867.9	82.9%	14.09
1991	1,017.6	840.1	82.6%	13.37
1990	1,054.2	869.5	82.5%	13.24

NOTE: The basis for industry classification has changed from the Standard Industrial Classification System (SIC) to the North American Industry Classification System (NAICS).
SOURCE: U.S. Department of Labor, Bureau of Labor Statistics.

U.S. MOTOR VEHICLE AND EQUIPMENT MANUFACTURING EMPLOYMENT, 1994-2004

Industrial Production and Capacity Utilization

INDUSTRIAL PRODUCTION INDEX FOR MOTOR VEHICLE AND PARTS MANUFACTURERS

	Industrial Production Index			
	Total		Motor Vehicle and Parts	
Year	Index	Percent Change	Index	Percent Change
2004	112.6	0.6	124.5	3.8
2003	111.9	0.0	119.9	3.6
2002	111.9	-0.4	115.7	9.5
2001	112.3	-4.3	105.7	-8.8
2000	117.3	4.5	115.9	-0.7
1999	112.2	5.3	116.7	10.9
1998	106.6	6.6	105.2	5.2
1997	100.0	8.5	100.0	7.9
1996	92.2	5.0	92.7	0.8
1995	87.8	5.7	92.0	2.9
1994	83.1	6.4	89.4	14.9
1993	78.1	3.7	77.8	10.5

NOTE: "Industrial Production" is an index benchmarked to 1997=100.
SOURCE: Board of Governors of the Federal Reserve System.

CAPACITY UTILIZATION FOR MOTOR VEHICLE AND PARTS MANUFACTURING

Year	All Manufac- turing	Percent Change	Vehicle & Parts Mfg.	Percent Change
2004	76.4	3.7	81.4	1.2
2003	73.7	0.3	80.4	0.5
2002	73.5	-1.3	80.0	7.2
2001	74.5	-7.9	74.6	-11.1
2000	80.9	-0.5	83.9	-2.2
1999	81.3	-0.9	85.8	6.7
1998	82.0	-1.0	80.4	-2.5
1997	82.8	1.8	82.5	3.0
1996	81.3	-1.8	80.1	-3.3
1995	82.8	0.2	82.8	-3.9
1994	82.6	3.0	86.2	10.8
1993	80.2	1.0	77.8	8.1

NOTE: "Capacity Utilization" is a percent of capacity.
SOURCE: Board of Governors of the Federal Reserve System.

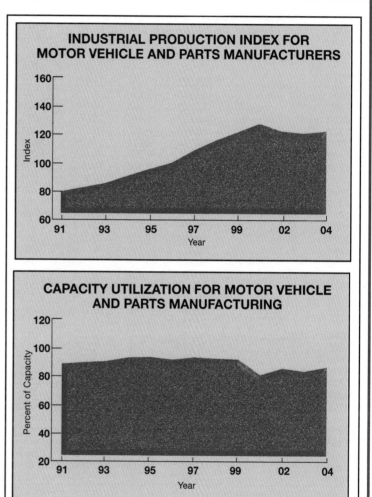

AUTO AND TRUCK OUTPUT (Dollars in Billions)

Year	Auto Output	Auto Percent of GDP	Truck Output	Truck Percent of GDP	Total Motor Vehicle Output	Percent of GDP	Gross Domestic Product (GDP)
2004	130.1	1.1	279.7	2.4	409.8	3.5	11,735.0
2003	130.6	1.2	259.6	2.4	390.2	3.5	11,004.0
2002	146.8	1.4	232.4	2.2	379.2	3.6	10,487.0
2001	141.4	1.4	203.1	2.0	344.5	3.4	10,128.0
2000	151.1	1.2	213.9	2.4	365.0	3.6	9,817.0
1999	150.4	1.4	221.5	2.4	371.9	3.7	9,268.4
1998	146.9	1.4	191.8	2.1	338.7	3.6	8,747.0
1997	144.6	1.5	175.1	2.0	319.7	3.5	8,304.3
1996	143.0	1.6	150.4	1.9	293.4	3.5	7,816.9
1995	138.6	1.8	139.3	1.9	277.9	3.7	7,397.7
1994	147.0	1.9	125.8	1.8	272.8	3.7	7,072.2
1993	128.7	1.8	103.9	1.6	232.6	3.4	6,657.4
1992	121.7	1.8	83.9	1.4	205.6	3.2	6,337.7

SOURCE: U.S. Department of Commerce, Bureau of Economic Analysis.

Corporate Profits and Research and Development Spending

SELECTED AUTOMOBILE MANUFACTURERS' REVENUES/NET INCOME (U.S. Dollars in Millions)

Year	DaimlerChrysler Revenues	DaimlerChrysler Net Income	Ford Revenues	Ford Net Income	General Motors Revenues	General Motors Net Income	Toyota Revenues	Toyota Net Income	Volkswagen Revenues	Volkswagen Net Income
2004	$192,319	$3,338	$171,652	$3,487	$193,517	$2,805	$163,637	$10,995	$120,438	$969
2003	171,870	564	164,338	495	185,837	3,822	128,965	6,247	106,839	1,263
2002	156,838	4,947	162,256	-980	177,324	1,736	107,443	4,177	91,165	2,723
2001	136,072	-589	160,754	-5,453	177,260	601	106,030	5,447	78,493	2,594
2000	152,446	7,411	170,058	3,467	184,632	4,452	119,780	3,783	79,746	1,922
1999	151,035	5,785	160,658	7,237	176,558	6,002	100,990	3,747	75,525	2,534
1998	154,615	5,656	143,350	22,071	155,445	2,956	88,473	3,442	80,395	1,343
1997	61,147	2,805	153,627	6,920	178,174	6,698	99,730	3,143	63,664	765
1996	61,397	3,529	146,991	4,446	164,013	4,963	101,177	2,426	64,491	437
1995	53,195	2,025	137,137	4,139	160,254	6,881	89,715	1,458	61,168	233
1994	52,235	3,713	128,439	5,308	154,951	4,901	91,317	1,227	50,930	95
1993	43,596	-2,551	108,521	2,529	138,676	2,466	95,063	1,643	44,774	-1,134
1992	36,897	723	100,132	-7,385	132,429	-23,498	80,128	1,875	53,977	93
1991	29,370	-795	88,286	-2,258	123,056	-4,453	71,731	3,140	48,826	713
1990	30,620	68	97,650	860	124,705	-1,986	59,962	2,878	45,429	725
1989	35,186	359	96,146	3,835	126,932	4,224	61,440	2,652	37,606	597
1988	34,421	1,050	92,446	5,300	123,642	4,856	—	—	—	—
1987	28,353	1,290	79,893	4,625	114,870	3,551	—	—	—	—
1986	24,569	1,389	69,695	3,285	115,610	2,945	—	—	—	—
1985	22,738	1,610	57,616	2,515	106,656	3,999	—	—	—	—
1984	19,717	2,373	56,323	2,907	93,145	4,517	—	—	—	—
1982	10,040	170	37,067	-658	60,026	963	—	—	—	—
1980	9,225	-1,710	37,086	-1,543	57,729	-763	—	—	—	—
1978	13,618	-205	42,784	1,589	63,221	3,508	—	—	—	—
1976	15,537	423	28,840	983	47,181	2,903	—	—	—	—
1974	10,860	-52	23,621	361	31,550	950	—	—	—	—
1972	9,641	221	20,194	870	30,435	2,163	—	—	—	—
1970	7,000	-8	14,980	516	18,752	609	—	—	—	—
1968	7,445	291	14,100	627	22,755	1,732	—	—	—	—
1966	5,650	189	12,240	621	20,209	1,793	—	—	—	—
1964	4,287	214	9,670	506	16,997	1,735	—	—	—	—
1962	2,378	65	8,090	481	14,640	1,459	—	—	—	—
1960	3,007	32	5,238	428	12,736	959	—	—	—	—

Note: DaimlerChrysler is Chrysler Corp. only prior to 1998.
SOURCE: Ward's Communications and company annual reports.

RESEARCH & DEVELOPMENT EXPENDITURES FOR SELECTED MANUFACTURERS
(U.S. Dollars In Millions)

Year	Daimler-Chrysler[1]	Ford	General Motors	Toyota	Volkswagen	Year	Daimler-Chrysler[1]	Ford	General Motors	Toyota	Volkswagen
2004	7,660	7,400	6,500	6,455	5,637	1992	1,053	4,332	5,917	—	—
2003	7,018	7,500	5,700	5,561	5,215	1991	955	3,728	5,887	—	—
2002	6,455	7,700	5,800	4,423	4,118	1990	908	3,558	5,342	—	—
2001	5,281	7,400	6,200	3,864	2,461	1989	958	3,167	5,248	—	—
2000	5,347	6,800	6,600	4,196	3,855	1988	866	2,930	4,754	—	—
1999	7,628	6,000	6,800	4,771	3,806	1987	773	2,514	4,361	—	—
1998	7,853	5,300	7,900	3,367	3,343	1986	732	2,305	4,158	—	—
1997	1,714	6,327	8,200	3,723	2,555	1985	609	2,018	3,625	—	—
1996	1,602	6,821	8,900	—	—	1984	452	1,915	3,076	—	—
1995	1,420	6,624	8,200	—	—	1983	365	1,751	2,602	—	—
1994	1,303	5,811	6,900	—	—	1982	307	1,764	2,175	—	—
1993	1,230	5,618	6,030	—	—	1981	250	1,718	2,250	—	—

(1) Data for Chrysler prior to 1998.
SOURCE: Compiled by Ward's Communications from company annual reports.

Use Tax Revenues by State

STATE MOTOR USE TAX REVENUES, 2004 (In Thousands)

State	Total State Tax Revenue	State Tax on Motor Vehicle Fuel	State License Tax on Motor Vehicles	State License Tax on Motor Vehicle Operators	Total Motor Vehicle Fuel and License Taxes	Percent Motor Vehicle of Total Taxes
Alabama	$7,018,242	$535,493	$172,815	$16,712	$725,020	10.3
Alaska	1,288,164	40,660	43,782	—	84,442	6.6
Arizona	9,606,318	671,765	161,398	16,069	849,232	8.8
Arkansas	5,580,678	453,148	109,831	15,875	578,854	10.4
California	85,721,483	3,324,883	2,155,042	187,395	5,667,320	6.6
Colorado	7,051,457	597,558	192,923	14,293	804,774	11.4
Connecticut	10,291,289	456,805	197,418	38,204	692,427	6.7
Delaware	2,375,482	112,435	33,592	205	146,232	6.2
Florida	30,767,561	1,823,349	1,124,851	151,774	3,099,974	10.1
Georgia	14,570,573	755,994	279,991	36,907	1,072,892	7.4
Hawaii	3,849,135	84,378	89,268	189	173,835	4.5
Idaho	2,647,790	218,019	107,269	7,042	332,330	12.6
Illinois	25,490,593	1,421,927	1,370,405	77,409	2,869,741	11.3
Indiana	11,957,470	802,168	158,542	211,999	1,172,709	9.8
Iowa	5,133,126	357,835	377,672	19,100	754,607	14.7
Kansas	5,283,676	428,985	161,497	14,841	605,323	11.5
Kentucky	8,463,400	476,605	205,314	11,205	693,124	8.2
Louisiana	8,025,507	560,769	114,090	11,236	686,095	8.5
Maine	2,896,759	220,410	81,740	7,109	309,259	10.7
Maryland	12,314,799	746,044	282,167	29,065	1,057,276	8.6
Massachusetts	16,698,723	684,242	292,688	90,605	1,067,535	6.4
Michigan	24,061,065	1,081,259	1,064,774	66,634	2,212,667	9.2
Minnesota	14,734,921	648,428	517,447	37,952	1,203,827	8.2
Mississippi	5,124,730	464,748	117,892	22,763	605,403	11.8
Missouri	9,119,664	726,705	254,740	16,559	998,004	10.9
Montana	1,625,692	197,605	144,651	5,082	347,338	21.4
Nebraska	3,639,811	302,899	88,780	8,210	399,889	11.0
Nevada	4,738,877	293,595	139,467	14,546	447,608	9.4
New Hampshire	2,005,389	129,913	84,431	13,051	227,395	11.3
New Jersey	20,981,428	546,952	398,691	34,669	980,312	4.7
New Mexico	4,001,780	210,863	121,246	5,855	337,964	8.4
New York	45,833,652	518,557	793,597	120,225	1,432,379	3.1
North Carolina	16,576,316	1,272,611	440,180	75,372	1,788,163	10.8
North Dakota	1,228,890	118,744	54,707	3,889	177,340	14.4
Ohio	22,475,528	1,541,151	713,149	67,504	2,321,804	10.3
Oklahoma	6,426,713	415,318	552,799	14,039	982,156	15.3
Oregon	6,103,071	404,547	418,903	31,752	855,202	14.0
Pennsylvania	25,346,869	1,785,200	792,430	60,209	2,637,839	10.4
Rhode Island	2,408,861	133,415	56,986	577	190,978	7.9
South Carolina	6,803,568	489,322	122,056	36,094	647,472	9.5
South Dakota	1,062,722	126,017	42,167	1,875	170,059	16.0
Tennessee	9,536,031	832,168	255,137	41,737	1,129,042	11.8
Texas	30,751,860	2,918,842	1,232,494	96,199	4,247,535	13.8
Utah	4,189,172	344,121	91,372	9,233	444,726	10.6
Vermont	1,766,719	85,994	62,566	4,175	152,735	8.6
Virginia	14,233,065	909,468	340,085	45,826	1,295,379	9.1
Washington	13,895,346	925,723	334,244	47,812	1,307,779	9.4
West Virginia	3,749,013	309,274	83,663	3,808	396,745	10.6
Wisconsin	12,531,098	1,028,516	330,291	30,759	1,389,566	11.1
Wyoming	1,504,777	69,975	50,784	1,907	122,666	8.2
Total	**593,488,853**	**33,605,402**	**17,412,024**	**1,875,547**	**52,892,973**	**8.9**

SOURCE: U.S. Department of Commerce, Bureau of the Census.

New Car Corporate Average Fuel Economy

NEW CAR CORPORATE AVERAGE FUEL ECONOMY PERFORMANCE BY MANUFACTURER AND MODEL YEAR (Sales Weighted Combined City/Highway Miles Per Gallon)

Manufacturer	Preliminary Sales Basis 2004	Final Sales Basis 2003	2002	2001	2000	1999	1997	1995	1993	1985	1974
DOMESTIC FLEETS											
Chrysler[1][2]	29.7	29.7	27.6	27.9	27.9	27.2	27.6	28.4	27.8	27.8	13.9
Ford[1]	26.5	27.9	27.8	27.7	28.3	27.6	27.2	27.7	28.8	26.6	14.2
General Motors[1]	29.0	28.9	28.6	28.3	27.9	27.7	28.2	27.4	27.4	25.8	12.1
Honda	31.1	34.4	32.4	32.7	31.4	33.5	28.5	—	—	—	—
Nissan	27.9	28.9	28.9	27.9	28.1	29.9	—	—	—	—	—
Toyota	33.2	28.1	33.6	34.2	33.3	28.3	28.8	28.5	—	—	—
IMPORT FLEETS											
Alfa Romeo	—	—	—	—	—	—	—	—	—	27.7	—
AMC-Renault	—	—	—	—	—	—	—	—	—	28.6	—
BMW	26.3	26.8	25.8	25.0	24.8	25.4	25.7	25.3	25.2	26.4	19.5
Chrysler	26.6	26.3	26.5	26.5	25.3	26.5	25.7	28.6	31.0	36.2	—
Ford	27.8	28.2	28.1	27.9	27.4	30.1	31.3	34.0	26.7	25.2	—
Fuji (Subaru)	27.2	27.6	27.6	27.8	28.2	27.7	28.3	28.9	29.6	32.6	25.7
General Motors	29.5	28.3	27.7	26.5	25.4	25.5	32.1	36.7	30.5	47.9	—
Honda	37.4	31.9	29.8	29.3	29.3	29.4	32.4	32.7	32.5	34.5	31.1
Hyundai	29.6	30.4	31.2	31.3	30.4	30.8	31.4	31.2	31.3	—	—
Isuzu	—	—	—	—	—	—	—	—	34.8	34.2	—
Kia	29.2	30.4	29.7	30.5	30.0	30.9	31.0	—	—	—	—
Mercedes-Benz	—	—	—	—	—	—	25.2	24.7	22.9	23.6	15.3
MG-Triumph-JaguarREaguar	—	—	—	—	—	—	—	—	—	19.3	21.3
Mitsubishi	—	—	—	29.4	29.4	30.0	30.0	29.9	29.4	31.9	—
Nissan	29.1	27.4	29.5	28.7	28.3	29.9	29.9	29.5	29.4	30.1	24.0
Peugeot	—	—	—	—	—	—	—	—	26.2	25.2	19.0
Saab	—	—	—	—	—	—	—	—	—	26.4	19.8
Suzuki	29.5	33.0	33.6	35.1	35.0	35.5	35.2	40.8	45.6	58.7	—
Toyota	32.4	32.4	29.3	30.6	28.9	29.9	30.1	30.4	29.1	33.5	22.5
Volvo	—	—	—	—	—	26.2	25.8	26.0	25.9	27.2	19.4
VW-Audi	28.7	29.8	29.2	28.5	28.8	28.2	29.0	29.0	27.2	30.5	25.9
Yugo	—	—	—	—	—	—	—	—	—	—	—

(1) Domestic fleet excludes captive imports after '79. (2) DaimlerChrysler Includes Mercedes-Benz and the Chrysler Group beginning in '99.
SOURCE: U.S. Department of Transportation.

NEW CAR CORPORATE AVERAGE FUEL ECONOMY (Sales Weighted Combined City/Highway Miles Per Gallon)

Model Year	Federal Standard	Domestic Fleet	Import Fleet	Total Fleet
2004 (prelim.)	27.5	29.3	28.7	29.1
2003	27.5	29.1	29.9	29.5
2002	27.5	29.1	28.8	29.0
2001	27.5	28.7	29.0	28.8
2000	27.5	28.7	28.3	28.5
1999	27.5	28.0	29.0	28.3
1998	27.5	28.6	29.2	28.8
1997	27.5	27.8	30.1	28.7
1996	27.5	28.1	29.6	28.5
1995	27.5	27.7	30.3	28.6
1994	27.5	27.5	29.7	28.3
1993	27.5	27.8	29.6	28.4
1992	27.5	27.0	29.2	27.9
1991	27.5	27.3	30.1	28.4
1990	27.5	26.9	29.9	28.0
1989	26.5	27.2	30.8	28.4
1988	26.0	27.4	31.5	28.8
1987	26.0	27.0	31.2	28.5
1986	26.0	26.6	31.6	28.2
1985	27.5	26.3	31.5	27.6
1984	27.0	25.6	32.0	26.9
1982	24.0	25.0	31.1	26.6

NOTE: After 1979, domestic fleet excludes captive imports.
SOURCE: U.S. Department of Transportation.

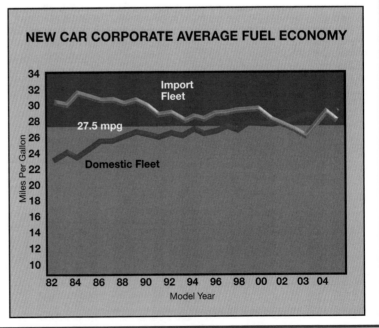

NEW CAR CORPORATE AVERAGE FUEL ECONOMY

New Light Truck Corporate Average Fuel Economy

NEW LIGHT TRUCK[1] CORPORATE AVERAGE FUEL ECONOMY
(Sales Weighted Combined City/Highway Miles Per Gallon)

	Federal Standard	Other[3]	Captive Import[4]	Total Fleet
2004	20.7	—	—	21.5
2003	20.7	—	—	21.8
2002	20.7	—	—	21.4
2001	20.7	—	—	20.9
2000	20.7	—	—	21.3
1999	20.7	—	—	20.9
1998	20.7	20.8	—	21.1
1997	20.7	20.4	—	20.6
1996	20.7	20.7	—	20.8
1995	20.6	20.5	—	20.5
1994	20.5	20.8	—	20.8
1993	20.4	21.0	24.3	21.0

	2-Wheel Drive			4-Wheel Drive		
	Federal Standard	Sales Weighted Average Domestic*	Import	Federal Standard	Sales Weighted Average Domestic*	Import
1991**	20.7	20.9[2]	23.0[2]	19.1	20.9[2]	23.0[2]
1990**	20.5	20.3[2]	23.0[2]	19.0	20.3[2]	23.0[2]
1989**	21.5	20.4[2]	23.5[2]	19.0	20.4[2]	23.5[2]
1988**	21.0	20.6[2]	24.6[2]	19.5	20.6[2]	24.6[2]
1987**	21.0	20.4	27.5	19.5	19.4	25.3
1985**	19.7	19.9	27.4	18.9	19.6	24.7[2]
1983**	19.5	19.6[2]	27.1[2]	17.5	19.6[2]	27.1

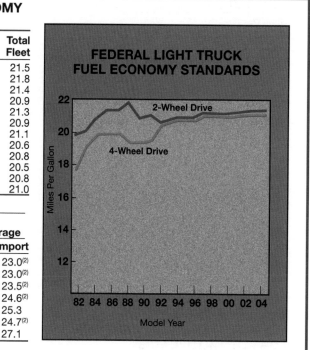

FEDERAL LIGHT TRUCK FUEL ECONOMY STANDARDS

*Captive imports are excluded.
**Manufacturers may elect to meet a single combined corporate fleet average of 19 mpg in 1983, 20 mpg in 1984, 19.5 mpg in 1985, 20 mpg in 1986, 20.5 mpg in 1987-89, 20 in 1990, and 20.2 in 1991.
(1) Light truck defined as 0-6,000 lbs. In 1979 and 0-8,500 lbs. in subsequent years.
(2) Combined 2-wheel and 4-wheel drive fleet average.
(3) Not a captive import light truck; 2 and 4 wheel drive combined.
(4) A light truck which is not domestically manufactured but imported by a manufacturer whose principal place of business is the United States; 2 and 4 wheel drive combined.
SOURCE: U.S. Department of Transportation.

NEW LIGHT TRUCK CORPORATE AVERAGE FUEL ECONOMY
PERFORMANCE BY MANUFACTURER[1] (Miles Per Gallon)

Manufacturer	Preliminary Sales Basis 2004	Final Sales Basis 2003	2002	2001	2000	1997	1995
BMW	21.5	20.0	19.2	19.2	—	—	—
Chrysler*	20.7	22.2	20.7	20.7	20.8	20.2	20.1
Ford*	21.1	21.3	20.5	20.5	20.4	20.0	20.8
General Motors*	21.2	21.3	20.5	20.5	20.3	20.5	20.1
Honda	24.5	24.7	24.9	24.9	26.1	26.9	—
Hyundai	24.1	24.4	25.2	25.2	—	—	—
Isuzu	23.0	22.3	21.1	21.1	21.5	19.6	20.3
Kia	20.5	19.7	22.9	22.9	24.4	23.7	24.4
Mazda	—	—	—	—	20.4	20.5	20.9
Mitsubishi	—	—	—	—	22.3	22.3	20.2
Nissan	21.1	21.9	20.7	20.7	21.2	22.3	22.4
Rover	—	—	—	—	17.0	17.2	16.3
Suzuki	22.9	21.9	22.0	22.0	23.8	27.4	28.1
Toyota	22.7	21.9	22.1	22.1	22.9	22.6	21.2
Volkswagen	19.3	21.3	20.5	20.5	19.1	18.5	19.6

*Captive imports are excluded.
(1) Trucks under 8,500 lbs. gross vehicle weight
SOURCE: U.S. Department of Transportation.

Gas Guzzler Tax Receipts, Automotive Fuel Prices and New Car Quality Improvements

NEW CAR GAS GUZZLER TAXES

Miles Per Gallon* At Least - Less Than	1980	1981	1982	1983	1984	1985	1986-90	1991 & Later
0-12.5	$550	$650	$1,200	$1,550	$2,150	$2,650	$3,850	7,700
12.5-13.0	550	650	950	1,550	1,750	2,650	3,200	6,400
13.0-13.5	300	550	950	1,250	1,750	2,200	3,200	6,400
13.5-14.0	300	550	750	1,250	1,450	2,200	2,700	5,400
14.0-14.5	200	450	750	1,000	1,450	1,800	2,700	5,400
14.5-15.0	200	450	600	1,000	1,150	1,800	2,250	4,500
15.0-15.5	0	350	600	800	1,150	1,500	2,250	4,500
15.5-16.0	0	350	450	800	950	1,500	1,850	3,700
16.0-16.5	0	200	450	650	950	1,200	1,850	3,700
16.5-17.0	0	200	350	650	750	1,200	1,500	3,000
17.0-17.5	0	0	350	500	750	1,000	1,500	3,000
17.5-18.0	0	0	200	500	600	1,000	1,300	2,600
18.0-18.5	0	0	0	350	600	800	1,300	2,600
18.5-19.0	0	0	0	350	450	800	1,050	2,100
19.0-19.5	0	0	0	0	450	600	1,050	2,100
19.5-20.0	0	0	0	0	0	600	850	1,700
20.0-20.5	0	0	0	0	0	500	850	1,700
20.5-21.0	0	0	0	0	0	500	650	1,300
21.0-21.5	0	0	0	0	0	0	650	1,300
21.5-22.0	0	0	0	0	0	0	500	1,000
22.0-22.5	0	0	0	0	0	0	500	1,000
22.5 & Over	0	0	0	0	0	0	0	0

NOTE: New car purchaser pays tax if car's combined city/highway fuel economy rating is lower than standard.
*Combined city/highway rating.
SOURCE: Internal Revenue Service.

GAS GUZZLER TAX RECEIPTS

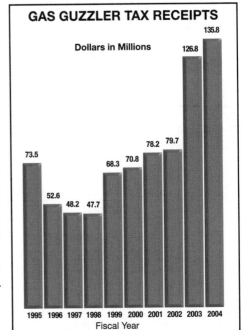

Dollars in Millions

Fiscal Year	
1995	73.5
1996	52.6
1997	48.2
1998	47.7
1999	68.3
2000	70.8
2001	78.2
2002	79.7
2003	126.8
2004	135.8

U.S. CITY AVERAGE RETAIL PRICES FOR AUTOMOTIVE FUEL
(Cents Per Gallon, Including Taxes)

Year	Unleaded Regular	Unleaded Premium	All Types[1]	Diesel
2004	188.0	206.8	192.3	192.1
2003	159.1	177.7	163.8	164.5
2002	135.8	155.6	144.1	142.6
2001	146.1	165.7	153.1	153.4
2000	138.2	169.3	156.3	151.1
1999	116.5	135.7	122.1	112.0
1998	105.9	125.0	111.5	104.5
1997	120.0	138.1	124.5	120.0
1996	123.1	141.3	128.8	123.6
1995	114.7	133.6	120.5	110.9
1994	111.2	130.5	117.4	112.0
1993	110.8	130.2	117.3	114.8
1991[2]	114.0	132.1	119.6	124.3
1990	116.4	134.9	121.7	134.3
1989	102.1	119.7	106.0	110.0
1988	94.6	110.7	96.3	104.6
1987	94.8	109.3	95.7	106.3
1986	92.7	108.5	93.1	99.9
1985	120.2	134.0	119.6	129.5
1980	124.5	N.A.	122.1	112.4

N.A.-Not available.
(1) Includes types of motor gasoline not shown separately.
(2) Price changed from "Full Service" to "Self Service".

AVERAGE RETAIL PRICE INCREASES FOR NEW CAR QUALITY IMPROVEMENTS
Requirements (Adjusted to 2004 Dollars)

Model Year	Safety	Emissions*	Other**	Total
2005	$193.11	$117.39	$0.00	$310.50
2004	37.16	21.80	24.00	82.96
2003	0.00	0.00	24.89	24.89
2002	0.00	0.00	66.61	66.61
2001	24.25	65.21	115.55	205.01
2000	14.64	0.00	0.00	14.64
1999	0.00	73.48	391.58	465.06
1998	0.00	49.62	170.03	219.66
1997	8.61	19.62	147.09	175.32
1996	15.64	83.67	83.35	182.66
1995	115.44	51.55	0.00	166.99
1994	181.23	38.85	137.94	358.02
1993	0.00	0.00	90.73	90.73
1992	36.14	0.00	234.77	270.92
1991	229.82	0.00	0.00	229.82
1990	196.88	0.00	42.59	239.47
1989	26.00	0.00	179.44	205.44
1988	74.93	0.00	206.34	281.27
1987	0.00	0.00	55.07	55.07
1986	33.20	0.00	192.59	225.79
1985	0.00	25.33	165.80	191.13
1984	-15.75	76.71	82.42	143.38
1983	0.00	86.65	84.96	171.62
1982	0.00	116.41	57.24	173.66
1981	6.13	666.86	85.61	758.60
1980	20.13	178.80	166.89	365.82
1979	9.41	19.81	46.65	75.87
1978	0.00	17.65	70.89	88.54
1977	13.22	27.20	72.09	112.50
1976	26.82	15.21	-10.81	31.22
1975	22.78	253.75	0.00	276.53
1974	248.84	3.24	20.58	272.66
1973	209.16	67.68	25.66	302.50
1972	4.90	14.69	29.37	48.96
1971	0.00	46.09	-60.64	-14.55

SOURCE: U.S. Department of Labor, Bureau of Labor Statistics.

Federal Exhaust Emission Standards for Cars and Light Trucks

FEDERAL EXHAUST EMISSION STANDARDS FOR CONVENTIONALLY FUELED PASSENGER CARS AND LIGHT TRUCKS (Grams Per Mile)

EPA Tier 1 Emission Standards for Passenger Cars and Light-Duty Trucks, FTP 75, (grams/mile)

Category	50,000 miles/5 years						100,000 miles/10 years[1]					
	THC	NMHC	CO	NOx diesel	NOx *gasoline*	PM	THC	NMHC	CO	NOx diesel	NOx *gasoline*	PM
Passenger cars	0.41	0.25	3.4	1	*0.4*	0.08	—	0.31	4.2	1.25	*0.6*	0.1
LLDT, LVW <3,750 lbs	—	0.25	3.4	1	*0.4*	0.08	0.8	0.31	4.2	1.25	*0.6*	0.1
LLDT, LVW >3,750 lbs	—	0.32	4.4	—	*0.7*	0.08	0.8	0.4	5.5	0.97	*0.97*	0.1
HLDT, ALVW <5,750 lbs	0.32	—	4.4	—	*0.7*	—	0.8	0.46	6.4	0.98	*0.98*	0.1
HLDT, ALVW >5,750 lbs	0.39	—	5	—	*1.1*	—	0.8	0.56	7.3	1.53	*1.53*	0.12

(1) Useful life 120,000 miles/11 years for all HLDT standards and for THC standards for LDT

Abbreviations:
LVW - loaded vehicle weight (curb weight + 300 lbs)
ALVW - adjusted LVW (the numerical average of the curb weight and the GVWR)
LLDT - light light-duty truck (below 6,000 lbs GVWR)
HLDT - heavy light-duty truck (above 6,000 lbs GVWR)

EPA Tier 2 Emission Standards, FTP 75, (grams/mile)

Bin#	50,000 miles					120,000 miles				
	NMOG	CO	NOx	PM	HCHO	NMOG	CO	NOx*	PM	HCHO
Temporary Bins										
MDPV[c]						0.28	7.3	0.9	0.12	0.032
10[a,b,d,f]	0.125 (0.160)	3.4 (4.4)	0.4	—	0.015 (0.018)	0.156 (0.230)	4.2 (6.4)	0.6	0.08	0.018 (0.027)
9[a,b,e]	0.075 (0.140)	3.4	0.2	—	0.015	0.090 (0.180)	4.2	0.3	0.06	0.018
Permanent Bins										
8[b]	0.100 (0.125)	3.4	0.14	—	0.015	0.125 (0.156)	4.2	0.2	0.02	0.018
7	0.075	3.4	0.11	—	0.015	0.09	4.2	0.15	0.02	0.018
6	0.075	3.4	0.08	—	0.015	0.09	4.2	0.1	0.01	0.018
5	0.075	3.4	0.05	—	0.015	0.09	4.2	0.07	0.01	0.018
4	—	—	—	—	—	0.07	2.1	0.04	0.01	0.011
3	—	—	—	—	—	0.055	2.1	0.03	0.01	0.011
2	—	—	—	—	—	0.01	2.1	0.02	0.01	0.004
1	—	—	—	—	—	0	0	0	0	0

NOTE: Tier 2 standards will be phased in between 2004 and 2009. For new passenger cars and light LDT's, Tier 2 standards will phase in beginning in 2004, with the standards to be fully phased in by 2007. For heavy LDT's and MDPV's, the Tier 2 standards will be phased in beginning in 2008, with full compliance in 2009.
*average manufacturer fleet NOx standard is 0.07 g/mi
a - Bin deleted at end of 2006 model year (2008 for HLDTs)
b - The higher temporary NMOG, CO and HCHO values apply only to HLDTs and expire after 2008
c - An additional temporary bin restricted to MDPVs, expires after model year 2008
d - Optional temporary NMOG standard of 0.195 g/mi (50,000) and 0.280 g/mi (120,000) applies for qualifying LDT4s and MDPVs only
e - Optional temporary NMOG standard of 0.100 g/mi (50,000) and 0.130 g/mi (120,000) applies for qualifying LDT2s only
f - 50,000 mile standard optional for diesels certified to bin 10

Federal Motor Vehicle Safety Standards

FEDERAL MOTOR VEHICLE SAFETY STANDARDS (FMVSS)

FMVSS NUMBER	Car	MPV	Truck	Bus	Equip.
100 SERIES Crash Avoidance					
101 Controls, Location & Identification	•	•	•	•	
102 Transmission Shift Lever Sequence	•	•	•	•	
103 Windshield Defrosting & Defogging	•	•	•	•	
104 Windshield Wiping & Washing System	•	•	•	•	
106 Brake Hoses	•	•	•	•	•
108 Lights & Reflectors	•	•	•	•	•*
109 New Tires for Passenger Cars(1)	•				
110 Tire Selection & Rims for Passenger Cars	•				
111 Rearview Mirrors	•	•	•	•	
113 Hood Latch System	•	•	•	•	
114 Theft Protection	•	•*	•*	•*	
115 Vehicle Identification Number (Location)	•	•	•	•	
116 Hydraulic Brake Fluids	•	•	•	•	•
117 Retreaded Tires	•				
118 Power-Operated Window Systems	•	•	•		
119 New Tires for Trucks, Buses, etc		•	•	•	•
120 Tire Selection & Rims for Trucks, Buses, etc.		•	•	•	•
121 Air Brake Systems			•	•	•
124 Accelerator Control Systems	•	•	•	•	
125 Warning Devices					•*
129 Non-Pneumatic Tires	•				
131 School Bus Pedestrian Safety Devices				•*	
135 Light Vehicle Brake Systems	•	•*	•*	•*	
200 SERIES Occupant Protection					
201 Occupant Protection in Interior Impacts	•	•*	•*	•*	
202 Head Restraints	•	•*	•*	•*	
203 Steering Wheel Impact Protection	•	•*	•*	•*	
204 Steering System Rearward Displacement	•	•*	•*	•*	
205 Glazing Materials	•	•	•	•	•
206 Door Locks & Hinges	•	•	•		
207 Anchorage of Seats	•	•	•	•	
208 Occupant Restraints	•*	•*	•*	•*	
209 Seat Belt Assemblies(2)	•	•	•	•	
210 Seat Belt Anchorages	•	•	•	•	
212 Windshield Mounting	•	•*	•*	•*	
213 Child Restraint Systems	•	•	•	•	

FMVSS/CFR NUMBER	Car	MPV	Truck	Bus	Equip.
214 Side Door Strength	•	•*	•*	•*	
216 Roof Crush Resistance	•*	•*	•*	•*	
217 Bus Window Strength & Emergency Release				•	
219 Windshield Zone Intrusion	•	•*		•*	•*
220 School Bus Rollover Protection				•*	
221 School Bus Body Joint Strength				•*	
222 School Bus Seats				•*	
223 Rear Impact Guards					•
224 Rear Impact Protection					•*
300 SERIES Post Crash Protection					
301 Fuel System Integrity	•	•*	•*	•*	
302 Flammability of Interior Materials	•	•	•	•	
303 Fuel System Integrity-CNG	•	•*	•*	•*	
304 CNG Fuel Container Integrity	•	•	•	•	
49 CFR PART NO. - Code of Federal Regulation (CFR) Parts					
— Importation of Motor Vehicles & Equipment	•	•	•	•	•
541 Theft Prevention	•	•	•	•	•
565 Vehicle Identification Number (Content)	•	•	•	•	•
566 Manufacturers Identification	•	•	•	•	•
567 Certification	•	•	•	•	•
568 Vehicles Manufactured in 2 or More Stages	•	•	•	•	•
569 Regrooved Tires	•	•	•	•	•
572 Anthropomorphic Dummy (Test Equipment)	•	•	•	•	•
573 Defect Reports	•	•	•	•	•
574 Tire Identification & Record Keeping	•	•	•	•	•
575 Consumer Information					
Truck-Camper Loading			•		
Uniform Tire Quality Grading	•				
Utility Vehicles		•*			
577 Defect Notification	•	•	•	•	•
579 Defect & Non-Compliance Responsibility	•	•	•	•	•
580 Odometer Disclosure Requirements	•	•	•		
581 Bumper Damage Limits	•				
582 Insurance Cost Information	•				
583 Automobile Parts Content Labeling					•
595 Retrofit On-Off Switches for Air Bags					•

1) Vehicle application is implied or is specified in other FMVSS.
*Application or requirements vary for specific vehicle types or Gross Vehicle Weight Ratings (GVWR).
PASSENGER CAR: Motor vehicle with motive power, except a multipurpose passenger vehicle, motorcycle or trailer designed for carrying 10 persons or less.
MULTIPURPOSE PASSENGER VEHICLE: Motor vehicle with motive power, except a trailer, designed to carry 10 persons or less which is constructed either on a truck chassis or with special features for occasional off-road operation.
TRUCK: Motor vehicle with motive power, except a trailer, designed primarily for the transportation of property or special purpose equipment.
BUS: Motor vehicle with motive power, except a trailer, designed for carrying more than 10 persons.
EQUIPMENT: Individual vehicle components or systems whether installed on a new vehicle or provided as a replacement.
SOURCE: National Highway Traffic Safety Administration.

Motor Vehicle Deaths by Type of Accident and Death Rates

MOTOR VEHICLE DEATHS BY TYPE OF ACCIDENT AND DEATH RATES

Year	Total Motor Vehicle Deaths	Pedes-trians	Other Motor Vehicles	Rail-road Trains	Pedal cycles	Animal drawn Veh. or Animal	Fixed Objects	Deaths from Non-collision Accidents	Per 10,000 Motor Vehicles	Per 100,000,000 Vehicle Miles	Per 100,000 Popu-lation
2002	44,000	5,700	18,200	300	700	100	13,500	5,500	1.81	1.56	15.7
2001*	43,700	6,100	18,400	300	800	100	12,800	5,200	1.86	1.57	15.7
2000*	43,354	5,900	19,100	321	800	100	12,300	4,800	1.92	1.58	15.8
1999	42,401	6,100	18,600	314	800	100	11,800	4,700	1.98	1.57	15.5
1998	43,501	5,900	19,700	309	700	100	12,200	4,600	1.94	1.59	16.1
1997	43,458	5,900	19,900	371	800	100	12,000	4,400	2.05	1.70	16.2
1996	43,649	6,100	19,600	373	800	100	12,100	4,600	2.07	1.76	16.5
1995	43,363	6,400	19,000	514	800	100	12,100	4,400	2.11	1.79	16.5
1994	42,524	6,300	18,900	549	800	100	11,500	4,400	2.11	1.80	16.3
1993	41,893	6,400	18,300	553	800	100	11,500	4,200	2.12	1.82	16.3
1992	40,982	6,300	17,600	521	700	100	11,700	4,100	2.11	1.83	16.1
1991	43,536	6,600	18,200	541	800	100	12,600	4,700	2.26	2.00	17.3
1990	46,814	7,300	19,900	623	900	100	13,100	4,900	2.43	2.18	18.8
1989	47,575	7,800	20,300	720	900	100	12,900	4,900	2.48	2.26	19.3
1988	49,078	7,700	20,900	638	1,000	100	13,400	5,300	2.60	2.42	20.1
1987	48,290	7,500	20,700	554	1,000	100	13,200	5,200	2.63	2.51	19.9
1986	47,865	8,900	20,800	574	1,100	100	3,300	13,100	2.63	2.60	19.9
1985	45,901	8,500	19,900	538	1,100	100	3,200	12,600	2.59	2.59	19.2
1984	46,263	8,500	20,000	630	1,100	100	3,200	12,700	2.69	2.69	19.6
1983	44,452	8,200	19,200	520	1,100	100	3,100	12,200	2.62	2.68	19.0
1982	45,779	8,400	19,800	554	1,100	100	3,200	12,600	2.77	2.88	19.7
1981	51,385	9,400	22,200	668	1,200	100	3,600	14,200	3.13	3.30	22.4
1980	53,172	9,700	23,000	739	1,200	100	3,700	14,700	3.29	3.50	23.4
1979	53,524	9,800	23,100	826	1,200	100	3,700	14,800	3.35	3.50	23.8
1978	52,411	9,600	22,400	986	1,200	100	3,600	14,500	3.41	3.39	23.6
1977	49,510	9,100	21,200	902	1,100	100	3,400	13,700	3.33	3.35	22.5
1976	47,038	8,600	20,100	1,033	1,000	100	3,200	13,000	3.28	3.33	21.6
1975	45,853	8,400	19,550	979	1,000	100	3,130	12,700	3.33	3.45	21.3
1974	46,402	8,500	19,700	1,209	1,000	100	3,100	2,800	3.44	3.59	21.8
1973	55,511	10,200	23,600	1,194	1,000	100	3,800	15,600	4.28	4.24	26.3
1972	56,278	10,300	23,900	1,260	1,000	100	3,900	15,800	4.60	4.43	26.9
1971	54,381	9,900	23,100	1,378	800	100	3,800	15,300	4.68	4.57	26.3
1970	54,633	9,900	23,200	1,459	780	100	3,800	15,400	4.92	4.88	26.8
1969	55,791	10,100	23,700	1,495	800	100	3,900	15,700	5.19	5.21	27.7
1968	54,862	9,900	22,400	1,570	790	100	2,700	17,400	5.32	5.40	27.5
1965	49,163	8,900	20,800	1,556	680	120	2,200	14,900	5.36	5.54	25.4
1960	38,137	7,850	14,800	1,368	460	80	1,700	11,900	5.12	5.31	21.2
1955	38,426	8,200	14,500	1,490	410	80	1,600	12,100	6.12	6.34	23.4
1950	34,763	9,000	11,650	1,541	440	90	1,300	10,600	7.07	7.59	23.0
1943-47ave.	28,458	10,570	7,490	1,660	490	120	820	7,120	8.60	10.52	20.8
1938-42ave.	33,549	12,430	9,500	1,624	748	140	1,048	7,848	10.41	11.49	25.4
1933-37ave.	36,313	14,484	8,630	1,598	540	214	1,034	9,464	13.50	15.55	28.6
1928-32ave.	31,050	12,300	5,700	1,850	—	274	700	9,100	12.10	15.60	25.3
1923-27ave.	21,800	—	—	1,200	—	—	—	—	11.10	18.20	18.8
1918-22ave.	12,700	—	—	—	—	—	—	—	13.90	11.90	—
1913-17ave.	6,800	—	—	—	—	—	—	—	23.80	6.80	—

* Revised.
SOURCE: National Safety Council.

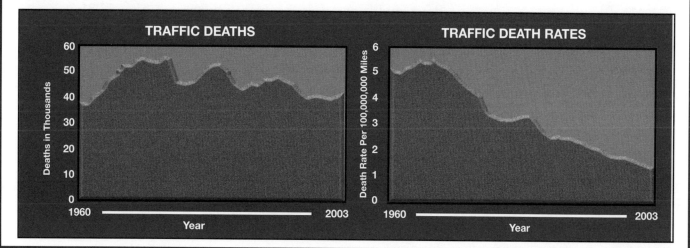

Motor Vehicle Traffic Deaths and Traffic Death Rates by State

MOTOR VEHICLE TRAFFIC DEATHS AND TRAFFIC DEATH RATES BY STATE

State	Traffic Deaths						Traffic Deaths Per 100,000,000 Vehicle Miles	
	2004	2003	2002	2001	2000	1999	2004	2003
Alabama	1,097	983	1,004	997	990	1,083	1.8	1.7
Alaska	101	95	85	85	103	76	2.0	1.9
Arizona	1,150	1,120	1,104	1,047	1,036	929	2.1	2.2
Arkansas	704	627	641	611	652	602	2.3	2.1
California	4,082	4,047	4,104	3,926	3,730	1,755	1.2	1.3
Colorado	629	629	732	736	679	N.A.	1.4	1.4
Connecticut	306	305	325	317	342	303	1.0	1.0
Delaware	140	144	126	136	128	103	1.5	1.6
Dist. of Columbia	45	70	50	72	52	46	1.1	2.0
Florida	3,257	3,179	3,137	3,013	2,998	2,867	1.7	1.8
Georgia	1,641	1,610	1,522	1,506	1,548	1,499	1.5	1.5
Hawaii	142	139	115	141	133	98	1.5	1.6
Idaho	260	293	265	259	275	278	1.8	2.1
Illinois	1,356	1,455	1,411	1,414	1,414	1,456	1.3	1.4
Indiana	947	787	792	909	892	934	1.3	1.1
Iowa	390	445	409	447	445	486	1.2	1.4
Kansas	461	472	510	494	461	532	1.6	1.6
Kentucky	964	931	917	850	824	808	2.0	2.0
Louisiana	906	896	865	957	937	826	2.0	2.1
Maine	196	205	191	191	167	177	1.3	1.4
Maryland	643	648	650	662	617	587	1.2	1.2
Massachusetts	476	462	459	477	433	412	0.9	0.9
Michigan	1,159	1,283	1,279	1,328	1,382	1,329	1.1	1.3
Minnesota	567	628	653	568	625	616	1.0	1.1
Mississippi	900	873	885	784	949	926	2.4	2.4
Missouri	1,130	1,232	1,203	1,098	1,157	1,089	1.6	1.8
Montana	229	262	268	230	237	220	2.1	2.5
Nebraska	254	293	307	246	276	295	1.3	1.6
Nevada	398	368	380	311	325	349	2.0	2.0
New Hampshire	170	126	127	142	126	141	1.3	1.0
New Jersey	731	733	786	745	732	727	1.0	1.0
New Mexico	522	437	458	464	437	461	2.3	1.9
New York	—	—	1,523	1,490	1,353	1,473	—	—
North Carolina	1,574	1,528	1,564	1,523	1,563	1,062	1.7	1.6
North Dakota	100	105	97	105	86	119	1.3	1.4
Ohio	1,286	1,278	1,301	1,379	1,249	1,337	1.2	1.2
Oklahoma	774	642	725	670	658	741	1.7	1.4
Oregon	456	511	436	487	451	414	1.3	1.5
Pennsylvania	—	—	1,618	—	N.A.	1,549	—	—
Rhode Island	83	104	84	81	81	88	1.0	1.3
South Carolina	1,046	968	1,053	1,061	1,061	1,064	2.1	2.0
South Dakota	197	203	175	171	173	142	2.3	2.4
Tennessee	1,317	1,198	1,159	1,188	1,235	1,225	1.9	1.7
Texas	3,654	3,826	3,722	3,727	3,519	3,123	1.6	1.7
Utah	296	309	330	291	376	346	1.2	1.2
Vermont	—	69	78	—	79	92	—	0.7
Virginia	922	942	913	935	930	843	1.2	1.2
Washington	563	601	660	649	630	628	1.0	1.1
West Virginia	410	377	437	376	410	396	2.0	1.9
Wisconsin	784	836	805	764	801	745	1.3	1.4
Wyoming	164	165	176	186	152	189	1.8	1.8
Total*	44,600	44,800	44,100	43,700	42,500	41,300	1.5	1.6

2004 Data shows preliminary figures
N.A.-Not available.
*Total includes both traffic and nontraffic motor vehicle related deaths.
SOURCE: National Safety Council.

Traffic Accidents and Fatalities

MOTOR VEHICLE TRAFFIC DATA

Year	Crashes	Injuries	Fatalities
2003	6,328,000	2,889,000	42,643
2002	6,316,000	2,926,000	42,815
2001	6,323,000	3,033,000	41,877
2000	6,394,000	3,189,000	41,821
1999	6,279,000	3,236,000	41,717
1998	6,335,000	3,192,000	41,501
1997	6,624,000	3,348,000	42,013
1996	6,770,000	3,483,000	42,065
1995	6,699,000	3,465,000	41,817
1994	6,496,000	3,266,000	40,716
1993	6,106,000	3,149,000	40,150
1992	6,000,000	3,070,000	39,250
1991	6,117,000	3,097,000	41,508
1990	6,471,000	3,231,000	44,599

SOURCE: U.S. Department of Transportation, National Highway Traffic Safety Administration.

TRAFFIC FATALITIES BY AGE AND SEX OF VICTIM, 2003

Age of Victim	Sex of Victim		
	Male	Female	Total
4 & under	332	275	607
5-9	328	263	591
10-15	839	532	1,371
16-20	4,093	1,909	6,002
21-24	3,299	1,061	4,360
25-34	5,044	1,657	6,701
35-44	4,774	1,947	6,721
45-54	4,112	1,676	5,788
55-64	2,536	1,216	3,752
65-74	1,609	1,107	2,716
75-98	2,135	1,779	3,914
Unknown	87	33	120
Total	29,188	13,455	42,643

SOURCE: U.S. Department of Transportation, National Highway Traffic Safety Administration.

TRAFFIC FATALITIES BY AGE AND PERSON TYPE, 2003

Age of Victim	Person Type				Total
	Drivers	Passengers	Pedestrians	Pedalcyclists	
4 & under	0	483	112	5	600
5-9	8	409	131	38	586
10-15	189	864	200	102	1,355
16-20	3,571	2,070	298	51	5,990
21-24	2,931	1,140	263	23	4,357
25-34	4,697	1,366	565	56	6,684
35-44	4,636	1,103	844	116	6,699
45-54	4,011	870	777	117	5,775
55-64	2,545	582	542	65	3,734
65-74	1,691	596	390	32	2,709
75-98	2,336	965	584	13	3,898
Unknown	25	44	43	4	116
Total	26,640	10,492	4,749	622	42,503

SOURCE: U.S. Department of Transportation, National Highway Traffic Safety Administration.

FATAL CRASHES BY HOUR OF DAY AND DAY OF WEEK, 2003

Hour of Day	Sun.	Mon.	Tues.	Wed.	Thurs.	Fri.	Sat.	Total
12 to 3 am	1,208	453	355	438	449	641	1,228	4,772
3 to 6 am	681	294	274	299	351	368	703	2,970
6 to 9 am	404	591	529	598	511	546	547	3,726
9 am to noon	477	508	530	524	525	563	640	3,767
noon to 3 pm	778	702	703	677	690	702	764	5,016
3 to 6 pm	959	848	857	852	884	1,015	957	6,372
6 to 9 pm	893	681	750	765	741	1,011	1,034	5,875
9 pm to 12 am	642	566	620	639	713	1,094	1,079	5,353
Unknown	88	48	31	42	45	44	84	401
Total	6,130	4,691	4,649	4,834	4,909	5,984	7,036	38,252[1]

(1) Includes 19 fatal crashes that occurred on unknown days.
SOURCE: U.S. Department of Transportation, National Highway Traffic Safety Administration.

Traffic Deaths in Selected Countries and Countries with Safety Belt Use Laws

STATES WITH STANDARD/PRIMARY SEAT BELT ENFORCEMENT LAWS*

Alabama	Maryland
California	Michigan
Connecticut	New Jersey
Delaware	New Mexico
District of Columbia	New York
Georgia	North Carolina
Hawaii	Oklahoma
Illinois	Oregon
Indiana	Tennessee
Iowa	Texas
Louisiana	Washington

* The safety belt use law may be enforced independent of another violation.
SOURCE: National Highway Traffic Safety Administration.

TRAFFIC DEATHS IN SELECTED COUNTRIES

	2003	2002	Traffic Fatalities Per 100,000 Registered Vehicles 2003	2002
Australia	1,621	1,723	13.2	14.2
Austria	931	956	21.2	22.1
Denmark	432	463	18.6	20.1
Finland	379	415	14.6	16.6
France	6,058	7,655	17.0	21.8
Germany	6,613	6,842	13.6	14.2
Hungary	1,326	1,429	42.0	48.0
Italy	N.A.	6,736	N.A.	17.9
Japan	8,877	8,326	12.2	11.5
The Netherlands	1,028	987	12.5	12.5
Norway	280	312	11.7	13.2
Poland	5,640	5,827	41.7	44.3
Portugal	1,546	1,675	29.5	31.8
Spain	5,399	5,347	22.9	23.2
Sweden	529	532	11.7	11.9
Switzerland	546	513	13.4	12.7
United Kingdom	3,658	3,431	11.2	10.7
United States	42,643	42,815	18.9	19.4

N.A.-Not available.
Note: Data varies significantly between countries both definitionally and quantitatively.
SOURCE: International Road Federation.

COUNTRIES WITH SAFETY BELT USE LAWS

Country	Effective Date	Country	Effective Date
Australia	1/72	Connecticut	1/1/86
Austria	7/76	Delaware	1/1/92
Belgium	6/75	District of Columbia	12/12/85
Brazil	6/72	Florida	7/1/86
Bulgaria	1976	Georgia	9/1/88
Canadian Provinces		Hawaii	2/16/85
Alberta	7/87	Idaho	7/1/86
British Columbia	10/77	Illinois	7/1/85
Manitoba	4/84	Indiana	7/1/87
Newfoundland	7/82	Iowa	7/1/86
New Brunswick	11/83	Kansas	7/1/86
Nova Scotia	1/85	Kentucky	7/13/94
Ontario	1/76	Louisiana	7/1/86
Prince Edward Island	1/88	Maine	12/27/95
Quebec	7/76	Maryland	7/1/86
Saskatchewan	7/77	Massachusetts	2/1/94
Czechoslovakia	1/69	Michigan	7/1/85
Denmark	1/76	Minnesota	8/1/86
Finland	7/75	Mississippi	3/20/90
France	10/79	Missouri	9/28/85
Germany	1/76	Montana	10/1/87
Greece	12/79	Nebraska	1/1/93
Hong Kong	10/83	Nevada	7/1/87
Hungary	7/77	New Hampshire	—
Iceland	10/81	New Jersey	3/1/85
Ireland	2/79	New Mexico	1/1/86
Israel	7/75	New York	12/1/84
Ivory Coast	1970	North Carolina	10/1/85
Japan	12/71	North Dakota	7/14/94
Jordan	12/83	Ohio	5/6/86
Luxembourg	6/75	Oklahoma	2/1/87
Malaysia	4/79	Oregon	12/7/90
Netherlands	6/75	Pennsylvania	11/23/87
New Zealand	6/72	Puerto Rico	1/19/75
Norway	9/75	Rhode Island	6/18/91
Poland	1/84	South Carolina	7/1/89
Portugal	1/78	South Dakota	1/1/95
Singapore	7/81	Tennessee	4/21/86
South Africa	12/77	Texas	9/1/85
Spain	10/74	Utah	4/28/86
Sweden	1/75	Vermont	1/1/94
Switzerland	1/76	Virginia	1/1/88
Turkey	10/84	Washington	6/11/86
United States and Territories		West Virginia	9/1/93
Alabama	7/18/92	Wisconsin	12/1/87
Alaska	9/12/90	Wyoming	6/8/89
Arizona	1/1/91	**United Kingdom**	1/83
Arkansas	7/15/91	**USSR**	1/76
California	1/1/86	**Zimbabwe**	7/80
Colorado	7/1/87		

SOURCE: National Highway Traffic Safety Administration.

INDEX

INDEX

WARD'S The POWER of Automotive Information

WARD'S COMMUNICATIONS™
THE POWER OF AUTOMOTIVE INFORMATION

Contact Ward's Information Products for pricing
or more information on the products below.

John Sousanis • **248.799.2622** • **jsousanis@primediabusiness.com**

Lisa Williamson • **248.799.2642** • **lwilliamson@primediabusiness.com**

Online Subscription Services

WardsAuto.com

All of Ward's in one online subscription --
news, data, analysis and more.

Call for pricing
(based on number
of users)

_____

Ward's AutoInfoBank™ on the web

Powerful web-based data reporting tool

_____

Forecast Report Products

Ward's AutoForecasts

Knowledgable forecasts on where the
automotive manufacturing industry is headed

Call for pricing
(multiple forecast
products available)

_____

Ward's Monthly Auto Data Reports

Call for details and pricing on these reports:
- Retail sales
- Production/factory sales
- Commercial vehicle exports
- Passenger car exports

Magazines

	US & Mexico	Canada	Airmail Overseas
Ward's AutoWorld®* 1 yr. (12 issues)	$57	$71	$85
Ward's Dealer Business®* 1 yr. (12 issues)	$40	$58	$85

Contact Customer Service for pricing
or more information on the products below.

Laurie Collins • **248.799.2645** • **lcollins@primediabusiness.com**

Newsletters

Ward's Automotive Reports®*
- ❏ One year (52 issues) with Yearbook .... $1,295 (airmail overseas, add $50)
- ❏ 13-week trial .... $245 (airmail overseas, add $12.50)

**Ward's Engine and
Vehicle Technology Update**®*
- ❏ One year (24 issues) .... $935 (airmail overseas, add $25)
- ❏ Half-year (12 issues) .... $475 (airmail overseas, add $12.50)

Reference Annuals

Ward's Automotive Yearbook®**
- ❏ 2005 Yearbook .... $495 (airmail overseas, add $30)
- ❏ 2005 Yearbook and CD-ROM set .... $785 (airmail overseas, add $30)
- ❏ 2004 Yearbook .... $475 (airmail overseas, add $30)
- ❏ 2004 Yearbook and CD-ROM set .... $765 (airmail overseas, add $30)

Ward's World Motor Vehicle Data™
- ❏ 2005 Data Book (Sept 05) .... $245 (airmail overseas, add $25)
- ❏ 2005 Data Book and CD-ROM set .... $450 (airmail overseas, add $25)
- ❏ 2004 Data Book .... $235 (airmail overseas, add $25)
- ❏ 2004 Data Book and CD-ROM set .... $435 (airmail overseas, add $25)

ALL ORDERS MUST INCLUDE APPLICABLE TAXES. If tax-exempt and not
a government agency, please provide copy of tax exempt certificate.
* Subject to sales tax in AL, CO, CT, FL, GA, IN, KS, KY, MO, SC, TN
and Canada.
** Subject to sales tax in AL, AK, CA, CO, CT, FL, GA, IL, IN, KS, KY, MA,
MI, MN, MO, MS, NE, NJ, NY, OH, PA, SC, TN, TX, WI and Canada.

Please make checks payable to: PRIMEDIA BUSINESS in U.S. funds, drawn on a U.S. bank.

Payment enclosed $ _____ Signature _____

Bill to my: ☐ VISA   ☐ Mastercard   ☐ American Express   ☐ Discover

Card number _____ Exp. Date _____

Name/Title (Please print) _____

Company/Division _____

Street Address _____

City _____ State/Province _____

Zip/Postal Code _____ Country _____

Phone _____ Fax _____

E-mail Address _____

Mail Orders to: Primedia Business - Ward's Communications • 13628 Collections Center Drive • Chicago, IL 60693-0136

Customer Service Inquiries: Contact Laurie Collins by phone: (248) 799-2645, by fax: (248) 357-0810, or email: lcollins@primediabusiness.com